Knocking on Heaven's Door

MARK OPPENHEIMER

Knocking on Heaven's Door

**American Religion in the
Age of Counterculture**

Yale University Press   New Haven and London

Published with assistance from the income of the Frederick John Kingsbury Memorial Fund.

Published with assistance from the Mary Cady Tew Memorial Fund.

Designed by Sonia Scanlon
Set in Minion type by Ink, Inc.
Printed in the United States of America by Vail-Ballou Press, Binghamton, New York.

Library of Congress Cataloging-in-Publication Data

Oppenheimer, Mark, 1974–
Knocking on heaven's door : American religion in the age of counterculture / Mark Oppenheimer.
    p.   cm.
Includes bibliographical references and index.
ISBN 0-300-10024-8 (alk. paper)
1. United States—Religion—20th century. 2. Counterculture—United States—History—20th Century. 3. United States—Social conditions—20th century. I. Title
BL2525.O66   2003
200'.973'09045—dc21   2003005802

A catalogue record for this book is available from the British Library.

The paper in this book meets the guidelines for permanence and durability of the Committee on Production Guidelines for Book Longevity of the Council on Library Resources.

10 9 8 7 6 5 4 3 2 1

CONTENTS

ILLUSTRATIONS

ACKNOWLEDGMENTS

I did not do this book alone, and I would not have wanted to.

I gladly thank Bill Sumners of the Southern Baptist Historical Library and Archive; William Limbacher of Hebrew Union College in Cincinnati; Jennifer Peters at the Episcopal Archives in Austin, Texas; Nancy Godleski, William Massa, and the other industrious souls at the Yale libraries; Leslie Reyman at Union Theological Seminary; Don Buske of the Archdiocese of Cincinnati; Frances O'Donnell at the Andover Harvard Theological Library; and the archival staffs of the Reconstructionist Rabbinical College and the Unitarian Universalist Association. Heather Huyck, thank you for sharing your files.

I received financial support from the Mellon Undergraduate Research Fund; the Andrew Mellon Fellowship of the Woodrow Wilson Foundation; the Franke Interdisciplinary Fellowship at Yale; the

Jacob Javits Fellowship of the Department of Education; Jonathan Edwards College at Yale (where Barbara Goddard was especially helpful); the Yale Graduate School of Arts and Sciences; the Center for the Study of Religion in America at Yale; and my grandfather.

I received documents, books, and counsel from Robert Imholt of Albertus Magnus College, Michael McGough, Paul Elie, Jim Sleeper, Nancy Ammerman, Betty Bone Schiess, and Sarah Ruth Hammond. Tandi Huelsbeck provided me with the transcript of her interview with the late James Stoll, which helped send me on my way back in 1995. Daniel Guralnick found me that apartment in Austin, vacated for the summer by that girl whose name I still don't know. Richard Kirschner, M. Kay Gartrell, and Daniel Rinella hosted me on my Virginia research trip. Lucy Wood was hospitable in Austin, as was Sarah Page Hammond in Nashville. Victoria A-T. Sancho lent me a computer at a crucial time. I thank Erica Freed for typing two chapters, and I thank Larisa Heimert, Susan Laity, Keith Condon, Dan Heaton, and the staff of Yale University Press.

I'm fortunate that my teachers are friends and my friends are teachers: Jamie Mercier; John Ratté, forever the headmaster; Jane Archibald, Curt Robison, and James Rugen at the Loomis Chaffee School; and Jon Butler, Paula Hyman, J. D. McClatchy, Robert Stone, Harry S. Stout, and Nicholas Wolterstorff at Yale. I extend gratitude to Willard Spiegelman.

Betsy Lerner helped. Bernie Davidow taught me a lot during my short stint at the *Hartford Courant*. Others who gave me time or ideas are Lila Corwin, Michael Alexander (whose book *Jazz Age Jews* was an inspiration), Joseph Kip Kosek, Rebecca Davis, Eric Gregory, Noam Pianko, and, especially, Lauren Winner. The members of the Gerber Colloquium in Religious Studies asked good questions. I learned from discussions with Esther Choo, Emmanuelle Depayre, Cyd Fremmer, Jonathan Pitt, Adam Ondricek, Andrew Slap, and Gerardo Vildostegui. I also thank Seth Lobis, Douglas McKay, and Derek Slap. Anne Bruder, of course.

I would like to thank in advance any readers who write to correct the factual errors that I am sure linger in the text. My e-mail is oppenheimer@aya.yale.edu, and paper mail may be sent to the publisher.

I did not earn my family, but I hope I deserve them: Walter Kirschner, Joanne and Thomas J. Oppenheimer, Daniel J. Oppenheimer, Jonathan Oppenheimer, and Rachel Anna Oppenheimer. If you disagree with anything in this book, I know you'll tell me at the dinner table. Home is something you somehow haven't to deserve.

Knocking on Heaven's Door

INTRODUCTION

American society in the late 1960s to the mid-1970s, the Nixon years, looked wild and unwieldy. Photographs, movies, music, and newspaper headlines show the United States in the birthing pains of a new cultural model, more liberal than any that had gone before. The new liberalism was keyed less to liberal politics than to more liberal assumptions about etiquette, clothes, language, music, and sexual mores. This book is about how countercultural movements, arising from this new liberalism, affected American religion.

Because writers and historians are attracted to extremes, the story typically told about Nixon-era religion focuses on cults, sects, Eastern religion, meditation, Moonies, Scientologists, communes. That way of thinking about American religion in the sixties corresponds to an equally simplistic way of thinking about sixties America at large: as a country of acid trips, antiwar protests, and tie-dyed T-shirts. But we must pull back from the extremes, to wash away the accumulated silt of our historical imagination—protests in Chicago! Dylan goes electric! the Beatles go mystical!—to understand that American culture, and in particular American religion, is the story not of the most exotic characters but of unknown characters living in exotic times.

Various countercultures, like feminism, gay rights, and pacifism, changed the ways in which Americans worshiped God. But the most important changes came in old, traditional denominations, not in sects, cults, communes, or movements from the East. Most new religious movements had few adherents and shrank quickly or even disappeared. Few adherents of the new religions were still devoted, regular practitioners a decade or two later. Rather, the vast majority of Americans who practiced a religion continued to do so within the organizational structures of the Roman Catholic Church, Judaism, or long-established branches of Protestantism. Even as believers were affected by American countercultures, even if they were reading *Ms.* magazine or smoking pot for the first time (two things most Americans never did), they remained Methodists or Lutherans, Catholics or Jews. The counterculture changed American religion through its insinuations into traditional denominations— complex groups that yield less-gripping photographs but deeper, more interesting stories.

To revise our understanding of American religion in the sixties, we must first understand that a coherent 1960s never existed.[1] Let's try a brief thought experiment. What movements made the sixties what it was? Your list will probably include civil rights, feminism, free speech, hippies and drug culture, and opposition to the Vietnam War, and maybe gay rights and sexual liberation, too. But wait. Martin Luther King's ascent occurred between the Montgomery bus boycott in 1955 and 1956 and the March on Washington for Jobs and

Freedom in 1963, after which his movement began to falter slightly; the heyday of the hippies was from 1965 to 1969, and the hippie was rumored to be passé in 1967, when a mock "Hippie Funeral" was held in San Francisco; *Ms.*, the landmark feminist magazine, began publishing only in 1972, three years after the Stonewall riots, which helped launch the gay liberation movement; the free speech movement at the University of California at Berkeley was in 1964; and the height of antiwar activism was from 1967 (the year of the first "mobilization" at the Pentagon) to 1970 (when four protesting students were killed by National Guardsmen at Kent State University in Ohio—and two more students, largely forgotten, were killed ten days later at Jackson State College in Mississippi). Abortion was decriminalized in 1973. In other words, a college senior who marched with King in Montgomery would have been forty years old by the time she began canvassing for support for the Equal Rights Amendment.

Meanwhile, according to polls, in 1968 Richard Nixon and George Wallace received more votes for president combined among twenty-one- to twenty-nine-year-olds, a presumably liberal sector of society, than did the Democrat Hubert Humphrey. In 1970 a national poll of college students found that only 11 percent of them described themselves as "radical or far left"—a substantial but not overwhelming number. Polls showed that the young disproportionately supported the Vietnam War. As late as 1967, only 5 percent of Americans had ever tried marijuana, and in 1964 a majority of American brides still said they were virgins until their wedding nights.[2]

So "the sixties" is not a very coherent concept. It lasted from 1955 to 1975, and it never turned a majority of any age group into leftists or libertines. In 1976 the Georgia moderate and Southern Baptist Jimmy Carter was elected president (with the help of many evangelical voters), after which the conservative Ronald Reagan, who as governor of California had attacked hippies and student activists, served two terms as president. Although some of President Lyndon

B. Johnson's Great Society survived, Americans in the 1980s became suspicious of the welfare state, and they began dismantling it in the 1990s. Americans became more tolerant of homosexuality, premarital sex, interracial relationships, and drug use—those would seem to be liberal positions. But in other ways, Americans became more conservative: less supportive of the United Nations, less trustful of government, less tolerant of high taxes.

The 1960s is thus a complex phenomenon, not easily reduced to political or social trends. On the other hand, it would be too easy to say that the 1960s—what we think of as *the sixties*—didn't exist. *Something* happened, whatever the exact dates. That something has to do with etiquette, clothes, language, music, and sexual mores. The country loosened up. If you look at the cover of an early Rolling Stones album like *The Rolling Stones,* you see that even the bad boys of rock wore suits and ties in 1964. The Beatles, even with their messy hair, also performed in suits when they landed in America that year. By the time they disbanded in 1970, they wore unkempt, fringed hippiewear. President John F. Kennedy carried himself coolly and regally; Richard M. Nixon, nobody's idea of a fun guy, appeared buffoonishly on *Laugh-In* in 1968. Martin Luther King and Malcolm X, ideologically so far apart, dressed with identical conservatism. But Black Panthers Huey Newton and Bobby Seale, emblems of the later 1960s, wore black leather jackets. In 1960 women still wore gloves on formal occasions, but by 1970 they did not. In 1960 Americans across the religious continuum, from conservative Southern Baptists to liberal Unitarians, wore suits or dresses to church; in 1970 it was acceptable in both denominations to wear khakis or blue jeans. By 1970 fewer people dressed for dinner. They were more likely to swear. Their ears had become used to, or at least resigned to, loud rock and roll music. Bank tellers and telephone solicitors switched from the formal "Mr." or "Mrs." to the informal use of customers' first names. People unbuttoned.

It is not clear why American culture was so malleable in the

1960s and 1970s. There have always been countercultures, but few so brazen or successful. The computer scientist and art critic David Gelernter has suggested that the intelligentsia of any society is countercultural but that only in the 1960s was the intelligentsia ceded so much power. Writing about Picasso's bohemian circle, the *Partisan Review* crowd of 1930s New York, and the Paris intellectual scene of Sartre, Genet, Beckett, and Beauvoir, Gelernter says that none of these groups much approved of organized religion, the military, constraints on sexual behavior, traditional sex roles, formality, or fancy dress—authority in general. "But illegitimacy didn't zoom up in 1905 Paris. No legal assault on public displays of religion took place in 1930s America. Nor did divorce rates explode or sexual restraints crack wide open or vulgarity become normal in popular culture; none of these things happened *until the intelligentsia took over*. And *then* they happened."[3] Gelernter explains, with some disgust, that in the 1960s the intelligentsia, by which he seems to mean bohemia, took over the university faculties for the first time. Institutions that had always been guardians of culture and conservators of tradition became scythes of rebellion, cutting down what had come before. There is some truth to what Gelernter says.

Others blame the Vietnam War: "No legacy of the 1960s had as long and embittering effect on the politics and culture of the United States as that left by the war in Vietnam," two liberal historians write. This explanation seems lacking. Did Vietnam turn people to the political left? The right? It is hard to say. Did people dress differently because of the war? It is hard to see how or why; the hippies began dressing wildly well before the war seized the country's consciousness. Did people listen to different music because of Vietnam? The folk revival began in the late 1950s, and *Bob Dylan* was released in 1962. The Grateful Dead antedated most Vietnam protest. Was Vietnam responsible for Betty Friedan's *The Feminine Mystique*, the founding document of contemporary feminism, published in 1963? Vietnam clearly had nothing to do with the important currents in visual arts; the era's most important dissident work, from Robert Frank's bitter antiracist photographs in *Les Américains* (1958, published in the United States in 1959) to Jasper Johns's flag series (begun in 1954) to the pop art of Ed Ruscha and Andy Warhol, was all completed before the assassination of President Kennedy.[4] The war's escalation surely drew more people to the counterculture, but the counterculture's iconography was already in place.

Whatever the reason, around 1968 the stylistic changes of the counterculture became apparent. Even if one looks at a photo of Ken Kesey and his Merry Pranksters in 1965, they still appear within the bounds of polite society. Their clothes are a bit outlandish, their hair unkempt, but it is not clear that any extraordinary shift in the American culture has occurred. But sometime between the Summer of Love in 1967 and the Woodstock festival in 1969, or between the death of King and the deaths at Kent State, even the conservatives began to dress down, talk more informally, and listen to different music. Those changes made it apparent that there was a counterculture afoot, bound to influence even the most staid religious denominations. And by the mid-1970s, the counterculture had become the culture.

The most effective countercultures have aspects beside the political.[5] In republics, there are always political dissenters. There is always a loyal opposition in Parliament, always pacifism during a war. But except under repressive regimes, political dissent can exist without challenging the culture. A real counterculture, then, will have elements other than the political. Leninists dressed differently from czarists and called each other by unusual names ("Comrade"). Supporters of Castro grew beards. What happened from 1968 to 1975 was less a political shift than a visible assertion of counterculture aesthetics.

In focusing on specifics like Jews' obsession with black men's Afros, Southern Baptists' fears of *Playboy* magazine, and how Simon and Garfunkel functioned in the Roman Catholic mass, we will only occasionally touch down on such grand themes as the meaning of *religion* or the definition of *counterculture*. Along the way we will meet the first openly gay minister in a mainline Protestant denomination, the all-time worst Christian feminist poet, and the famous evangelist to the hippies of Sunset Strip. We will briefly glimpse notables like the novelists Ken Kesey and Philip Roth, and we will learn about thousands who, influenced by them, wrought important changes in the way Americans practice religion: taking communion from female priests, for example, or praying not in a synagogue but in a crowded living room with the baby crying.

Because religion in the United States must make its own way, freed of government supports and government prohibitions, free to rise or fall by its own lights and strengths, it is more changeful than religion in, say, Sweden or England. The Lutheran Church in Sweden is not much affected by rebellious youth culture or the fall of foreign governments; the Church of England is anemic whether the radio is playing the Beatles or Oasis. But American religions must constantly sell themselves, and the ones that last are the ones that discover ways to exert imaginative sway. Cults and sects can be brief flashes, the brainchildren of charismatic leaders with unusual and provocative ideas; in order to make the transition to durable religion, however, a group must take account of the culture (and any prominent counterculture) at large. Looking at Nixon-era religion not through cults and sects, but rather through the counterculture's manifestations in mainline denominations, should point the way toward a new kind of church history: one that understands how the counterculture functioned not on the fringes of society—on communes and around gurus—but in the traditional denominations that must interact with America, or die.

And these groups were, after all, the ones that defined religion in America. Even if Will Herberg's book *Protestant, Catholic, Jew* had never crystallized for us the idea that all Americans belonged to one of those three traditions, we would have made the assumption any-way.[6] Protestants crafted our government and presided over its political, business, and cultural institutions. In the nineteenth century, sizable numbers of Jews arrived and prospered. There was anti-Semitism, including a violent wave in the 1930s, but persecution of Jews in the United States ebbed in the 1950s and 1960s. Gentile critics celebrated Jews' successes in art and literature. Jews like Abraham Ribicoff of Connecticut won elections in states with small Jewish populations. (Ribicoff was most famous as a senator from 1962 to 1980, but as early as 1954 he had defeated the patrician John Davis Lodge for governor.) Catholics, who in the nineteenth and early twentieth centuries had become the majority in some cities, also moved from urban ghettos to the suburbs. They achieved educational parity with Protestants. In 1960 they helped elect a Catholic president.

As Catholics and Jews achieved greater success in the United States, they identified more, not less, with their religions. Sixty-one percent of Americans polled in 1955 said that they belonged to a religious congregation. Church membership grew faster than the population at large in the 1950s, from 57 percent of the population to 63 percent.[7] Jews, Protestants, and Catholics in the postwar years were proudly and devotedly religious, more than before or since. In numbers, anyway, American religion was thriving.

In a country where Mormonism and Christian Science began, and which had seen small vogues for séances, Rosicrucianism, and Buddhism, we would still expect some underground religious experimentation. In the 1950s and early 1960s, Alan Watts's books on Buddhism sold well, as did *Vedanta and the West*, a 1945 collection of essays about Hinduism edited by the English writer Christopher Isherwood, with contributions from Watts, Aldous Huxley, Jawaharlal Nehru, and the Indian poet Rabindranath Tagore.[8] Watts had the imprimatur of drug enthusiasts Timothy Leary and Richard Alpert (soon to be guru Baba Ram Dass), who wrote the preface to the 1962 book *The Joyous Cosmology*, in which Watts argues that drugs could induce many of religious mysticism's effects.[9] The Japanese Zen Buddhist D. T. Suzuki lectured to large campus audiences in the early 1950s, and some students found parallels (unintended by Suzuki) with the popular existentialism of Albert Camus and Jean-Paul Sartre.[10] Beat writers like Jack Kerouac dabbled in Zen and then rewrote it for a popular audience.

There is a perception that, because of competition from alternative religion, traditional denominations drastically hemorrhaged members from the 1960s onward. The 1960s did begin a period of major decline for liberal Protestantism, a decline that sharpened into a precipitous fall by the end of the century. From 1990 to 2000, the United Church of Christ and the liberal branch of Presbyterianism, for example, each lost more than 10 percent of their members. But many American religions survived the 1960s and 1970s with their membership rolls intact or even swelling. Conservative churches, of course: the Church of Jesus Christ of Latter-day Saints (the Mormons) continued to grow, as did Pentecostal groups like the Assemblies of God. From 1963 to 1976 the Southern Baptist Convention grew by 2.5 million members.

Some liberal and moderate churches grew, too. In 1963 there were 992 Unitarian churches in the United States, with 147,000 members; there were 23,000 Roman Catholic parishes comprising 43 million members; and there were 7,155 Episcopal churches with 3.3 million members. All those membership figures went up in 1965, and again in 1967, and again in 1968. By 1976 Unitarians had grown 30 percent since 1963, and Catholics 15 percent, although the Episcopalians had begun their slide. In other words, while most mainline traditions were losing members, conservative churches were growing, as was the very liberal Unitarian church and (helped along by immigration) the Catholic Church, conservative in some ways but quite liberal in others.[11] The general picture of mainline religious decline is fair but not complete. The nuances matter.

For example, church attendance across denominations has been steady throughout the century. When asked in a Gallup poll, "Did you, yourself, happen to attend church or synagogue in the last seven days, or not?" about 40 percent said yes in 1939, 1975, and 1998. There was a spike to 49 percent in 1958—but that was an unusual peak, rather than the norm.[12]

Decline is a slippery concept. Since the middle of the century, liberal Protestants and Jews have had the lowest birth rates, fewer than two children per couple, while conservative Protestants have had the highest birth rate of any white group. In other words, if Congregationalists and Southern Baptists both had zero attrition, the former would still eventually disappear while the latter would keep growing.[13] And it's more complicated still. *Membership* means different things in different religions. For Catholics the numbers refer to how many people have been assigned to parish rolls by the church hierarchy. For Unitarians membership means joining a local church or society, which then reports its numbers to headquarters in Boston. Jews like figures that reflect national censuses rather than synagogue membership lists—they usually want to know how many Jews there are, not just how many Jews are praying on the Sabbath.

So it is helpful to look at other gauges of vitality. Some Jews are converts, and a majority of Unitarians are not cradle Unitarians. The same is true of Quakers. Do these high rates of conversion strengthen the religions? And when we look at Catholics, we need to note the decline in vocations to the priesthood and the angry fights over the Mass; it would be too simple just to say that membership kept rising and so all was well. For Episcopalians the story was even bleaker than the declining attendance would suggest. In the late 1960s confirmations, infant baptisms, and adult baptisms all dropped precipitously; church school enrollment fell by a quarter from 1965 to 1971.[14]

These endlessly complicated numbers and considerations don't mean that understanding American religion is hopeless; rather, they mean that numbers cannot tell the whole story. The extraordinary work done by sociologists and pollsters in the past fifty years is indispensable, but it is not definitive.[15]

Because the Nixon years are seen as an incubator for alternative religion, we should defend in some depth our focus on denominational religion. The vast majority of Americans have continued, throughout this century, to lead religious lives circumscribed by denominations. Even though the baby boomers are seen as compulsive church-hoppers, they are usually hopping from one denominational church to another—from a Methodist church to a Baptist, for example. Yes, there are many unaffiliated congregations in this country, from evangelical Bible churches to Jewish havurot, or small worship groups. But they are the small minority, as they were throughout the 1950s, 1960s, and 1970s.

The alternative groups we identify with the late 1960s were far smaller than imagined, and some historians, easily infatuated with the new and the sexy, have been led badly astray. One great scholar of Baptism wrote a book in the late 1970s in which he indicated that there were substantial numbers of Hell's Angels, Satanists, and witches at large in America. But in fact there were at times only several hundred Hell's Angels, and there has never been reliable evidence of widespread Satanism or paganism. Like so many others, this scholar was gulled by Carlos Castañeda's Yaqui books, works of crank "anthropology" in which Castañeda describes his supernatural experiences while using peyote under the tutelage of a Mexican shaman. (At one point, he says, he literally turned into a crow.)

"In this Fourth Great Awakening, as in all awakenings," the historian writes, "the line between science and magic, the real and the unreal, has temporarily disappeared. People are ready to believe almost anything.... Was astrology a science or a religion? Did Rosicrucians know secrets of the universe that scientists did not know? Is Uri Geller [who said he could bend spoons with his brain waves] a mountebank, or does he have extraordinary powers? Were 'space probes' any more scientific than the search for Noah's Ark? Americans read avidly about the magic regions of Tolkien's Hobbits and just as avidly read reports of the Army's interests in UFOs. Interest in spiritualism, astrology, and Ouija boards flourished in the 1960s. . . . The search for another order of reality in these 'outlandish' activities marked the failure of the ordinary religious institutions to provide satisfactory answers about the mysterious, the unknown, the unexplainable, and of course it also marked the failure of science to do so."[16]

Given the spurious reasoning—science was explaining *more* in the 1950s and 1960s than ever before, and Americans appeared quite committed to their churches—we should not be surprised by the faulty conclusions. Despite Uri Geller's popular television appearances and college students' interest in J. R. R. Tolkien's *Lord of the Rings,* it is not true that Americans were "ready to believe almost anything." At least, no truer than usual, and certainly not true of the Americans who joined the Southern Baptist Convention and the Roman Catholic Church in increasing numbers. We should note, too, a powerful class bias: dabblers in Rosicrucianism, when they existed, were found on liberal college campuses; but most Americans either do not go to college, or they go to state schools with more conservative cultures. The University of Alabama and Ole Miss were probably not centers of "spiritualism, astrology, and Ouija boards."

Had droves of Americans been hitching rides on the paisley bus of religious experimentation, those experimental religions would have swollen to great size. But they never did. Perhaps Transcendental Meditation (TM) and Silva Mind Control "together . . . involved over a million persons"—but only if you believe their publicity materials. If you believed Yogi Bhajan, his Healthy-Happy-Holy Organization, which received much press coverage in the early 1970s, had "several thousand committed members"—which means that, depending on one's definition of "committed," in reality it may have had several hundred.[17]

According to more disinterested research, few Americans joined experimental religious groups. In a longitudinal study of undergraduates at the University of California at Berkeley from 1970 to 1974, sociologists found that only 2 percent of Jewish students entered college with "Eastern/mystical" beliefs, and by junior year only 4 percent had them. Of Protestant and Catholic juniors, only 3 percent had Eastern/mystical beliefs. These were typical students at one of the most liberal campuses in the country—92 percent of the Jewish juniors had used drugs, as had 75 percent of their Gentile classmates—but there was almost no measurable religious experimentation.[18]

A one thousand–person survey conducted in 1973 in California's Bay Area—again, this is the time and place we would most expect to find experimental religion—asked whether respondents knew "a lot," "a little," or "nothing" about Hare Krishna, Zen, Yoga, Scientology, est, Jews for Jesus, and Transcendental Meditation. Only 1 percent said they knew a lot about Hare Krishna; 61 percent knew nothing. Three percent knew a lot about Zen Buddhism, 27 percent knew a little, and 70 percent knew nothing. Almost 8 percent, the highest number, had participated in yoga, 5.3 percent in TM, and 2.6 percent in Zen. In other words, in a famously liberal, iconoclastic city, a random sampling of the population revealed low, even minuscule, levels of familiarity with prominent alternative religions.[19]

Like hippie culture, alternative religion had influence beyond its numbers, of course. In the age of radical chic, to use Tom Wolfe's famous term, uptight establishmentarians were proving their hipness, looking for chances to take a walk on the wild side. Ministers of staid Protestant denominations went on retreats that used "encounter sessions" drawn from "transactional analysis" of the "human potential movement" to put them in touch with their ids. In 1971 the General Assembly of the United Presbyterian Church voted to donate $10,000 to the legal defense fund of Angela Davis, the Black Power avatar and communist charged with murder, kidnapping, and criminal conspiracy. Preachers adopted black and hippie lingo when proselytizing on the wrong side of the tracks. "After Jesus busted outa the grave he met two of his gang on the road," reads a paraphrase of the Emmaus story used by a New York prison chaplain. "Man! Were they ever spooked and surprised. They ran like crazy to the place where the other guys were. And started to tell who they seen. Before they could say much, bingo! Jesus was there. . . ."[20]

But if traditional Christians were influenced by the cults and sects, the false prophets and pyramid schemes, and the cool cat aesthetics of the time, then we should look for that influence in the church on the town green, or in the suburban synagogue. We should study traditional religions, because they remained the spiritual homes for most Americans. Christians and Jews may have experimented, but mainline churches and synagogues were the laboratories.

One might argue that by excluding the preponderance of cults, sects, and communes from this study, we are denying them the status of "religion." That is correct—but for the purpose of clarity, not condescension.

Unfortunately, what Ludwig Wittgenstein famously wrote about the word *game* applies to religion, too: any description will be too narrow. If we describe a game as a competition, we exclude solitaire; if we describe a game as a relaxing activity, we exclude polo or big-game hunting; and so forth.[21] Similarly, if we describe religion as a set of rituals, we exclude solitary prayer or contemplation, which William James thought was the essence of religion itself. If we describe religion as appeal to the supernatural, we exclude many Unitarians and Confucians. The Christian theologian Stanley Hauerwas once said that when he says Christianity is true, what he means is that he will die for it; in other words, his religion is defined by a certain level of commitment. But that definition would exclude the vast majority of American Methodists, Congregationalists, Lutherans, and Reform Jews, very few of whom would choose death before conversion.

For our purposes, then, we shall aim at comprehensiveness by defining religion in both a positive and a negative sense. Positively, religion is commitment to a set of beliefs that requires meaningful sacrifice. A belief that you must tithe, or donate of a portion of your income to your church or faith community, is religious. It is religious to believe that you must sacrifice your first-born child to the gods; the townsfolk who stone their neighbor to death to increase the harvest yield in Shirley Jackson's short story "The Lottery" are acting religiously (even if the victim doesn't consent to being their sacrifice). The belief that you must pray three times a day is a religious belief.

But we shall also adhere to a formula of what practices are *not* religious. To get to that formula, we first note that in the United States, religion is aggressively social: people "belong" to a particular congregation, synagogue, or mosque. This is unusual for Muslim immigrants, to take one example; in the old country, they would stop by whatever mosque was closest for prayers, but here they have adopted the American model of joining, "belonging to," a certain mosque—paying membership dues, being on a mailing list, serving on committees. What this joining or belonging means is that while many people pass through periods of religious seeking, often shopping at different churches, they finally settle into membership at one. For Catholics, this membership is determined by parish boundaries; for Jews, membership is often determined by the existence of only one synagogue in the area. But even for Protestants, it is highly unusual to belong to more than one church, or to bring one's children to a different Sunday school each week. Thus our negative definition of religion: we know that an American has picked a religion when we see that she does not have two religions. Or, to put it another way, religion excludes its competitors.

We can see this idea best by looking at the messianic Judaism movement, or Jews for Jesus, as some members are known. They are usually Jewish by birth, but have accepted Jesus Christ as their lord and savior. They say that they're Jewish *and* Christian. They still observe Jewish dietary laws, for example, and celebrate Jewish holidays. Now in a sense, all Christians (and Muslims) are Jews. They all accept the Hebrew Bible, or Old Testament, as divine. But in the United States, Jewish converts to Christianity who say that they are still Jews do not really strike us as Jews. This is true even though, theologically, their Christian community regards them as Jewish, as does their Jewish community, which considers anyone with a Jewish mother Jewish. For most of us, to look at them worshiping Jesus is to figure that they are no longer Jews. It is not that we know a Jew when we see one; rather, we know that they are not Jews when we see them being Christian.

It helps to remember that the term *religion* implies what Wittgenstein called a "family resemblance"—*Familienähnlichkeiten* was his word. In my family, we all look alike, but no one attribute defines Oppenheimerness. We don't all have brown eyes, though most of us do; we don't all have small feet, though five of the six of us do. But if you saw us together, you could tell we were related. Religions, too, share attributes—they look alike—but no one attribute is the essence of a religion. So one of the only things we can say for sure about a Jew is that he is not a Christian. One thing we can say for certain about a Presbyterian is that she's not a Methodist or a Baptist.

Combining both our positive and negative definitions of religion, then, we may say that a religion is a sacrificial system whose adherents do not ascribe to another religion.

This definition of religion could have some funny implications, especially in post-1960s America. Fans of the late-sixties television show *Star Trek* are often so devoted to its legacy that they spend their nights and weekends watching reruns, collecting and cataloguing memorabilia, quarreling in Internet chat rooms over the correct interpretation of an episode, and attending conventions where they meet other Trekkers or Trekkies (there is some disagreement over which name is preferred). *Star Trek* is the totalizing fact of their lives. It requires quite real sacrifices. Now: how many of these people are also devoted members of the local Presbyterian church? Very, very few, it would seem. Just as very few true Deadheads, who spent their summers following the Grateful Dead on tour around the country, were also Orthodox Jews. Again: religions require sacrifice *and* exclude other religions.

We should not run from this definition. Perhaps Deadheads and Trekkers do have religions of their own. Anyone who has met a committed Trekker has no trouble believing this. What's more, defining religion this way allows us to include Unitarians and Episcopalians, Jews and Catholics, in the same study. Catholicism comes from baptism, Judaism from descent, and Unitarianism from ascription to certain humanistic principles—but they are all religions, all memberships people have in one community instead of another. And the more devoted people are to a religion in America, the more apparent it is that they belong to that religion alone.

This definition has particular ramifications for any discussion of the counterculture, because it excludes all the religions in the 1960s and 1970s that served as accoutrements, add-ons to improve quality of life without asking for real membership. It excludes most "New Age" religion like Gestalt therapy, primal-scream therapy, and some types of Buddhist meditation. It excludes people who practiced syncretism or hodgepodge. It excludes, for example, the famous leftist activist Jerry Rubin, who said, "In five years, from 1971 to 1975, I directly experienced est, Gestalt therapy, bioenergetics, rolfing, massage, jogging, health foods, tai chi, Esalen, hypnotism, modern dance, meditation, Silva Mind Control, Arica, acupuncture, sex therapy, Reichian therapy, and More House."[22] Rubin wasn't religious; he just had a lot of free time. Our definition implies membership, not just dabbling or curiosity. There was a lot of seeking going on in the Nixon years, and no doubt it proved meaningful and positive for thousands of people. But not all seeking was religious seeking. Some of it was therapeutic, or spiritual—but that is not our topic here.

The kind of particularist, exclusionary membership that we are discussing is, in a pluralist country that requires no membership at all, an important family resemblance. Jews may not be Unitarians, just as Catholics are never Baptists, but they all have something in common. At a time when tradition was suspect, people who chose to stay within their church or synagogue communities were making affirmative commitments to historical faiths and families. A rabbi and a priest meeting on the street in 1970 would have had a lot to talk about. They would have felt similarly besieged and misunderstood. They would have wondered whether any of the children would still be stopping by ten years later. There is good reason, then, to study Jews, Catholics, and Protestants side by side.

In a country that has birthed hundreds of new religions to join the hundreds it has imported, we must narrow the field of study. In this book, Unitarians, Southern Baptists, Jews, Roman Catholics, and Episcopalians, just five groups, are asked to stand in for "American religion" as a whole. There is good reason to choose these five. They are similar enough to offer useful points of comparison. Each has a national presence. None is young. All five are well established— three are Protestant churches of early-modern Europe, while Judaism and Catholicism are far older. And yet they are different enough to permit meaningful insights. Jewish and Baptist congregations choose their own pastors, while Catholic bishops assign priests to parishes. Catholics and Episcopalians have a history of lay religious orders, while Jews and Unitarians do not. And so forth. These are five traditions, all mainstream enough to seem "normal"— adherents can run for office without having to explain their religion, as a Scientologist might have to—yet all quite different, each with worship services, theologies, and histories that could not be mistaken for those of any of the others.

Really, though, the stories chose themselves. A vocally gay Unitarian minister, the first in any Protestant denomination. A small group of women asking that their call to the Episcopal priesthood be heard—and being mocked by the sworn opponents of "priestesses." Antiwar protesters in a church, the Southern Baptist Convention, that saw peaceniks as hippies, hippies as the end of the world. The disappearance of the Latin Mass, leaving mournful Catholics to be comforted by guitars and tambourines. Jews, many from middle-class families and with Ivy League degrees, identifying themselves as the new niggers, growing their hair into "Jew-fros" and blaming their synagogue rabbis for being assimilationist Uncle Toms—or "Uncle Jakes," as they called them. In their tensions between a conservative nation and its loud, countercultural minority, these stories tell stories much bigger than themselves.

If *religion* is a slippery word, then *counterculture* is even more vexatious. People use it to congratulate themselves. As the Italian novelist and semiotician Umberto Eco writes, "Counter-culture is an overused term which, like Resistance, is invariably mentioned so as to reflect well on the person using it. Nobody is against the Resistance, and nobody nowadays would dare suggest that there was anything negative about counter-culture."[23] Eco's not entirely right; not everybody favors the counterculture. But he is right that *counterculture* is generally used to make the speaker look humane and progressive. As such, the term is maddeningly vague.

So Eco bravely endeavors to clarify the word:

> Counter-culture is thus the active critique or transformation of the existing social, scientific or aesthetic paradigm. *It is religious reform.* It is the heresy of whoever confers a licence upon himself and prefigures another church. It is the only cultural manifestation that a dominant culture is unable to acknowledge and accept. . . . Counter-culture comes about when those who transform the culture in which they live become critically conscious of what they are doing and elaborate a theory of their deviation from the dominant model, *offering a model that is capable of sustaining itself.*[24]

In other words, counterculture, entirely typical of political or religious reform, of Marx or Luther, is threatening because it is self-sustaining. The Marxist is more threatening than the draft dodger not because he's more violent (he may not be) or because he's more sincere (he may not be) but because he has an alternative model that can entirely replace capitalist democracy.[25]

This definition of counterculture, as offering a self-sustaining alternative model of culture, means that counterculture need not be liberal, or even particularly scholarly. It means that Barry Goldwater was more countercultural than John F. Kennedy, Timothy Leary more than Peter, Paul and Mary.[26] Václav Havel was countercultural. Dissidents are countercultural. So are members of the Resistance. This kind of counterculture, embodying a self-sustaining critique, will be threatening.[27]

Just as Eco predicts in his essay, counterculturalists provoke schism. Most Episcopalians did not abandon their church after it ordained women, but some did, and they joined splinter churches like the Anglican Church of America and the Anglican Episcopal Church. The Second Vatican Council produced small schismatic Catholic churches. The Cooperative Baptist Fellowship was founded in 1991 in opposition to the uniform conservatism of the Southern Baptist Convention. Some Unitarian churches, upset by the liberalizations of the 1960s and 1970s, specifically identify as Unitarian Christian churches now.

There are parallels in secular culture. Bob Dylan's decision to "go electric" at the 1965 Newport Folk Festival was countercultural in the folk music community, which prized acoustic, nondistorted guitar. It provoked schism, it ended friendships. Electric guitar was a self-sustaining critique of folk music; it provided an alternative model, which has thrived indifferent to the old ways. Campaign finance reform is not counterculture—it is reform. Communism, on the other hand, is countercultural in a democratic capitalist country; it questions the very assumption of the free market and offers a self-sustaining alternative.

All five religious groups survived the countercultural challenges without major schism, however, which means either that the reformers were indeed not counterculturalists; that the religions adopted the counterculturalists' model; or that the counterculturalists lost. Gay Unitarians, for example, defied the sexual norms of modern Western civilization, but their religion deferred to them, while peace activists in the Southern Baptist Convention were straight-laced, clean-cut, and clean-shaven—and were quickly forgotten. Is it possible that even their mild dissent appeared, in a denomination that had come to prize uniformity, counterculturalism of the most threatening kind? Was it more dangerous to threaten Southern Baptists with pacifism than to threaten Unitarians with homosexuality?

If so, then the Southern Baptists' fears, which surfaced in all religious groups facing internal dissent, were based partly on images in the media and popular culture. What made countercultural activists so threatening was not their political liberalism. Jimmy Carter was to the left of center politically, as Lyndon Johnson had been. Both had received many Southern Baptist votes. But they were not countercultural. Carter and Johnson supported the culture. So, in fact, did Martin Luther King Jr., whose doctorate in theology, natty clothes, and reliance on patriotic tropes ratified all the assumptions of American politics. But when Cassius Clay rejected two symbols of the United States—its European names and service in its military—Muhammad Ali became a counterculturalist.

American leftists were as diverse as conservatives, and some sought to redeem the American state rather than to undermine it. But conservatives' fear was generalized and did not make these fine distinctions. They saw on television not the Port Huron Statement (the founding document of the quite patriotic New Left) or the Black Panthers' platform (which was never so radical as the Panthers looked) but beads, beards, and bongs.

When Allen Ginsberg, Ken Kesey, and Ralph "Sonny" Barger Jr., the president of the Hell's Angels, met at Barger's house in Oakland,

Allen Ginsberg, Ivy League–educated homosexual Jewish Hindu poet, plays his finger cymbals at a Human Be-in in San Francisco, 1967. Photograph by Michelle Vignes.

California, in November 1965, it was perhaps the greatest countercultural summit ever. Ginsberg was the homosexual Jewish poet who had chanted his angry poem "Howl" on college campuses in the late 1950s and, in his late-1960s second vogue, would try to levitate the Pentagon and exorcise its warmongering demons.[28] Kesey was the precocious author of *One Flew over the Cuckoo's Nest* who had traveled the country in his Day-Glo-painted school bus with a gaggle of LSD users known as the Merry Pranksters, filming their shenanigans—nothing much lewder than skinny-dipping while on acid, unfortunately—and offending the locals everywhere. Tom Wolfe immortalized Kesey in his book *The Electric Kool-Aid Acid Test*. Barger presided over the nation's most notorious band of outlaw motorcyclists, apocryphally known for pillaging towns and raping women.[29]

The three men had much, and yet little, in common. Ginsberg was an influential and famous poet. He was also a Columbia-educated New Yorker and an operator who schmoozed with ACLU lawyers and Democratic politicians, in whose presence he sometimes burst into spontaneous chanting of mantras and chiming of his finger cymbals. Kesey was a Stanford-trained litteratus, married (though not faithfully) with children, who spent most of his time on his ranch in northern California. Barger and his Angels were not the lawless hooligans people thought they were, but they were something even unlikelier: working-class patriots who supported the war in Vietnam and were wary of racial integration. And all three were equally terrifying to the Babbitts of small-town America. All three did lots of drugs, had unconventional careers, and looked weird. It did not matter that Sonny Barger had telegrammed President Johnson to volunteer the Hell's Angels' services in the war: "We feel that a crack group of trained gorrillas [sic] would demoralize the Viet Cong and advance the cause of freedom. We are available for training and duty immediately."[30] He was still clearly a counterculturalist, as they all were. For they all lived their lives as affronts to the khaki-and-penny-loafer order of things. They lived as critiques of the dominant culture.

It had nothing to do with whom they supported for president or their views on the welfare state. Compare these two descriptions, one of the Hell's Angels and the other of the Youth International Party, the Yippies, who clashed with Chicago police outside the 1968 Democratic National Convention. Here's Hunter S. Thompson: "The Hell's Angels' massive publicity [in 1965]—coming on the heels of the widely publicized student rebellion in Berkeley—was interpreted in liberal-radical-intellectual circles as the signal for a natural alliance. Beyond that, the Angels' aggressive, anti-social stance—their *alienation,* as it were—had a tremendous appeal for the more aesthetic Berkeley temperament. Students who could barely get up the nerve to sign a petition or to shoplift a candy bar were fascinated by tales of the Hell's Angels ripping up towns and taking whatever they wanted. Most important, the Angels had a reputation for defying police, for successfully bucking authority, and to the frustrated student radical this was a powerful image indeed. The Angels didn't masturbate, they raped." And here's Jerry Rubin, a founder of the Yippies: "Our goal is to send niggers and longhair scum invading white middle class homes, fucking on the living room floor, crashing on the chandeliers, spewing sperm on the Jesus pictures, breaking the furniture, and smashing Sunday school napalm-blood Amerika forever."[31]

Now which of the two groups is conservative and which is liberal? The keen student of the late 1960s will note that Rubin refers to the United States as Amerika, with a *k,* which was a left-wing descriptor. But otherwise, there is nothing in the two descriptions to clue us in that the Hell's Angels comprised many military veterans and tended to support the war in Vietnam, while Rubin angrily opposed the war. Or that the Hell's Angels hated communism, while Rubin's followers admired Marx.

The Hell's Angels, Yippies, and hippies shared a *style,* even if they did not always know it. Allen Ginsberg wrote a poem to the Hell's Angels imploring them to see all that they had in common with the hippies: "If you dig POT why don't you dig that the whole generation who don't dig the heat war also dig pot and consciousness & spontaneity & hair & they are your natural brothers." Ginsberg presumes that if people shared predilections for pot, spontaneity, and long hair, then they were "natural brothers." The Angels, like the hippies and Yippies, opposed the culture not with published tracts but with clothes, music, dirty words, hair, and drugs. "There was no theology to it," Tom Wolfe wrote of Kesey and his Merry Pranksters, "no philosophy, at least not in the sense of an *ism.* There was no goal of an improved moral order in the world or an improved social order. . . . On the face of it there was just a group of people who shared an unusual psychological state, the LSD experience."[32]

An unusual psychological state—that's what the Merry Pranksters, the Hell's Angels, and the followers of Ginsberg had in common. They saw the rest of society as having a *usual* psychological state, one under the hegemony of the "technocracy." The average working stiff was a pawn of corporate society, or, worse, what President Eisenhower had called the military-industrial complex. He was Sloan Wilson's "man in the gray flannel suit" or William Whyte's "organization man," always concerned about others' opinion of him, with no moral compass of his own.[33]

In our five case studies, the religious activists shared a distrust of the usual; they refused to believe that what was usual was always correct. They always said they were honoring their religious traditions and the accumulated wisdom of the past, but they refused to be bound by precedent. Their opponents would answer back that one may not always pick and choose among traditions, that the wisdom of the ages is not so easily divisible.

The religious activists in mainline Protestant and Catholic churches and in Jewish synagogues were rarely identifiable as druggies, bikers, or violent street-theater anarchists. But in their rejection, or loosening, of the bounds of precedent and in their presentation of alternative, self-sustaining styles—informal folk music, a priesthood integrated by sex, outdoors Mass, praying in blue jeans, changing the words of traditional prayers—they took cultural permission from radical countercultural elements. When the English historian Arnold Toynbee called the hippies "a red warning light for the American way of life," he was expressing the same worry for American society that many Episcopalians and Catholics felt for their churches.[34]

Americans always think they are in decline; that is the Puritans' gift to us.[35] In the 1960s, the threat of decline, whether in church or in society, was embodied, yes, by political dissent, but moreover by styles, aesthetic or linguistic or musical, that challenged the usual.

As we proceed, we will consider theology and doctrine, but we must also consider that content is inseparable from form. Even if Episcopalian feminists said they were asking only for the right to be priests, in religion there is no such thing as *only*. Ask a low-church

Episcopalian whether the "only" difference between his church and the higher-church rival across town is the smell of incense. Or ask a Jew whether the "only" difference between his old synagogue and his new prayer group is that the latter meets in a fraternity's TV lounge. Nostalgic Catholics do not want "only" to hear the Mass in Latin. A break with a formal or aesthetic aspect of tradition can have stirring implications for faith and worship. A change that seems only superficial, a mere change of appearance, can inaugurate a new, changed relationship with God. The aesthetic counterculture, the counterculture of style, which might seem like window dressing, could be the most radical counterculture of all, akin to Christendom in Rome. And it could insinuate itself, cunningly.

How the religions either fought or acquiesced—that is what we aim to learn. I propose several broad answers.

First, these mainline religions matter in any discussion of the counterculture because they did, in fact, engage the counterculture. They remained vital loci of argument, attuned to the changes going on across the land. Sometimes their attention was suspicious in nature, as with many Southern Baptists. Or they could be willing converts to the countercultural vision, as with Unitarians and sexual liberation. But all of our case studies reveal a mainline religious world that lived the excitement of the counterculture, often more vitally than New Age movements did. Was it more interesting to be debating the ordination of Episcopal women or to be living in a Hare Krishna temple, with its rote schedule and constant visits to airports to proselytize? Mainline religion in the 1960s and 1970s was not only more important, because of its overwhelming superiority in numbers, than New Age or alternative religious movements, but it was involved in its own spirited changes, too. Mainline religion in the 1960s, whatever its falling membership totals, must be taken seriously. And old-style, denominational, church history is more important, and more fun, than might be supposed.

Second, what was countercultural in the mainline religions was often aesthetic, rather than political or theological. American religions underwent little theological or doctrinal change in the 1960s and 1970s. What changed was the form, not the content, of the religious traditions. Different music, clothing, and decor became permissible. Women earned the right to preach or lead services, and to participate in the planning of liturgy; for both the supporters and critics of such changes, the most important fact was how different the worship service now *looked* or *felt,* rather than any new ideas being taught.

Third, this aesthetic change could, in itself, be subversive. Even if it did not always involve new teaching, it could still create a new religious experience, an alternative, self-sustaining model. For example, liberal and conservative Catholics agree that changes in the appearance of the Mass, such as the priest's facing the pews, radically altered the laity's experience of Catholicism. Furthermore, hearing the Mass in the vernacular is wholly other than hearing it in Latin. God Himself seems different.

Finally, the case of American religion during this period allows us to make certain arguments about "the sixties" in general. It seems, for example, that the Vietnam War did not play as important a role in the counterculture as we have been led to believe. And, by contrast, that the civil rights movement played an even more important role than we've been led to believe. If the counterculture was mainly aesthetic, much of the aesthetic change was directly influenced by black style and rhetoric. Middle-class Episcopal women, Jewish college students, and gay Unitarians were just some of the activists who drew directly on tropes created by African Americans; their counterculture depended on the black example.

Religion is not the whole of the American experience, but its voice shouts loudly above the national din. The United States is the world's longest-lasting experiment in religious liberty under a democratic, religiously neutral government. We might expect American religion to be free and ever-changing. We might expect that in times of national rancor, religion would register the shocks and tremors. We would be right.

ONE

Unitarians and Gay Rights

The thirty-three-year-old Unitarian minister James Stoll did not "come out," if by that we mean a singular, dramatic event. He went on a coming-out tour. He first announced his homosexuality on September 5, 1969, to Student Religious Liberals, the association of college Unitarians, at their convention in Laforet, Colorado. The next spring, on May 10, 1970—Mother's Day—he gave a speech called "On Being a Homosexual" at Honolulu's First Unitarian Church, where Stoll knew the pastor, the Rev. Gene Bridges, from the antiwar movement. At about the same time, Stoll discussed his homosexuality at churches in Sepulveda and Burbank, California.[1]

The Rev. James Stoll was the first minister of any American religious denomination, and probably in the world, to publicly admit his homosexuality.[2] Stoll came out of the closet before the Stonewall riots, before AIDS, before scholars considered it important to "out" Walt Whitman or Noël Coward or Langston Hughes, before they tried to out Emily Dickinson. *Gay* could still be used to mean happy. The most important openly homosexual American was Allen Ginsberg, whom most Americans had not heard of. People did not suspect others, least of all ministers, of being homosexual.

Stoll was a minister of the Unitarian Universalist Association, and his act was the first to help make the Unitarians the most welcoming denomination for homosexuals. Unitarians were first to have an openly gay minister; first officially to condemn discrimination against homosexuals; and first to take official church stances on matters of especial importance to the gay and lesbian community. After Stoll's coming out, gay Unitarians soon organized into the first powerful gay religious organization. Stoll was a controversial man who promoted the decriminalization of marijuana (at a time when few did) and who had lost his last pulpit after making sexual advances toward pubescent boys; soon after coming out, Stoll vanished from the Unitarian scene. But the Unitarians embraced his vision of gay liberation, and when Stoll died twenty-five years later, he was, within his denomination, so ordinary as to be forgotten.[3]

Religions can be conservators of tradition, wary of change. But Unitarians have a tradition of change, a tradition of discarding tradition. With a long history of assimilating radical dissent, from atheism to pacifism to feminism, Unitarians look at counterculture favorably, or at least tolerantly. The Unitarians greeted an unusual challenge, homosexuality, with uncommon openness. We begin with the Unitarians not because they are typical, but because they provide a simple reminder: that religion, so often in step with American culture and mores, need not be.

Unitarians have a long history of dissent. In 1579 Fausto Sozzini wrote a tract, published in Rascow, Poland, promoting worship of Christ as a *man,* chosen by God but not part of the Godhead. Heretically, Sozzini denied the triune god. There were not, he said, the Father, the Son, and the Holy Ghost; there was a Father, to whom Jesus the Son was inferior. Sozzini's followers, the Socinians, worshiped in Poland until 1658, when the Polish legislature banned the sect. Rather than convert, many Socinians sought refuge in the Unitarian community of Transylvania, whose Unitarian king, John Sigismund, tolerated religious diversity.

So Unitarianism, from the beginning, attracted liberals for two reasons. First, it challenged an essential point of Roman Catholic doctrine that most Protestants dared not go near—more than any other sect, it put the *protest* in Protestant. Second, a challenge to the Trinity, which had always been one of the murkier points of Christian theology, difficult for even the devout to grasp, seemed like a forceful assertion of reason against pure dogma.

Unitarianism, stifled on the Continent, spread to England. In 1689 the Act of Toleration excluded English Unitarians from its protection (a rather pointed omission, in such a liberal season), but Unitarians found a home in the Dissenting churches. In 1719 the Dissenters split into two groups, the more liberal of which moved toward the old anti-Trinitarianism. Unitarianism thus existed in certain English precincts throughout the eighteenth century, and American divines read about it. In 1805 Henry Ware, who had found persuasive the writings of English Unitarians, was elected Hollis Professor of Divinity at Harvard. The controversy around his unorthodox beliefs divided the local religious community into two camps: the normal Trinitarian Congregationalists and the Unitarians.[4] Unitarianism spread, and in 1819 the Reverend William Ellery Channing preached the sermon "Unitarian Christianity," the famous "Baltimore Sermon," listing four defining features of American Unitarianism: first, that the Bible is subject to criticism, just as other books are; second, that the Trinity is a fiction; third, that Jesus was human, not part of the Godhead; and finally, that there is a god of "moral perfection," a god who is infinitely good and not wrathful.

Unitarianism in the early republic was a pointed rebuke both to Catholics, so invested in the Trinity, and to Protestants' Calvinist notions of original sin and predestination. It had just the right program to please liberals and humanists, and to offend everybody else. Early on, it showed its potential as a countercultural philosophy, for Ralph Waldo Emerson, Henry David Thoreau, Horace Mann, the abolitionist Senator Charles Sumner, the protofeminist Margaret Fuller, the asylum reformer Dorothea Dix, and the poet Julia Ward Howe all became Unitarians.[5]

By the middle of the twentieth century, fewer and fewer Unitarians would refer to themselves as Christians. The religion was becoming, like modern Quakerism, a religious sanctuary for people offended by strict dogma. Unitarian churches also became halfway houses for intermarried Jewish and Christian, or Protestant and Catholic, couples. In 1961 the Unitarians completed a merger with the Universalists, a small Christian denomination marked by the belief that all people would ultimately get to heaven. The ideals of the new Unitarian Universalist Association were said to be "summarized"—though not dictated—by "the Judeo-Christian heritage." In place of actual Christianity was a noble ideal of "love to man [and] brotherhood, justice and peace . . . in every land." The Unitarian Universalist first principle says nothing of God, but affirms, poetically, "the inherent worth and dignity of every person."[6]

By the 1960s many Unitarian societies (they had often forsaken the word *church*) were liberal enough to sponsor pagan celebrations of the winter solstice or to host Hanukkah celebrations. The Unitarian society in Schenectady, New York, offered an astrology discussion group. The few Unitarian Christians left were uninterested in the Bible and, like the Universalists, dismissive of the concept of sin. In 1972 one Unitarian scholar lamented this biblical illiteracy: "The lack of notable Unitarian Universalist Bible scholars in our time is perhaps a reflection of the widely-held liberal philosophy that the Bible has little in the way of unique inspiration that cannot be found in other literary productions," he wrote in the *Unitarian Universalist Christian* magazine. "There is a feeling that since it is no longer regarded as a divine oracle which can provide solutions to every problem, it need not preoccupy our attention."[7]

These Unitarians were not the first to drift away from the Bible's harbor: William Ellery Channing had focused on the teachings of Jesus but ignored most other Scripture; the non-Unitarian deist Thomas Jefferson had produced a bowdlerized version of the New Testament in which all signs of irrationality—miracles, for example—had been omitted; and Catholics, of course, have long placed more emphasis on church liturgy than on the words of Scripture. What was new about this repudiation of the Bible was that modern Unitarians could not agree on what would replace it. Most Unitarians were reluctant to accord special place to the teachings of Jesus, and no consensus had developed around, say, Kantian ethics or even the Ten Commandments. "The inherent worth and dignity of every person" is vague even by the vague standards of most religious dicta, and it would become clear that Unitarians had little basis on which to declare anything positively wrong, except for intolerance itself.

Discussions about the treatment of blacks, women, or homosexuals lacked the language of sin, and they would be argued according to Unitarians' intuitions.

Those intuitions were no longer theologically based, but they had some basis. Unitarian churches usually had the distinction of being the most liberal church in town. The only interracial couple might well attend the Unitarian church, as might some barely closeted gay bachelors. Even before it was okay to be gay, Unitarians were more likely to wink and not ask questions, just live and let live. A Unitarian preacher probably would not disdain you for having long hair. The draft resister would feel comfortable in a Unitarian church. In Sunday school, children could express doubt about God. Having been abolitionists and feminists when no one else was, Unitarians had a tradition of contorting tradition. Even if Unitarianism was not quite countercultural according to our definition—a self-sustaining alternative to regnant cultures—it was, in much of America, as close to counterculture as one could get.

Unitarians were not alone in discussing homosexuality in the Nixon years. While Unitarianism was a logical, perhaps inevitable, spawning ground for gay rights activism, John J. McNeill, a Jesuit and the leading Catholic gay activist, first wrote on the subject of gay religionists in 1970. Dignity, the organization for Catholic homosexuals, had a national convention in 1973.[8] Integrity, the group for homosexual Episcopalians, was founded in 1974. But the first Episcopal priest to admit his homosexuality publicly was Malcolm Boyd, in 1976, a full seven years after James Stoll, and he and McNeill were frightfully controversial in their churches.[9] The gay Unitarian, meanwhile, was becoming prosaic, almost clichéd.

Shortly before his death in 1994, James Stoll told an interviewer, "I had served a congregation in eastern Washington State for seven years. And in February of '69 I resigned and was planning on going on to another church. They gave me a six-month sabbatical, which I spent in Berkeley. And that turned out to be true fate, because spring of '69 in Berkeley was when the roof came apart. You know, People's Park . . . and the first vestiges of gay liberation in the Bay Area as well as, of course, Stonewall, and I . . . realized I had to make a choice and either spend my life in the closet or come out and deal with the consequences." The consequences may have seemed ominous: in 1969 homosexuality was still scandalous. Homosexual acts were illegal in many states, and homosexuality was considered rank perversity or, in the view of the American Psychiatric Association, a pathology.[10]

When Stoll came out in Colorado at the convention of Student Religious Liberals, the college-aged Unitarians, he got national attention. Young, radical Unitarians would already have been familiar to anyone who had read Tom Wolfe's *The Electric Kool-Aid Acid Test*, which described the detour Ken Kesey and his Merry Pranksters had made in 1965 to a Unitarian conference in Asilomar, a California state park near Monterey. Wolfe specifically mentions the teenagers' enthusiastic reaction to Furthur, Kesey's Day-Glo school bus. And Kesey's mistress, Carolyn Adams, better known as Mountain Girl, later the wife of the Grateful Dead's Jerry Garcia, "had been brought up as a Unitarian herself and had been a member of the real hope of the church, the LRY, the Liberal Religious Youth," the association of high school–age Unitarians.[11]

It seems that no copy of the Colorado speech has survived, but in late 1969 Stoll set forth his ideas in a letter to *Context*, the collegiate Unitarians' newsletter. He first recounts his history as a self-loathing gay man, then draws comparisons with other oppressed people. "No homosexual," he writes, "gets much joy out of making love because he's been told by reliable sources that he's sick, weird, and all those other words that we all know. God, do I know them. Maybe you now have some sense of what it means to hear the word 'Nigger' and know that means you. Now, maybe you'd better learn that there are many different groups of 'Niggers' in this country . . . Mexican Americans, poor people, women and yes, homosexuals."[12]

Before becoming Ken Kesey's mistress and then Jerry Garcia's wife, Carolyn Adams, known as Mountain Girl, was—as Tom Wolfe was careful to note—raised a Unitarian. Photograph by Gene Anthony.

Stoll's letter suggests a preacher's gift for shaping rhetoric to its audience. He knew that others could relate to his plight when seen in the context of those more familiar causes. Gay liberation was in its infancy, but Stoll frames it as an extension of current movements; he must have known that apposing homosexuals and other oppressed groups would persuade Unitarians to see things his way. Furthermore, the students reading the newsletter were more radical than their parents were. They would identify with a speaker who saw their fights as his own.

Stoll went to the students because "that's the level at which he communicated most comfortably," said Richard Nash, a Unitarian who became active in gay rights, "and the youth identified with him. . . . So he was already well accepted at those liberal events." Stoll refined his hip message in speeches to churches and liberal groups across the country. He was rumpled and obese, and he looked nothing like the stereotypical preacher, rather more like an outcast or a town eccentric. In interviews and from pulpits, he preached a new, young doctrine of gay liberation. Interviewed by a newspaper in Hawaii, Stoll, who in 1965 had marched in Alabama from Selma to Montgomery with Martin Luther King, alluded to blacks' struggle against bigotry. "He said people tend to remember, just as they remember when they called a black 'nigger,' all the times they've used the word 'queer.' [Stoll's] purpose is to help people realize the similarity between the fight for civil rights and the fight for sexual rights." Stoll couched his avant-garde theme in popular lingo: "Homosexuality is not bad. It's a groove," he preached in 1970, at First Unitarian Church in San Francisco.[13]

After the San Francisco sermon, Stoll considered starting a group for gay Unitarians. "I knew there was a potential there for a lesbian and gay group that might have avoided many people getting involved with MCC, which I never found particularly meaningful," he said in 1994.[14] (The MCC was the Metropolitan Community Church, a gay and lesbian church with an evangelical Christian style, very un-Unitarian.) But Stoll never returned to the ministry. He spent several years as an itinerant guest preacher and a lecturer on behavioral psychology, his first field of study, and then left the Unitarian scene. He worked in the mental health and drug abuse treatment fields and became active with the American Civil Liberties Union, serving as its San Francisco chapter president in 1993 and 1994.

But others, like the Rev. Richard Nash, had taken up the homosexuals' cause. A former parish minister and a veteran of the progressive Unitarian Universalist Service Committee, Nash arrived in Los Angeles in 1969, where he began working odd jobs, including selling luggage at Bullock's. "I had moved to L.A. in September 1969 and identified with the Gay Liberation Front here.... It was the aftermath of the Stonewall riots."[15] The famous Stonewall riots had begun in New York City on June 28, 1969, when New York police

The Rev. James L. Stoll was a complicated figure: an activist, a self-aggrandizing showman, and probably a pederast—but also a gay rights pioneer. Reprinted with the permission of the First Unitarian Society of Chicago.

raided the Stonewall Inn, a gay bar in Greenwich Village. Police had long raided gay bars: before conventions or fairs or sporting events, in response to complaints, or just for fun. They would arrest the revelers—sometimes on bogus charges, sometimes for real legal violations like solicitation, cross-dressing, or same-sex dancing—imprison them for one night, and sometimes assault them. On June 28 the drag queens, junkies, hustlers, and party boys—Stonewall catered to a poor, underworld gay community—resisted arrest, and a brief riot spilled onto the street, featuring a mix of anger and camp. Some drag queens threw high heels at the cops; others formed a chorus line and did a can-can dance. Protests continued intermittently for five days. That show of resolve gave birth to the Gay Liberation Front, led to the gay pride parade (today New York's largest annual parade), and, most important, received a lot of media attention.[16]

Though Nash and Stoll did not meet until they had both come out (Nash came out in 1971), and despite Nash's claim that "what [Stoll and he] did was very much separate," they were both inspired by Stonewall, and they shared an interest in other progressive causes, like civil rights. "I was flexing my muscles," Nash says. "And black liberation has been proceeding for a while . . . we [gay-rights advocates] pretty much patterned ourselves after them."[17] Nash naturally connected his struggle to the blacks', and the mutuality of their interests soon proved useful.

Noticing the absence of any forum for gay religionists in the Los Angeles area, Nash and Floyd Hof, another Unitarian, organized a conference "for people whose sexual orientation is gay and whose religious orientation is liberal," according to the press release for their event, "Getting Our Thing Together." "The purpose of this unusual conference, according to the Reverend Richard Nash, one member of the conference's convening committee, is to bring together men and women who are both gay and liberals in religion. 'We think the time is ripe,' he said, 'to get ourselves together, to discover what kind of continuing association we want, and to join forces to achieve common aims.'" The press release says that "about ten workshops will be offered in the afternoon, and they will be selected by the conferee's preferences from among the following topics: 1. Homosexuality: Sickness or Alternative Lifestyle. 2. Gay Priorities. 3. Developing a Gay Culture with Alternatives. 4. Gay Relationships. 5. Bisexuality. 6. Discrimination among Homosexuals. 7. Special Problems of the Female Homosexual," and so on.[18]

Even as the gay activists were talking young—getting their "thing" together, reveling in the gay "groove"—they were organizing old. They now had denominational support. On July 4, 1970, at its General Assembly in Seattle, the Unitarian Universalist Association had passed a resolution, written by Nash, condemning discrimination against homosexuals and bisexuals. The General Assembly recognized that "a growing number of authorities on the subject now see homosexuality as an inevitable sociological phenomenon and not as a mental illness [and that] there are Unitarian Universalists, clergy and laity, who are homosexuals or bisexuals"; it urged that "all peoples immediately bring to an end . . . all discrimination against homosexuals, homosexuality, bisexuals, and bisexuality."[19]

Despite the gesture of solidarity from headquarters, Nash and Hof had still not convinced everyone. Witness an interesting addendum to the press release for their conference: "The following statement is one that was prepared for all publicity used by representatives of the First Unitarian Church of Los Angeles and the Gay Religious Liberals Conference Committee: 'Since there is diversity on the subject of homosexuality, the church does not sponsor the Conference of Gay Religious Liberals. The planners of the conference have come to a mutual agreement with the Board of the First Unitarian Church of Los Angeles regarding the use of these facilities for a Press Conference, November 8 and a Gay Religious Liberal Conference on December 12. The Conference Committee wishes to make it clear that use of Church facilities does not imply church endorsement.'"[20] Only months after the national body had passed a resolution promising an end to church discrimination against homosexuals, a big-city Los Angeles Unitarian church refused to allow a gay group, led by Unitarians from the congregation, to use the building unless they assured people that they had received only use of the building, no actual encouragement. The effect must have seemed as a scarlet letter to Nash. It certainly reinforced, in his mind, the need for the conference.

By January 1971 the country's first organization of gays in a nongay religion had been founded in Los Angeles. The Gay Fellowship began to meet weekly almost immediately after the initial conference, and it attracted gay religionists from around the area. The founders were Unitarian, and from the Gay Fellowship came the drive for a national umbrella group for gay Unitarians.

Nash was growing bolder. He was planning to give a sermon discussing gay liberation that March at the Unitarian fellowship in West Covina, California, where he had been preaching monthly. Usually, upcoming sermons and their topics were published in the newsletter of the First Unitarian Church in Los Angeles, whose new minister,

Peter Christiansen, was trying to stock the West Covina fellowship with young married couples (the fellowship in West Covina was too small to have its own minister). But Christiansen was afraid that heterosexuals would see the topic and not attend. Even more worrisome was the possibility that gay men and lesbian women *would* attend, and enjoy themselves, and keep coming—discouraging the desirable heterosexual couples. The board tried to persuade Nash to change his topic, but ultimately, Nash said, acceded to the Unitarian tradition of pulpit freedom. "On the morning of the sermon, [the church] was overflowing, the largest crowd in the [fellowship's] history, and once they saw the crowd, the board was pleased." Nash made it clear in the sermon that he was gay, but he did not finish his sermon that morning, and he told them, "If you want to hear the rest, you'll have to invite me back."[21] The second sermon, also on gay liberation, was given in May 1971.

Nash and Hof's press release had been published by the *Unitarian Universalist World,* the main Unitarian magazine, which had always been silent about all things homosexual. "At that time," Nash writes, "Elgin Blair of Toronto was encountering a wall of resistance from the Unitarian church there, which he had approached on behalf of a gay group he helped organize, for meeting space. [Blair] read the article, recognized our common efforts to come up front, and wrote."[22] Blair and Nash became fast correspondents, and together they planned a gay delegation to the 1971 General Assembly in Washington, D.C. The *World*'s coverage of the Los Angeles conference helped Nash and Hof compile a mailing list that continued to grow.

On May 10, 1971, Nash and Blair sent a form letter to all members of their list. "Would you be interested in joining other gay UU's to get our thing together?" Nash writes. "Could we count on you to contribute time or creativity or money to this effort? Elgin Blair from Toronto and I are developing plans for capitalizing on the chance presented by the GA to begin the organizational process.

Your thinking would be valuable to us. . . . Elgin and I both came up front within the denomination several months ago. We have each separately already been working to heighten the awareness within the denomination of gay oppression and gay liberation. The job will be easier if instead of 2, there are 20 or 200 or 2000 to do it together. For some it is relatively easy to step forward. By doing so we create the climate which makes it easier for others. For some it's still dangerous." So that no gay Unitarian would miss the message, Nash and Blair took out an advertisement in the *World* of June 1, 1971. "Are you a GAY UU? DO you agree it's time to get our thing together? . . . If you're gay, we want to hear from you."[23]

The General Assembly began Sunday, June 6, 1971, at the Shoreham Hotel in Washington. Nash's plan was "to bring as many gays as possible out of the woodwork and to begin organizing . . . for effective action within the denomination. Just what kinds of meetings—business and social—will have to wait to be planned on the scene."[24] He had secured a booth, to be staffed by himself and Blair, at the convention hall. They would distribute buttons, flyers, and literature from the "homophile," or gay rights, movement. They would hope for people to stop by.

By the end of the 1960s, the General Assembly had become, according to one minister, "something like a circus or a medieval fair; or a cross between a meeting of the American Philosophical Association and Humanistic Psychology Association. There was one act after another, a cast of colorful characters in costume, refreshment booths, and hawkers for cause after cause."[25] Two of those colorful characters, Nash and Blair, stood in front of a large sign that read, "GAY IS GROOVY." Wearing buttons that read, "I AM GAY, HOW ABOUT YOU?" the two men passed out posters, fliers, cartoons, pamphlets, and copies of Nash's two Los Angeles sermons. They entreated people to stop and talk, and by the end of the week, their new Unitarian Universalist Gay Caucus had fourteen members.

Fourteen Unitarians' choosing to, in effect, come out constituted a success.[26] The Rev. Thomas Mikelson, who was at that General Assembly, writes, "In 1971 I had never met people who were openly gay and politically organized. At the G.A. they seemed to be every-where. Their colorful PR buttons were also everywhere. They were raising consciousness. . . . I was moved more than I can communi-cate at finding a continental church meeting at which gay people could openly politick. . . . It tested many people's limits of tolerance but the basic environment was supportive. I learned that these peo-ple already had a UU Gay network extending across the continent and that they had their own newsletter which I began to receive."[27] Mikelson's recollection may be hyperbolic: it is doubtful that the gays were "everywhere," and the newsletter had not yet begun publi-cation. But the exaggeration is itself significant, for it reflects Mikel-son's excitement and surprise at the new homosexual presence.

For Unitarians were simultaneously afraid of homosexuality and poised to accept it. They were afraid of homosexuality because they were Americans, and Americans still did not talk about such things. The few homophile groups, like the Mattachine Society and the Daughters of Bilitis, were small and obscure; they were not, in other words, gay or lesbian equivalents of the National Association for the Advancement of Colored People. The American Civil Liber-ties Union was still uninterested in gay rights. When asked about attitudes toward homosexuality, Unitarian ministers of the late 1960s and early 1970s described a range of responses. When the Rev. Emily Champagne wanted to bring James Stoll to her southern Cali-fornia church to speak about being gay, church members rebuffed her. So she called another minister to suggest that he open his pulpit to Reverend Stoll. "[He] acted real cool about it," Champagne said, "but I found out later he was extremely upset, and he called a num-ber of his congregation . . . and said, 'What's going on with Emily?' I called another minister who just blasted me. I couldn't believe it." But then she called yet another minister, the Rev. John Baker in

Sepulveda, and he immediately said yes.[28] The Rev. Gene Bridges had no problem bringing Stoll to Honolulu, and the Rev. W. Edward Harris, who was at Arlington Street Church in Boston, said of Stoll's coming out, "It didn't make a big impression on me."[29]

In some churches, like the famously liberal Arlington Street, homosexuality was no big deal; in other churches, it was a touchy subject, even a decade later. When Harris was at All Souls Church in Indianapolis in the 1980s, a vote to make the church a "welcoming congregation"—welcoming to homosexuals—almost did not pass. But by 2002 the church was renting its space to the Metropolitan Community Church, the evangelical gay group.[30] Churches on the coasts—or far off the coasts, in Hawaii—had members who were openly gay, or known to be gay, but that did not mean they talked about it; and, after all, there were no openly gay ministers before James Stoll. Churches in the South and the heartland tended to be more reserved or hostile. In Dallas the Unitarian church agreed to rent space to the Metropolitan Community Church, but only after much controversy.[31]

The Rev. Fred Campbell, pastor of a church in Little Rock, Arkansas, from 1967 to 1975, said this about his congregation: "As far as I remember gay issues were still so far out in the bushes that we did not imagine they were to become of importance. The key question in my interview for the job was, 'Would you guarantee us not to grow a beard if we call you as our minister?'"[32] Still, in the conservative milieu of Little Rock, the Unitarian church was where the liberals worshiped; when a black man joined Campbell's church, nobody objected. Campbell, like almost all the Unitarian ministers interviewed for this chapter, considered himself more a humanist than a Christian. But theological liberalism did not yet imply any beliefs about gay rights.

That was true even for ministers who were themselves homosexual. Consider, for example, the twenty-five-year career of the Rev. Charles Slap, minister to churches in Davis, California; West

The Rev. Charles Slap was born Jewish, became Unitarian, and dabbled in the paranormal before dying of AIDS-related illnesses in 1992. Reprinted with the permission of Derek Slap.

Lafayette, Indiana; Springfield, Massachusetts; and Schenectady, New York. Born Jewish, Slap banished the manger from the Springfield church's Christmas Eve service. (His director of religious education bought him a tie that read, "Bah humbug!" which he made a point of wearing every Christmas thereafter.) One of his sons describes Slap's conception of God this way: "He said God or the force is like water and we are the swimmers. We're surrounded by it but we don't control it. The three criteria: the experience makes you look inside yourself, then makes you feel universal love (agape), and then it calls you to action. The action may not be something you want to do. You say this must be done and I must do it. That is a full religious experience." God as "water," or a force that prompts one to action, is not traditional Christian theology, but it resonated with Unitarians. Yet despite his willingness to test theological boundaries, Slap was not publicly frank about his homosexuality until after his divorce in the mid-1980s. He died of AIDS-related illnesses in November 1992.[33]

The Rev. Ken MacLean, a minister in Boston; Knoxville, Tennessee; and Bethesda, Maryland, came out only after his wife of forty years died. "I was married for almost forty years," MacLean said, "and my wife died the year after I left Cedar Lane [the church in Bethesda]. And three years after that, I told my family [I was gay] and wrote a letter to the whole congregation at Cedar Lane and told them I'd fallen in love with a man. . . . And so that letter went out to one thousand people, and I got a very warm response. I got sixty-five or seventy letters. Every one was supportive."[34] But that was in the 1990s. In the 1970s MacLean, like Slap and dozens of other prominent homosexual Unitarians, was married; others were single and discreet.

The Unitarian Universalist Association may have been uncomfortable with homosexuals, but it could not have been shocked by their activism. Gay liberation was but one way the counterculture tested the Unitarian conscience.

On the first night of the 1971 Washington General Assembly, the Gay Caucus (whose membership grew sevenfold during the week, from two to fourteen, and probably stood at three or four on that Sunday evening) retired at the hotel to "a long meeting of the BAC (Black Affairs Council) Support Group. Strategies to win support for BAC funding preoccupied that meeting, as they were to most of the week."[35] The Black Affairs Council was the official department at church headquarters of the Black Unitarian Universalist Caucus. And as civil rights inspired gay liberation, the Black Caucus's activism made it a role model for the nascent Gay Caucus.

It is therefore significant that on the first night in Washington the gay activists met amicably with the blacks. The blacks were sympathetic and cooperative, but they had more pressing matters at hand. For the Black Affairs Council was trying to win back from the denomination money that it had worked hard to lose. In 1968 the General Assembly in Cleveland had voted 836 to 327 "for full support and funding of BAC, recommending to the UUA Board of Trustees one million dollars for the black empowerment organization to be spread over a four year period with annual allocations of $250,000. BAC's program was designed to allocate funds to various social action programs in ghetto communities and to establish pilot projects in disadvantaged environments around the country."[36] In November 1969, however, the denomination faced its most serious budget shortfall since the merger. Cutting one million dollars from its budget proved difficult, and the board cut spending on all fronts. The Black Caucus fared well, losing only one-fifth of its original annual allocation: it was to receive $200,000 for 1971 instead of the promised $250,000.

The board cut allocations fairly, and it asked the Black Affairs Council to shoulder only its fair share of the burden. But in those tense times, with more idealism than liquid money, the blacks felt cheated. "The issue is that this is one more case in which whites decided for blacks what they can do and what they cannot do," said Heyward Henry Jr., the national chairman of the Black Caucus, who called the cut "institutionally racist."[37] Dissatisfied with the church's protestations of poverty, the Caucus voted to disaffiliate the Black Affairs Council from the church.

As the 1970 General Assembly approached, many BAC members began to reconsider their drastic action. Disaffiliation meant giving up all claims to church money. When the reality of self-sufficiency set in, Henry began to sound a note of regret: "We cited the precedent of the Unitarian Universalist Service Committee having disaffiliated for essentially the same reasons we disaffiliated . . . but at no point did we say our complete financial relationship with the UUA would be like that of the UUSC"—the Unitarian Universalist Service Committee, which had complete financial independence.[38] In other words: emancipate us, but keep giving us our weekly allowance.

After boycotting the 1970 General Assembly in Seattle—where the approved budget contained no money for the Black Affairs Council—BAC members realized the disastrous implications of their actions and determined to win back funding at the 1971 assembly in Washington. Admitting the impotence of a boycott, blacks attended the Washington assembly to seek money, life support for the Black Affairs Council. Their efforts failed. The delegates in Washington voted to remain estranged from the council, approving a budget with no funds for it.

The Washington assembly, while a failure for the blacks, was a victory for gays. Nash, Blair, and company met with Heyward Henry, the radical black leader, who was an old acquaintance of Nash's. Henry's support of the gay cause lent the gay activists courage and a newfound legitimacy. It is important to recognize how deep the activist roots go: recall that Henry, in May 1970, "cited the precedent of the Unitarian Universalist Service Committee" in explaining the blacks' separatism. Not only did the reference to the Service Committee, a Unitarian social action group with a long, liberal history, place Henry in a leftist tradition, but it forged yet another link in the activist world that both Henry and Nash inhabited—for Nash, from 1965 to 1969, had been employed by the Service Committee.

During his tenure at the committee, beginning in 1965, Nash had overseen the elimination of approximately half the bloated organization's thirty-four programs. He had started an urban service initiative to provide education, health, and recreational services to inner-city groups. He had also directed funds toward an antiracism program in Oakland, California. Nash's leadership had brought the group into the sixties, so to speak. The activist urban initiatives that came to characterize the Service Committee were Nash's legacy. When he left, he went to Los Angeles hoping to work for a program similar to the one his office had supported in Oakland. He did not get that job, but did, of course, find another cause. He switched from black activism to gay activism.[39] Heyward Henry, then, drew inspiration from the activist organization where Richard Nash had spent his formative years, and Nash's new gay activism was supported by the Black Caucus run by Henry. And now they were together at the 1971 General Assembly, plotting strategy.

Although there were few women in the Gay Caucus, the women's movement cleared brush for the homosexuals. Unitarian churches were frequent meeting places for pro-choice and women's groups, and the Unitarian Universalist Women's Federation was becoming radically feminist; it bore no resemblance to the ladies' auxiliaries affiliated with so many churches and synagogues. Before *Roe v. Wade* was decided in 1973, Unitarian women rallied to oppose antiabortion laws, which existed even in some liberal states. On February 11, 1970, a characteristic women's federation event took place at Boston's Arlington Street Church, later a center of gay activism. At the time, Massachusetts still had an antiabortion law, and at the meeting women planned a campaign to educate people about the law's specifics. Many of the lesbians and female bisexuals who later moved into positions of leadership in the Gay Caucus were members of the Women's Federation.[40]

Less evident links, too, connected the women's and gay movements. Churches develop unique characters: ministers and congregants switch churches because one church has gotten "too liberal" or "too alternative" or "too conservative." When women (or blacks) began to use a church as their activist base, when they began to meet and recruit members at the church, the church took on an activist character. Reformers would be drawn to a welcoming church or minister. The Arlington Street Church exemplified this phenomenon. About 1970, the Women's Federation had a strong presence at Arlington Street, which hosted leftist political meetings and consciousness-raising sessions. The Boston chapter of Daughters of Bilitis, a women's homophile group, met there. The church became a center of support for the Equal Rights Amendment. Its gay and lesbian presence grew. For many years, Eugene Navias, the closeted gay man who helped develop the innovative, gay-friendly Unitarian sex education program, was affiliated with Arlington Street.[41] The crossover between women's groups and lesbian groups meant that as the former grew in strength, the latter benefited; the church that nurtured one would nurture the other.

The church nourished more than two movements. Having moved left under the Rev. Jack Mendelsohn's leadership in the 1960s, the Arlington Street Church hosted regular meetings of the Women's Federation, the Daughters of Bilitis, the Samaritans for Suicide, various antiwar groups, and Dignity, the association of gay Catholics.

The women's movement also presaged the gay movement's interest in the social construction of "gender," the idea that what seemed "masculine" or "feminine" was not biologically determined. Unitarian feminists, as they asked for new responsibilities and rights, reassessed theology and politics in light of gender theory. The 1973 continental conference of Student Religious Liberals examined the theme of androgyny in one of its workshops. And as young Unitarians explored issues of gender and sexuality, their parents and teachers responded with the *About Your Sexuality* curriculum, developed by Deryck Calderwood in 1971. Calderwood had been working on *The Invisible Minority,* a curriculum about homosexuality that had been dropped by the educational publishers who had first commissioned it.[42] Eugene Navias, who was in the Department of Religious Education, liked Calderwood's work and convinced Robert West, then president of the denomination, to help Calderwood publish *The Invisible Minority.* Having been brought in-house, Calderwood became the natural choice to write the new sex education curriculum.

About Your Sexuality was the first sex education program to affirm that gay sex was natural and should not be criminalized; many Unitarians remember the curriculum, which was shared with parents as well as children, as a catalyst for the discussion of gay rights. In the summer of 1971, as he was founding the Gay Caucus, Richard

Nash joined the Department of Religious Education curriculum team. He became one of the chief reviewers of sex education material used by the church.

The Department of Religious Education sent *About Your Sexuality* to ministers and educators, Unitarian and not. One disgruntled reviewer, John Preston, director of the Minnesota Council for the Church and the Homophile, wrote to Eugene Navias that "the purpose of the curriculum is to convey an 'it's OK to be sexual' message. That message, though, is not carried through when it comes down to specific areas of sexual activity. Then the message becomes: 'it's OK to be heterosexually sexual; if you are homosexually sexual, have hope, you might become bisexual. . . . I personally find this situation more destructive than that of a totally negative statement."[43]

The question was taken up in an issue of the Gay Caucus's newsletter. In a broadside probably written by Nash, the author quotes Hugo Holleroth, curriculum editor of the Department of Religious Education: "Re-reading the Same-Sex part of the course now is a hurtful experience to me, because it is referring to the lifestyle of newly-acquired friends but the way it is referred to reflects certain compromises which we felt at the time we had to make."[44] The piece says that Nash concurred with Preston's criticism and worked with Holleroth and Navias to revise the curriculum; the revised version appeared in 1973.

The gay newsletter continually paid attention to sex education, and the caucus considered tolerant sex education curricula a gay issue. Stoll, in his letter to the Student Religious Liberals' publication, spoke for many when he lamented the way in which his upbringing had left him ashamed and hateful of his homosexual urges. Sex education represented a way to help others to avoid that sense of shame. And the debate surrounding *About Your Sexuality* invigorated the Gay Caucus. Richard Nash, Eugene Navias, Deryck Calderwood, and Elgin Blair were drawn together around this issue. Once it was recognized that there was an identifiable gay position on sex education, the Gay Caucus was asked to participate in the preparation of sex education materials, which may have been why Nash was asked to join the Department of Religious Education. This invitation gave the caucus a tangible issue, sex education, that prompted the leaders to correspond with their members across the country.[45]

Congregationalists, Presbyterians, Episcopalians, and others became interested in women's liberation, sex education, civil rights, and other progressive movements, but it seemed that Unitarian churches couldn't say no to anything. The Unitarian Universalist Psi Symposium, founded in 1970, received no denominational funding, but by 1973 it boasted about a dozen chapters at Unitarian churches and fellowships, comprising people interested in psychic and paranormal phenomena. "For the first time we are attracting Blacks and Chicanos to the church," beamed a minister from southern California, discussing the Psi gatherings.[46] One Unitarian said, "If Unitarian Universalists mean what they say about welcoming truth from any variety of sources, then they should be open to the well-documented data of ESP."[47]

"Welcoming truth from any variety of sources"—this was by the early 1970s a characteristic feature of Unitarianism. It seems doubtful that any other American religion would open its minds to this kind of paranormal exploration. But having discarded the Christian narrative, disposed of the concept of sin, and become a culture of intellectual and racial toleration, could Unitarians disdain homosexuals? If so, on what grounds?

Unitarians had welcomed abolitionists, pacifists, and blacks. "Welcoming" was part of what Unitarians were. The Metropolitan Community Church, the evangelical Christian church for gay men and lesbians founded in 1969, had difficulty finding meeting spaces. While their charismatic, evangelical Christianity held no appeal for gay Unitarians, Unitarian churches offered space to Metropolitan Community Churches in Philadelphia, Dallas, and Riverside, California. In Denver, a Metropolitan Community Church minister and his lover exchanged vows of union in the local Unitarian church.[48]

Unitarians were returning a favor, really. At the 1971 Washington General Assembly, Metropolitan Community Church members had billeted Elgin Blair and Richard Nash; one might say that the Gay Caucus was born in the care of the Metropolitan Community Church. Having gained a foothold in their own church, gay Unitarians lent a hand to their evangelical brethren. But the relationship could be strained. One cannot know today how many Unitarian churches refused to share their fellowship halls; history doesn't record the negative evidence that way.[49] In Dallas there was the dispute over the Metropolitan Community Church. Elisabeth Michnick of First Unitarian Church in Toronto wrote to Eugene Navias to inquire warily about the church's position toward "homophile groups."[50] But wherever gay men and women even requested the use of Unitarian fellowship halls for functions, they forced the churches to reckon with the existence of homosexuals, and with their own consciences. When the Rev. Thomas Mikelson's church in Iowa hosted a gay and lesbian dance in 1971, how long could it be before it would sponsor one?

Soon the churches discovered that when they allowed gay and progressive groups to use church space, those groups fed members into the churches. Irreligious homosexuals, men and women who had abandoned religion as hopelessly intolerant, found themselves in churches for their weekly meetings of the Daughters of Bilitis, the Gay Liberation Front, or the National Organization for Women. They came to realize that some religious groups welcomed them after all. Consider Julia Lee, who committed herself to helping the Gay Caucus after a lifetime of lapsed Judaism, or the three board members of the Mattachine Society, a prominent homophile group, who joined the caucus chapter in Buffalo, New York.[51] Recall what Richard Nash said of his coming-out sermon: instead of driving people away, that Sunday's topic attracted the greatest crowd in the history of the fellowship. The realization of this untapped potential for gay membership helped Unitarians' actions fall in line with their Unitarian consciences.

The Unitarian Universalist Gay Caucus found its strength not in numbers but in passion. The 14 founding members at the 1971 General Assembly yielded ten delegates to the 1972 General Assembly. By 1973 the national membership had grown from 14 to 250.[52] Blanchon "Skip" Ward, a courtly, Southern Unitarian from Pineville, Louisiana, who joined the caucus at the 1972 Dallas General Assembly, became part of a leadership triumvirate with Richard Nash and Elgin Blair. He said Nash was the leader: "[Nash] was an inspiration to us. He certainly was an inspiration to me. I learned from him. I stood on his shoulders, so to speak. . . . [Elgin] was the solid worker type, sort of kept things on an even keel for the caucus. He was not the brilliant thinker like Dick Nash was. Dick was a brilliant theoretician, I believe is the word, and Elgin and I were more the workers. Elgin was always doing something like passing out literature, staffing a booth, always working quietly behind the scenes."[53] In June 1972 Nash appointed Ward caucus treasurer; with Nash as coordinator and Blair as editor of the newsletter, the three men guided their caucus through the waters of church politics.

In a 1977 history of the Gay Caucus, Blair lamented that "much effort was spent on creating materials to explain gay issues to straight congregations, but very little was provided to help sustain gays in services of their own. . . . In most cases Caucus groups failed to develop the growth groups and other processes to help us overcome the years of internalized self-hatred many of us have suffered and have yet to overcome."[54] But there was no template for what a gay group should do, and most gay Unitarians had never been part of a group like this one. Many had been out for only a few years, or months; some of them had only recently admitted to themselves that they were gay.

Through July 1973 most of the caucus's newsletters carried some news of Nash's fight with the California legal system. Nash had been arrested in 1971, shortly after the Washington General Assembly, charged with soliciting a prostitute. He pleaded innocent, and two years later, the charge was finally dismissed. In the meantime, the case became rather famous in gay circles, and gay activists, not all of them Unitarian, donated money to Nash's defense fund.[55] The newsletter also discussed gay events at Unitarian churches, new chapters of the Gay Caucus, political events of interest to the gay movement, and gay movements in other religions, and it periodically ran polemics by the caucus leaders and profiles of caucus members. One senses, reading these early dispatches, that the gay rights movement had so much energy, be it anger, joy, or the simple intoxication of newfound liberation, that it wanted to discuss everything and everybody.

Then the caucus found a purpose, one even more inspiring than liberal sex education curricula. Eager for more money and influence to effect its various goals—pulpit services relevant to gay men and lesbians, social work in the gay community, education—Nash, Blair, and Ward decided to seek a church office, funded and staffed with the denomination's money and located at its Beacon Street headquarters.[56] The idea came from Leo Laurence, who wrote for the *Advocate*, the national gay weekly. Nash liked the idea and brought a proposal for an Office on Gay Affairs to the 1972 Dallas General Assembly. Nash and the others found little support for their resolution, and they quickly decided not to push for passage (which would have been nearly impossible anyway, since it was not on the official assembly agenda). Deciding instead to plan ahead for the 1973 assembly, the Gay Caucus produced the pamphlet *Why an Office on Gay Affairs?* probably written by Nash. Echoing the Black Caucus's exasperated tone, the pamphlet asks for the office so that "Gay Unitarian-Universalists . . . sick of shouldering the burden of others' prejudices [might] deal effectively with anti-Gay attitudes and practices within our denomination."[57]

Following denominational rules, Nash sought, in the winter of

1972–1973, the sponsorship of five Unitarian congregations to get his resolution on the 1973 General Assembly agenda. According to Nash, five congregations did agree to sponsor, but only four reported their sponsorship to headquarters at Beacon Street. As a result, the caucus had to round up 150 signatures of Unitarians, with no more than 10 being from any one church or fellowship. By April 2, 1973, Nash and his people succeeded, getting more than 400 signatures from forty-five congregations. Having gotten their resolution on the agenda, the Gay Caucus still had to fight a vocal opposition, which included the denomination's president, Robert West. The agenda was sent to delegates with the resolution for an Office on Gay Affairs, but with a rider indicating that the board of directors unanimously opposed the resolution.[58]

At the General Assembly, the opposition was loud but ineffectual. The Rev. Don Harrington, the well-known progressive pastor of the Community Church of New York, opposed the creation of a new office. His main concern was money, but in his remarks, he inflammatorily called homosexuality "abnormal." "I raised a technical question," Harrington said years later. "As I look back upon it, it was rather stupid of me. What I objected to was calling gay a norm. I said it's apart from the norm. This immediately raised a question—'Well, that's denigrating people, calling them abnormal.' I said I didn't say 'abnormal,' I said it's not a norm. . . . At every point, I felt special steps had to be taken to make sure there was not discrimination against gays. But I got tagged with the 'abnormal.' So I said, 'Do you also feel, for example, that the relatively few cases of bestiality, that this is a norm too?' And some people said yes! And it got very heated."[59] Few people rushed to side with Harrington, whose remarks about bestiality had obscured the financial issue.

The denominational board, for its part, proposed an alternate resolution, with less bite, which West and his supporters hoped would preempt the caucus's more radical proposal. But the night before the vote on the alternate resolution, a spy smuggled a copy to

Nash, who was able to campaign against it before it was even brought to a vote. Using the intelligence of two moles—Hugo Holleroth, Nash's old friend from the sexual education curriculum team, and another man, a closeted, married gay man whose identity Nash has never revealed—the caucus and its partisans managed to outpolitick their opponents. On June 2, 1973, the alternate resolution was defeated, 277 to 216, but the caucus's resolution had been amended (to the caucus's dismay) to omit funding for the new office it would create. It passed on a hand vote, with observers guessing a two-thirds majority.[60] There was now a homosexual office, but no money to put a homosexual staffer inside it.

Many have charged men like West and Harrington with homophobia, and there may be some truth to that charge; Harrington, in particular, is remembered as hostile to gay rights. Thirty years later, West was eager to defend his good name. A former insurance salesman, West had spent six months in law school and two years in the navy, but he was more liberal than he believed the insurance, legal, or military professions would allow, and he decided to become a minister. "I was raised Methodist," he said.

> I was president of a Baptist youth club, I sang in a Presbyterian choir, I was married in an Episcopal church, and I was ordained Unitarian in a Jewish synagogue in 1957 in Knoxville. . . . I remember Jim [Stoll] speaking at the General Assembly where we approved this, and I thought he did a very good job. I was opposed to the wording of that resolution that passed. I felt very strongly that the entire time I'd been president, we'd tried hard within our money and staff to address gay and lesbian concerns. . . . When I was chairman of the religious education advisory committee before I became president, I was responsible for [*About Your Sexuality.*] When questions came up of including gay and lesbian lifestyles in that kit, I said certainly, and we did. . . .

And when budget cuts came, I held onto these programs. [But] I said very clearly that given the total situation of the UUA, we should not spend that amount of
money on a single issue.[61]

There were sound reasons, having nothing to do with spiteful-
ness, to oppose the creation of this new office. First, some Unitarians
did cling to a Universalist or Unitarian Christian heritage that might
have been at odds with homosexuality. There is language in the Bible
that disapproves of homosexuality, and Christians who take the
Bible seriously may genuinely oppose homosexual acts on doctrinal
grounds. Second, the psychiatric profession still considered homosexuality an abnormal malady; the American Psychiatric Association
deleted the entry for homosexuality from its diagnostic manual only
in December 1973, just after the Unitarians created their gay office.[62]
Third, most Unitarians were white liberals who admired Martin
Luther King; they were integrationists. They had been dismayed by
the militancy and bad faith of the black activists several years earlier.
Creating special offices to serve balkanized interest groups, while
common by the 1990s, could seem improper, fruitless, and even un-
Christian in 1973. Finally, the Unitarian Universalist Association had
not recovered from its fiscal crisis, and President West and his board
bore responsibility for the financial health of the denomination.
They knew that interest group follows interest group, with pursuant
demands for offices and eventual demands for money—which the
Unitarians did not have.

In 1974, its financial difficulties somewhat abated, the assembly
voted to fund the wisely retitled Office of Gay Concerns—"Office of
Gay Affairs," someone quipped, sounded like a dating service.[63] Arlie
Scott, a lesbian (though not a Unitarian), became the first director.
Gay Unitarians now had a gay-friendly sex education curriculum,
several openly gay ministers, and a lesbian paid to represent their
interests.

As Skip Ward said, the change has been "tremendous. Almost 180 degrees."[64] Gay liberation is today a fact of life more for Unitarians than for any other traditional American religionists. The change has not been accidental. Over the years, as their allegiance to the Bible lapsed, Unitarians developed into not so much a religion as a culture; the characteristics of the culture were toleration, skepticism, and progressive politics. In some conservative communities, the Unitarians were so unusual that they functioned as a counterculture.

The progressive stances, the liberal bent, the gay dances, and the organizing meetings—all these prodded Unitarians toward affirmation of sexual minorities. When the radicals, liberals, feminists, and, ultimately, homosexuals came knocking, all religions had to respond. The United Church of Christ ordained an open homosexual, William Reagan Johnson, in 1972, and, like Reform Judaism, officially deplored homophobia in 1977. The United Methodist Church ruled in 1979 that homosexuals could serve as pastors.[65] But the Unitarian character forced Unitarians to answer first, and they answered the ordination question simply: they never debated it. It was taken for granted that homosexuals could be ordained. The General Assembly never took up the question.

Although Unitarians had a responsibility to ask the question, their principles did not dictate the answer. The answer—tolerance and affirmation—was inevitable for other reasons. Having a history of liberalism, the Unitarian Universalist Association became a natural site for new progressive causes. The feminist, antiwar, and, above all, civil rights movements appealed to the Unitarians, and when the gay rights movement was born, its activists naturally allied with other reformers. The elusive James Stoll, probably a sexual predator but also the Simón Bolívar or Martin Luther King of gay Unitarians, borrowed a rhetoric of oppression from black power activists. The different progressive movements traded tactics and people, and gay Unitarian reformers took strength from their better-entrenched allies. Furthermore, the liberalism of the Unitarian church attracted young radicals, people with new ideas about sexuality and with experience in the civil rights, antiwar, and feminist movements. These youngsters were generally alienated from religion, but, like Mountain Girl, comfortable with Unitarianism.

James Stoll would have found them eventually, but the warm audience he found in Unitarianism was unique. At the turn of the decade, Stoll was a pioneer. Within five years, when gay activism surfaced in other religions, he was a throwback within his own. Feminism, antiwar protest, and all the other countercultural movements had become normal for Unitarians; not all Unitarians agreed with these activists, but they had to put up with them. That is what Unitarians did: put up with people. They embodied the paradox of liberalism, tolerant of everything except intolerance. Wherever the culture demanded conformity, Unitarianism was a counterculture, a self-sustaining alternative.

We begin with Unitarians because they were so unusual. They provide an example of how a counterculture (gay rights) functions in a culture (Unitarianism) that itself tends toward counterculture. It is easy to see how the Unitarian history of abolitionism, women's rights, and skepticism would shape a denomination that allowed its children to party with Ken Kesey and gave them the country's most liberal sex education curriculum. Gay Unitarians were reformers in a denomination that itself embodied reform. So yes, there was opposition to the Office of Gay Concerns, mostly from southern and midwestern churches. But they could make their case only in the most instrumental terms ("We don't have the money") or in the crassest insults ("What next, bestiality?"). After civil rights and women's rights, gay rights arrived, and if it had less support, it had all the same momentum. There was no countervailing force, no friction to slow its march. As one Unitarian wrote, salvation for a Unitarian is anything that "provides for victory over estrangement."[66] You could oppose the Gay Caucus, but you'd find no traction to stand fast against it.

TWO

Roman Catholics and the Folk Mass

"There is a singing group in this Catholic church today," writes Annie Dillard,

a singing group which calls itself "Wildflowers." The lead is a tall, square-jawed teen-aged boy, buoyant and glad to be here. He carries a guitar; he plucks out a little bluesy riff and hits some chords. With him are the rest of the Wildflowers. There is an old woman, wonderfully determined; she has long orange hair and is dressed country-and-western style. A long embroidered strap around her neck slings a big western guitar low over her pelvis. Beside her stands a frail, withdrawn fourteen-year-old boy, and a large Chinese man in his twenties who seems to want to enjoy himself but is not quite sure how to. He looks around wildly as he sings, and shuffles his feet. There is also a very tall teen-aged girl, presumably the lead singer's girlfriend; she is delicate of feature, half-serene and petrified, a wispy soprano. They straggle out in front of the altar and teach us a brand new hymn.

It all seems a pity at first, for I have overcome a fiercely anti-Catholic upbringing in order to attend Mass simply and solely to escape Protestant guitars. Why am I here? Who gave these nice Catholics guitars? Why are they not mumbling in Latin and performing superstitious rituals? What is the Pope thinking of?[1]

Guitars—to answer Annie Dillard's question—were not exactly what the pope was thinking of, but rather what some liberal American Catholics hoped the pope was thinking of. Or what traditional Catholics feared he was thinking of. American Catholics once thought their religion was timeless, perfectly designed to withstand the corrosive pressures of the world outside its cathedrals. But in the United States, religion must constantly sell itself, and so it must change to suit the new moods. Adapting to the culture is a chore incumbent on all American religions—except, it was once thought, if the religion was Catholicism.

At the Third Plenary Council in Baltimore in 1884, American bishops decided that every diocese must provide Catholic schooling for its young, so that they could withstand decadent, pagan America. Pius X, pope from 1903 to 1914, urged Catholics to resist modernist thought and to be suspicious of American pluralism. It was not sheer mythology that the Catholic Church had an unbending quality, with its eyes focused more on the eternal horizon and less on the fashions of the day. Annie Dillard had some right to expect, in Catholicism, refuge from "Protestant guitars."

The writer William F. Buckley Jr. loved that his natal church resisted trends. In Catholicism even dead languages never really died. Listen to Buckley's description of his sister's Latin funeral mass, held in 1967, after the official abolition of the Latin Mass in America: "And so on Jan. 18, in the sub-zero weather of a little town in northwestern Connecticut, in the ugly little church we all grew up in, the priest recited the Mass of the Dead, and the organist accompanied the soloist who sang the Gregorian dirge in words the mourners did not clearly discern . . . and yet we experienced, not only her family but her friends . . . something akin to that synaesthesia which nowadays most spiritually restless folk find it necessary to discover in drugs, or from a guru in Mysterious India."[2] Buckley's description of the Mass as an experience of synaesthesia—sensory confusion, as in the ability to hear colors—is apt, suggesting the totalizing effect of the old Mass: incense, colors, chants, the touch of the communion wafer to the tongue, the taste of the wine, all merging in the moment.

The reforming Protestants had tried to strip Christianity of these adornments and return it to the Word, with an occasional communion and some spare hymns. The Congregational service, for example, was simple, which meant that there were few places for tinkering. No one cared much what happened with the hymnody, or what paintings were on the wall; the Puritan ancestors had not wanted paintings anyway. But Catholicism still expected to touch all the senses, and the fuller the worship service, the more aspects to fuss over. The more tradition-bound the worship service, the more the fussing would be noticed and felt. A change in the Catholic liturgy would be felt, then, not as a slow shifting, the way the Mississippi can over time move land from one side of a state's border to the other, but as a breach in the dam.

That sensitivity to symbol is why Catholics sounded most hysterical as they watched unthinkable things happen in the late 1960s. It is why even the priestly collar, just a little white band, assumed tremendous significance. Garry Wills writes, "I asked a priest, one who had been among the first to demonstrate, whether his bishops wanted him, at first, to stay in clericals or to picket less obtrusively in lay attire. 'Are you kidding?' he answered—'That would have been like asking a Southern redneck if he prefers to have his twelve-year-old daughter get pregnant with a white man or a black one.'"[3]

Andrew Greeley, another Catholic sympathetic to liberal reforms, writes of three activists of WITCH, the Women's International Terrorist Conspiracy from Hell, putting a loud, shrieking curse on the sociology department at the University of Chicago in 1969, drawing frightened secretaries and researchers out of their offices to see what the commotion was. WITCH may have been a put-on, but Greeley does not seem so sure. He also quotes with alarm Huston Smith's description of MIT religion seminars that discussed the *I Ching,* yoga, Zen, astrology, UFOs, auras, drugs, and even brown rice.[4] Greeley worries about devil worship: "The popularity of *Rosemary's Baby,* the new adventures into witchcraft . . . lead one to believe that the diabolic is at least being experimented with."[5]

Rumors about Satanism in the late 1960s, like the satanic ritual abuse of the 1980s, were more myth than fact, but if so sane a scholar as Greeley could be so discombobulated, then Catholics were in the midst of a true crisis of confidence. The absolute numbers of Catholics never fell, but other indicators were worrisome. In 1963 about 72 percent of American Catholics went to Mass every week, but by 1974 that figure had fallen to about half, at a steady decline of 2 percentage points a year. The rate for those younger than thirty years old was less than 40 percent.[6] From 1960 to 1970 enrollment in Catholic schools declined, as did the conversion rate. Vocations to the priesthood were diminishing (even though, as a result of population growth and immigration, there were actually more American priests in 1970 than in 1960). Greeley estimated that during the decade "as many as 10 percent of the priests in the country" had left the priesthood.[7]

The priests who remained served parishioners increasingly dissatisfied with the church and vocal about their dissatisfaction; sometimes these laypeople left the church, but those who stayed often funneled their energy into reforming the central experience of Catholic life, the Mass. They changed the Mass in ways that saddened Annie Dillard and William F. Buckley, and in ways, conservatives feared, that could lead down a path to drug abuse, and maybe Satanism. Liturgical reform was the chief ambition of Catholic liberals and the chief fear of Catholic traditionalists. When Catholics of all persuasions remember that era, they talk about the Mass.

In 1959 Pope John XXIII announced the Second Vatican Council, which he charged with the task of *aggiornamento,* or updating. He believed that the church needed to lose its fear of modernity, start talking with believers of other religions, and permit innovation in its liturgy. Vatican II, as it came to be known, met from 1962 to 1965 in Vatican City. The bishops who met periodically for those three years eventually promulgated sixteen documents, which are the chief legacy of John XXIII, who died in 1963. (But it is a common mistake to see the liberal church reforms as a creature only of John; for example, it was his successor, Pope Paul VI, who in 1966 ended the traditional requirement to abstain from the eating of meat on Fridays.)[8]

The Vatican II documents did not exist in the realm of distant theory, as, say, an obscure Talmudic ruling might for the average Reform Jew. Catholics followed Vatican II in Catholic and secular newspapers. Whether one was a lace-curtain Irish banker who read the *New York Times* or a Polish beat cop in Chicago who occasionally read the parish newsletter, one knew about Vatican II and probably had some curiosity about what it would mean. Certain effects, like the decision to celebrate the Mass in the vernacular rather than in Latin, or the priest's turning toward the congregation rather than standing with his back to it, were easy to understand. Other decrees bore mysterious meanings. *Lumen gentium,* the Dogmatic Constitution of the Church, announced a new biblical metaphor to describe the people's relationship to the church: the People of God. Older descriptions of the Catholic Church—sheepfold, Body of Christ, bride—appeared in the document, but People of God was a new and conspicuous metaphor. The Decree on the Apostolate of the Laity, from 1965, affirmed that "the laity derive the right and duty to the apostolate from their union with Christ the head." In other words, lay Catholics had some apostolic duty, some obligation beyond the sacraments of confession, communion, marriage, and so forth. What would this mean?[9]

Conservatives anticipated change with leeriness. "I remember," writes William F. Buckley, "just before the word went out from Rome, reading the menu on a TWA flight. Immediately below the tenderloin-of-steak listing appeared in small type some such wording as, 'Roman Catholics on this flight, by agreement reached between TWA and the Vatican, are exempted from dietary obligations on Fridays.' . . . I had thought Friday abstinence—I think it is safe to say that *most* Catholics so thought it—a very slight deprivation, yet one that served as a palpable reminder that Friday had a special significance for us."[10]

We should remember that the hostility between reformers and

traditionalists was not new, just amplified. Nor was lay participation new. But since the death of Jesus, Christians have been unsure how much the layman is supposed to submit to the clergy and the church hierarchy. Paul, the popes, Calvin, and others have asserted their right to guide the faithful; wherever the laity has agitated for freedom, as in the French Revolution or the Anabaptist reformation, there have been clerics, and traditionalists, to resist.

Nineteen sixty-five, writes the English novelist Evelyn Waugh, "was a bad year for me in a number of ways—dentistry, the death of friends, the 'aggiornamento' . . ." Conservative Catholics influenced by French Archbishop Marcel Lefebvre saw Vatican II (especially its document *Dignitatis Humanae,* the Declaration on Religious Freedom) as endorsing pluralism and abandoning the church's ideal of the confessional state. The Lefebvrists also worried that Vatican II had loosened the traditional political alliances that had helped defeat liberalism, socialism, and modernism, and they regretted that Vatican II did not formally condemn communism. The sedevacantists, even more extreme, judged Vatican II heretical and considered all the popes who enforced its decrees heretics. They believed that the Apostolic See was in fact vacant. Then there were those who believed that an extraordinary satanic fraud had been perpetrated: the real pope was imprisoned somewhere in the Vatican, while an actor presided over the Council and destroyed the church.[11]

The Lefebvrists, like most nostalgians, were creating, not remembering, a past. The authoritarian Vatican they remembered had never exercised total power. Vatican II was another episode in a long, cyclical history of power shifts toward and away from the Holy See.[12] Dorothy Day, the founder of the Catholic Worker movement, saw the glory of Catholicism not in papal power but in the trials and triumphs of Catholic laypeople. She was influenced by the Dutch-French Decadent novelist J. K. Huysmans, who belonged "to the tradition of 'aesthetic Catholics' which included Baudelaire and others who 'savoured above all in religion the charms of sin, the grandeur of sacrilege.'" That is the same tradition described decades after Day by Camille Paglia, who writes of being held spellbound as a child by the sensuality of the saints' statues, like the one of St. Lucy holding out her eyeballs on a platter. "The garishness, the grotesquerie is so different from the experience of someone who is Protestant," she writes. "No Protestant person of my memory has ever had *that* in a sacred space."[13] For Catholics like Paglia, the essence of Catholicism has never been its clerisy or its laws, but the individual's experience of its sublime art and iconic stories.

Throughout Catholic history, there has been Catholicism that did not rely on clericalism. For example, Dorothy Day and Peter Maurin, her partner in the Catholic Worker movement, were influenced by personalism, a philosophy, derivative of Nietzsche, opposed to both capitalism and collectivism. Still other Catholics were attracted to the Mystical Body of Christ doctrine, according to which a united humanity could stand against godless, modernist individualism. In the nineteenth century, the idea of the Mystical Body was used by clerics to disparage all the church's secular enemies—naturalism, socialism, liberalism, and modernism—but the doctrine was put to more liberal use, too. The Mystical Body heightened Catholics' sense of agency, of social responsibility, and so encouraged them to become more active in society beyond the church.

The Mystical Body became, for liberal clergy, an important metaphor. A Benedictine monk from Minnesota, Dom Virgil Michel, returned from Europe in the 1920s to popularize the Mystical Body. Paul's metaphor of the *mystici corporis,* he argued, linked liturgy, social action, and community to characterize the work of Christ in the world. Michel's Liturgical Press and his journal *Orate Fratres* spread this conception, which helped fuel a liturgical renewal movement, emphasizing the vitality and relevance of Catholic liturgy, as well as a willingness to experiment with it. In 1943 Pius XII formally endorsed the Mystical Body idea in his encyclical *Mys-*

tici Corporis, and by the late 1950s a liturgical revival was fully under way—five years before Vatican II's first document. This liturgical revival emphasized lay piety, and it used the Mystical Body to conceive the church more spiritually, against the idea of the church as an instrument of papal authority.[14]

In other words, despite what the opponents of Vatican II thought, lay involvement and activism had a long history. It was the history not of an abstract theory but of lay organizations, publications, and vocations. From the Knights of Columbus to the cult of St. Jude in Chicago, from the Hibernians in Boston to the National Council of Catholic Men, the National Council of Catholic Women, the Young Christian Workers, the National Catholic War Council of 1917, and its descendent, the United States Catholic Conference of 1966, American Catholics have been nearly as active as Protestants and Jews in religious organizations.[15]

This history of lay activism, now affirmatively endorsed by Vatican II, coincided with other liberalizing trends in American Catholicism. Seminarians in the 1950s and 1960s were being exposed as never before to biblical criticism, and Catholic laypeople, like all Americans, had access to cheap, mass-market books, even books their priests had not recommended. The works of the Protestant anti-Nazi Dietrich Bonhoeffer, the existentialists Albert Camus and Jean-Paul Sartre, the Protestant theologians Paul Tillich and Karl Barth, and the controversial Catholic priest and paleontologist Pierre Teilhard de Chardin all reached beyond academia and toward the Catholic populace by way of paperbacks, and through annual conventions, Newman Club programs, college classrooms, the liberal Catholic press, and so forth.[16]

As Vatican II convened, American Catholics had one of their own, John F. Kennedy, in the White House. His bride, Jacqueline Bouvier Kennedy, was a Catholic. Catholics were assimilating, moving out of Catholic neighborhoods and abandoning the old parish. They had pulled even with the rest of the population in college attendance, and they were getting pluralist, not Catholic, educations: only about one-third of Catholic collegians in 1961 were in Catholic schools. For those who remained in Catholic schools, Catholic education was becoming less exotic, more mainstream. The Catholic theologian John Courtney Murray was on the cover of *Time* magazine in 1960—twelve years after the Protestant theologian Reinhold Niebuhr's appearance, six years before the famous "Is God Dead?" cover story. The education received at Georgetown or Holy Cross, or any of the lesser-known Catholic schools, was, by midcentury, largely secular.[17]

Catholics were now Americans, and not just because of Kennedy. It was something ineffable. Catholic burghers were American burghers—and Catholic hippies were American hippies. If the Catholic countercultural ethos of the 1960s was, as one observer put it, a kind of neo-Romanticism, characterized by a poetic vision, a mistrust of routine and discipline, a reverence for nature, a volkish ethnic consciousness, and millennial expectations, then it closely resembled the general American counterculture.[18] Being urban and attending college at the same rate as the rest of the population, Catholics were full participants in the American countercultural experiment.

Catholics never flew the banner of civil rights as proudly as Protestants did, but they did not ignore the issue either. Several hundred priests, sisters, and brothers were at the historic 1965 march on Selma, Alabama. (The local ordinary, Archbishop Thomas Toolen, did not approve, saying that they "should be home doing God's work.") There had been American nuns on a picket line even in the early days of Vatican II: in 1963 a group of Franciscan sisters in Chicago had marched, in their habits, in front of the Loyola University building that housed the Illinois Club for Catholic Women, which banned blacks. The Glenmary Sisters in Cincinnati were known for their attention to the race problem in the mid-1960s, as were the sisters of the Immaculate Heart of Mary in Los Angeles, who in 1967 and 1968 traded their habits for civilian clothes and "explor[ed] heretofore forbidden areas of the secular city from pop art to non-violent direct action"—to the displeasure of Cardinal Francis McIntyre. By the time the dispute was resolved, 150 of 540 sisters had left religious life altogether, and 285 others had become the largest group of American religious ever to be "laicized"; they were formally released from their vows, and they reconstituted as the Immaculate Heart Community, an intentional community of lay-women, one with a counterculture vibe.[19]

Catholics' worldliness, their sense of being part of an international culture, made them less reflexively patriotic than many conservative Protestants; but the Catholic Church had always been rigidly anticommunist, so on balance they supported the Vietnam War at least as much as other Americans did. Catholics fought and died there out of proportion to their numbers in the white population. But they also produced a disproportionate share of antiwar activists. The Berrigan brothers, priests Philip and Daniel, are the best known, but David Miller, a member of the Catholic Worker movement, became the first American to burn his draft card publicly and serve time in prison for Vietnam draft resistance. On November 9, 1965, Roger Laporte, a graduate of the Jesuits' Le Moyne College and an admirer of the Berrigans and Dorothy Day, expressed his feelings by sitting in front of the United Nations General Assembly Building and setting himself on fire.[20]

The sexual revolution flourished more at Bennington and Oberlin than at Providence College and Notre Dame, but Catholics thought deeply about the changes in sexual mores. Two issues in particular forced Catholics to examine their consciences. First, in 1968 Pope Paul VI issued *Humanae Vitae,* which reaffirmed the church's opposition to artificial birth control. "Every marital act," he wrote, "must remain open to the transmission of life." American Catholics were already disobeying this teaching, of course. The number of

Catholics with eight siblings was not what it once had been.[21]

Second, the modern women's liberation movement began. As women sought career parity with men, and as other religious traditions began ordaining women, liberal Catholics began to wonder whether the spirit of Vatican II might open the priesthood to women. "What will happen," one woman asked in 1965, in the liberal Catholic magazine *Commonweal,* "to the women in these other denominations, women who turn to the study of theology, pass the examinations, and in the subjective certainty of a vocation ask for the office of pastor, and in the Catholic church for the priesthood? . . . Tradition, which in this case has already been abandoned by many of the churches of Protestant countries taking part in interconfessional dialogue, is not an insuperable obstacle even in the Catholic church." In the same journal, Mary Daly, a prominent and radical Catholic feminist, wrote that "Catholic women are becoming more and more aware that something is out of joint. . . . When St. Paul told women to be silent in the churches, he was speaking in a normal manner for a Jew of his time. . . . Today, however, the anti-feminist tradition within the church is having a hard time finding firm legs to stand on. . . . It seems inevitable that the question of the ordination of women in the Catholic church will be raised, sooner or later."[22]

Catholics knew the church was dividing. In 1969 the picture was bleak, according to one observer: "priests defying their bishops; theologians defying the pope; religious leaving their convents; nuns and seminarians picketing; Catholic coeds demanding the pill; Catholic universities 'going secular,' being torn by controversies over academic freedom, and so on and so on." But in our examination of Catholic liturgical reform, we must, again, remember that Catholic laypeople did not all of a sudden, in 1965, discover their voice. Their history in America and elsewhere was already cacophonous; some of the voices were dissenting, some were just different. Catholics had role models for rebellion, too. Jack Kerouac, the great Beat writer, was born Jean Louis Lebris de Kerouac in 1922, son of French-Canadian Catholic parents who had immigrated to Lowell, Massachusetts. The Berkeley free speech activist Mario Savio was an Italian-American Catholic. The antiwar activist Tom Hayden and the gritty, realist writer Robert Stone, author of the Vietnam classic *Dog Soldiers,* were Catholics. Flannery O'Connor, too, of course.[23] Thoughtful historians and critics have tried, with some success, to locate these men and women in the Catholic tradition. All of them were born well before Vatican II, and they had dual educations, one catechetical, the other not. For twentieth-century American Catholics, both educations, equally, made them the Americans they became.

In his dyspeptic book about bad church music, Thomas Day tells the story of a friend at a mass in the early 1970s: "The time came around for the Handshake of Peace. . . . My friend turned to the elderly lady at this point and, holding out his hand in friendship, said, 'May the peace of the Lord be with you.' The old lady scowled. She looked at the proffered hand as if it were diseased. 'I don't believe in that shit,' she replied and, without missing a breath, went back to the quiet mumbling of her rosary."[24]

There is a tendency to think that this woman was typical in the world before Vatican II: raised on a Latin Mass performed by priests who expected no noise from the pews. But Catholics in certain parts of the world, Day notes, had a rich tradition of singing and praying aloud. In Germany and Poland, for example, the Mass was often accompanied by enthusiastic singing. And it is hard to imagine total lay silence in an Italian culture that had produced Verdi's *Requiem.* But in the United States, where the tone had been set by Irish priests, the quiet, controlled, ascetic Mass had become the norm. Here, "the flashy organ playing in French churches or thunderous hymns in the churches of Bavaria (not to mention the orchestras for High Mass) were unmistakable signs of decadence."[25] Bach and Mozart were not part of the American liturgical experience.

There had been liturgical reforms before—perhaps the first

"reform" was Pope Pius V's standardizing the Tridentine Mass in his *Missale Romanum* of 1570—but Americans had always been liturgically timid, accepting at face value the *Motu proprio* of Pope Pius X in 1903, which had established "a sort of trinity of song acceptable to the Church: Gregorian chant . . . Renaissance *a cappella* polyphony, and modern polyphonic composition." So the Constitution on the Sacred Liturgy, passed overwhelmingly by Vatican II in late 1962 and promulgated December 4, 1963, was thus particularly freighted for the American church. Article 121 of the *Sacrosanctum Concilium* section charges Catholic composers with a sacred task: "Composers, filled with the Christian spirit, should feel that their vocation is to develop sacred music and to increase its store of treasures. Let them produce compositions having the qualities proper to genuine sacred music, not confining themselves to works that can be sung only by large choirs, but providing also for the needs of small."

At first, some composers believed that even music composed in this new, liberal spirit should grow organically from Gregorian chant, be somehow derivative of it. But as the changes in the Mass were phased in, from the First Sunday of Advent, 1964, to the First Sunday of Advent, 1965, it became apparent that the Mass would have an entirely new feel. The priest was facing the communicants. He was speaking English. The new Mass was often punctuated by hymns to be sung by the congregation. "No longer the familiar sound of inaudible petitions and thank-yous offered to holy ones for favors sought and received," one historian writes. "Now everyone was asked (and expected) to participate 'fully and prayerfully.'"[26]

Critics declared the new Mass stillborn. "An aesthetic fiasco," said one in 1966. "The idea of recruiting the congregation into hyperactive participation simply hasn't worked," said another.[27] So many people accepted this wisdom that Thomas Day titled his 1990 book *Why Catholics Can't Sing*. But it is interesting that the critics do not agree on whether there is too much singing (by obnoxious folkies), too little (by a displeased silent majority of Catholics), or too little good singing (by a people not acculturated to singing out loud). If critics had such varying takes on the Vatican II liturgical experiment—not just in interpretation, but on the very facts of the matter—maybe there was no typical experience. And the evidence does suggest a variety of experiences. Some priests eagerly adopted the changes and encouraged experimentation, and others did not. Some laypeople felt newly liberated to sing, while others rued the thought.

Nobody, however, could ignore the changes. They could detest Vatican II, but they could not pretend that it hadn't happened. For in the United States, new plainsong hymnals appeared, beginning around 1965, and they sold widely. *The People's Mass Book, Our Parish Prays and Sings, The Hymnal of Christian Unity,* and others were adopted by hundreds of parishes, and there is no Gregorian chant in them. Except for the church's official imprimatur on the copyright page, they look like Protestant hymnals.[28]

Even if one's home parish eschewed the new liturgical options, one could no longer get a uniform experience across the world. Before Vatican II, a Catholic could travel everywhere and find masses that, in many basic elements, looked and sounded alike. But after 1965 a mass might be in Latin, or in Spanish, or in English, or in Lithuanian—it all depended on the priest, the neighborhood, the ethnic makeup of the parish, and the general temperament of the worshipers. This new pluralism extended beyond the United States. During Holy Week 1969 the Golconda priests in Colombia created a scandal by celebrating the traditional Good Friday liturgy with a twist. The words "I thirst" were rendered as "I thirst for justice, for equality, for freedom from want, for education." "Why hast Thou abandoned me?" was replaced by a child's saying, "I'm hungry."[29] Not all experiments were so daring as to change the words of Jesus, but even obedient Catholics were varying the Mass according to taste.

New ideas came from the ambient culture, and in the United

States, in the late 1960s, this meant folk or rock music. "Guitar mass" became a standard joke, sure to provoke rolled eyes and smirks. "I can remember," Thomas Day writes, "attending those first parish 'folk masses' back in the 1960s. . . . At the entrance they sang *Michael, Row the Boat Ashore*. At the Offertory there was *Kumbaya*. . . . Hands clapped. Guitars twanged." What Day describes as "Ego Renewal put to music" or "egotistical and narcissistic folk songs" may be more charitably understood as many Catholics' being in sync with both American culture and the spirit of Vatican II.[30] Having at last reached educational and socioeconomic parity with the rest of America—having fully emerged from psychic and geographic ghettoes—Catholics were fully attuned to American popular culture. They were hippies, Yippies, Jesus People, and commune dwellers, just like other Americans; or they were soldiers who fought in Vietnam and Republicans who voted for Nixon. They were Americans.

So when it came time for the Mass to change, American visual and musical aesthetics informed the changes. One writer summed it up well in 1972: "American Catholics are for the first time in their history aware of theological controversies that touch the most basic doctrines of Roman Catholicism. . . . On the other hand American Catholics have 'come of age' in their society." Guitar masses were the result. Hardly everybody approved, but by that point Catholics were used to disagreeing with the pope—on birth control, divorce, and so forth. One cheeky young Catholic, a Fordham University graduate and Yale Law student, said in 1967 that "on liturgical matters, I don't think anybody cares any longer what the Pope says."[31]

The seminaries, far from being bastions of tradition, were important incubators of Catholic folk music. Between 1965 and 1970, four leading Catholic folk composers or publishers studied at St. Thomas Seminary in Louisville, Kentucky: Joe Wise, Dan Onley, Pat Mudd, and Charlie Dittmeier. At St. Mary's Seminary in Baltimore, one could find, at various times, Mudd, Dittmeier, Jack Miffleton, Skip Sanders, Neil Blunt, and Tom Parker. Carey Landry and

The Catholic troubadour Joe Wise performs in Saginaw, Michigan, about 1968. Reprinted with the permission of Joe Wise.

publisher Dan Onley both studied at Catholic University in Washington, D.C. If one adds four more names—Ed Gutfreund, Sr. Miriam Therese Winter, Eric Sylvester, and Ray Repp—one has a fairly complete list of the leaders of the Catholic folk music movement.[32]

The music they wrote could make the Mass exciting and strange. Instead of sitting, standing, and kneeling, the new music might encourage swaying in a circle. The music might, on occasion, be accompanied by interpretive dance or drumming. And, perhaps most powerfully, the music provided opportunities for women to lead the congregation. Folk music is gender-blind. Women could play guitar and lead songs, just as men could. Folk music based on the blues even allowed a black voice into the Mass: Joe Wise, a leading Catholic folk composer, was a protégé of the black priest Clarence Rivers, who had heard Wise play in Memphis and had given him three thousand dollars to record his music. Wise made a monaural demo tape, later found a publisher, quit his job running a coffee shop, and toured with his blues- and gospel-inflected folk songs.

Songs by composers like Wise, Sr. Miriam Therese Winter and the Medical Mission Sisters, and the Cincinnatian Ed Gutfreund are typical folk not only in their musical influences, but in their language and tropes, too. Their songs feature, for example, the symbolism of nature, weather, and the earth's bounty. When Winter sang, "I saw raindrops on my window" ("Joy Is Like the Rain," 1965), or Wise sang, "Spirit filled yet hungry we await your food" ("Take Our Bread," 1966), they were simultaneously hailing the religious dimensions of nature and the political environmentalism of the times. These themes are even more explicit in Gutfreund's "Encircle Us" (1978): "feast on the bread of life again. . . . God comes to nourish and feed ev'ryone." Bread, of course, has earthy connotations and special Christian meaning, referring to the communion wafers. Gutfreund titled one of his songs "Your Bread Is for the World."

Catholic folk songs also emphasized the primacy of intimate relations over distant, obedient ones—symbolism analogous to

Sister Miriam Therese Winter, a Medical Mission Sister whose folk melodies became new Catholic standards, sits with her guitar in Jerusalem, ca. 1974. Reprinted with the permission of Miriam Therese Winter.

choosing lay leadership over clerical diktats. In the lay spirit of Vatican II, the God of these songs is kinder and gentler, more a benevolent father than a judgmental overlord. Joe Wise—himself a rather gentle soul, who retired to the Arizona desert to lead journal-writing workshops and paint watercolors—makes this point by treating man's and woman's relationship with God as a partnership: "Yours as we stand at the table you set," he sings in "Take Our Bread." "We are the sign of your life with us yet." For Miriam Therese Winter— later a professor of "liturgy, worship, spirituality, and feminist studies" at Hartford Seminary—God is a facilitator of human amity, one who "ask[s] us to care for each other."

Finally, Catholic folk songs encourage, in addition to naturalism and familiarity, a noncreedal universalism. Their religion is not about doctrine or catechism but about the generalized spirit. Whereas traditional Catholic liturgical music reminds people of the complexity and fanciness of Catholic ritual, these folk songs could easily be sung in a Methodist, Lutheran, or Presbyterian church. Ed Gutfreund's "Alleluia, Praise to the Lord" (1978) does not mention Jesus, resurrection, or atonement. It could appeal to Muslims or Jews. It could be Unitarian.[33]

These composers and singers, often nurtured in seminaries (and often leaving the seminaries before becoming priests), were dedicated to radical transformation of the Mass, and they benefited from three other groups also devoted to innovations. The first group comprised all the priests predisposed, even before Vatican II had ended, to experiment with the liturgy. (As early as 1964, the *National Catholic Reporter* ran a story about Sacred Heart, the "hootenanny parish" in Warrensburg, Missouri: "hardly a Sunday goes by, say the ushers, but a stranger will nervously edge up to one of them during Mass and whisper, 'Pardon me, but is this a Catholic church?'") The second group comprised the publishers. Almost as soon as Catholics began composing sacred folk music, there were publishing houses devoted to its dissemination. In Chicago there was Dennis Fitzpatrick's F.E.L.,

"Friends of the English Liturgy," which published the *Young People's Folk Hymnal*. In Cincinnati there was the World Library of Sacred Music, publisher of the *People's Mass Book* and the tremendously popular song sheets of Joe Wise; Ray Bruno's Epoch Universal Publications; and Dan Onley's North American Liturgy Resources.[34]

The third group, of course, comprised those Catholics who wanted to jettison the old Mass, replacing it with something unusual, contemporary, and new.

Catholics worship at their neighborhood parish. If you're Catholic, and you move from an urban Catholic ghetto to an airy suburb, you become a member of the parish that includes your new suburban neighborhood. You might have sentimental connections to the old church, but it's not yours anymore, because parish membership corresponds to geography. You may still drive in for Mass at the old church, but when you are married, when your children are baptized, and when you are buried, it is in the new parish. You may get special permission to have the old family priest do the mass—and such permission can be easy to obtain—but the general rule is that you have a new priest, a new church, a new religious home. Historically, there has been only one important exception. Bishops often divided racial and ethnic groups into different parishes. And after Vatican II, there was a new logic to the ethnic parishes: if people were to hear the Mass in the vernacular, then it made sense for all native speakers of, say, Lithuanian to be grouped into a Lithuanian parish, where they could hear a Lithuanian Mass. Such parishes were "extraterritorial."[35]

In the late 1960s another kind of exception was made. In a Catholic city like Cincinnati, with so many educated, middle-class, acculturated Catholics, Vatican II scraped away the happy flora to expose serious fault lines in the church community. Some Catholics wanted a fresh, updated Mass, with folk songs, congregational singing, and lay participation; others wanted the Mass to look as familiar as possible; and many wanted something in between. Those who wanted an experimental Mass with new music found each other, at first by accident and then by word of mouth, and in 1968 they got an extraterritorial parish based not on race, not on native tongue, but on worship style.

The Community of Hope was not the only extraterritorial congregation founded on worship style, but it was the first, and it was one of only two to have official parish status (the other was the Community of Christian Service in Dayton, Ohio). Atlanta's Community of Christ Our Brother began to meet in 1967, and later there were the Bea Community in Dayton, Ohio, and the New Jerusalem community, a charismatic spin-off from the Community of Hope—but none of these got parish status. Numerous smaller groups of lay Catholics began, in the 1960s, to meet without official sanction of the church, not unlike the countercultural Jewish havurot we will soon meet. The Cathedral of St. Francis de Sales in San Francisco, not an extraterritorial parish, drew hundreds of Catholics away from their home churches by offering an informal mood and new music in the liturgy. (One week, a mime mimed a sermon. Another week, children celebrated a "Peanuts" comic strip mass.[36]) But the Community of Hope was unique in its combination of size, longevity, vigor, and official sanction.

The Community began in the fall of 1968 when some Franciscan brother candidates at St. Anthony Friary in Cincinnati got their supervisor, Fr. Joseph Frommeyer, to ask Archbishop Karl J. Alter for permission to hold a special, nontraditional, 11:00 a.m. Mass for teenagers. Alter gave permission, and on December 8, 1968, the brother candidates and friars hosted about ten laypeople for a guitar Mass. Lay guitarists soon joined the group, then some friends and relatives, and soon a number of women religious, or nuns, became active. In January 1970 Fr. Ulmer Kuhn began to serve as "priest-coordinator" of the small worship group.[37]

By May 1970, the membership rolls of the Community of Hope included 284 people: fifty-one families and about seventy "singles."

They came from forty-seven geographical parishes. The parents worked in professions like real estate, carpentry, architecture, and bus driving. Nineteen of the families had three children, while seven families had two and seven families had four. One family had ten children. Five of the parents had Ph.D.s. Of the singles, the most commonly represented ages were eighteen and twenty-five, with eight members apiece. The singles represented a wide variety of occupations, including thirty-one students, fourteen teachers, four nurses, one barber, one lithographer, and one reservation agent for Delta Airlines. Twelve of the singles had master's degrees, but none had a Ph.D. In short, the group had grown by 1970, two years after its founding, to almost three hundred middle- and working-class Catholics with a wide range of education levels. Few families were religiously observant enough to have lots of children, but they were culturally Catholic enough to prefer three or four children to zero or one. Many were of German ancestry. They were pretty typical Cincinnatians.[38]

At first, Community members remained affiliated with their geographical parishes, but they soon began to think of the Community as their religious tribe, and they wanted to celebrate sacraments like baptism, marriage, and first communion with Father Kuhn and the Community. In August 1970 Kuhn wrote to Archbishop Paul Leibold to say that with about three hundred regular attendants at the friary on Sundays, not having parish status was beginning to present problems. One woman, Nancy Emmerich, had already been granted permission, by her own pastor and by the archdiocese, to have her wedding performed by Kuhn at the friary on August 29. Since her request had been granted, two couples had asked that their children be baptized at the friary. "I realize that your permission is required," Kuhn wrote to Leibold. "I'm asking your permission to have these two baptisms. Also, I'm asking your advice on how to handle such requests if they come in the future—as I'm sure they will."[39]

Leibold wrote back, granting permission for the baptism of John and Mary Kahles's baby. He then added a rather testy note: "I do not know who is responsible for this growing Community you describe; but it would seem that if some priest wants to accept the responsibility for the spiritual care of these people he would make it known and we could discuss . . . giving this Community some kind of status. Evidently these people are accepting the service of the church; it is not too clear how they are fulfilling their responsibilities to the church."[40]

Rather than squelching some attempt to form an extraterritorial parish, Leibold suggested it. He believed that bringing these nontraditional worshipers under the care and supervision of the archdiocese would ensure greater fidelity to Catholic tradition, as well as greater control by the archbishop. Better to have an eccentric nonterritorial parish, Leibold believed, than to lose these Catholics to agnosticism, or to the breakaway clusters of Catholics in the libertine, renegade, "underground" church.[41]

Taking the hint, Kuhn wrote to the Father Provincial and Definitorium two weeks later to describe his congregation and make a request. "There is a core group of 350 people," he wrote, inflating the previous month's figures by one-sixth. "We have eight liturgy committees who rotate in assisting with the planning of the liturgy each Sunday. . . . We have a ten-week Adult Education Program in progress with some sixty registrants. Pre-School religious instructions begin October 4, for five and six year olds." He then asked for provisional nonterritorial status, to be evaluated for renewal at the end of one year. Nine months later—Catholic bureaucracies are still bureaucracies—Kuhn received a letter from Archbishop Leibold granting the Community of Hope parish status, with the understanding that members would continue to support financially the parishes whose services, like parochial schools, they were using.[42]

The eight liturgy committees that Kuhn mentions were at the heart of the Community of Hope, but members had other reasons for joining, like attention to children, intimate community, lay participation, and the voluntary nature of belonging to the Community.

"As we became involved, our children enjoyed it, and we became withdrawn from the geographical parish," said Ron Hilvers, an early member. He also enjoyed "its informality, the enthusiasm of the people—they wanted to be there. . . . I feel these were for the most part people who felt frustrated by the lack of action in their traditional parishes. They couldn't carry out the mandates of Vatican II because of the reluctance of traditional Catholics and pastors who for centuries had done things one way." Ron Discepoli, another early member, said, "The parish we came from was a very large parish. . . . You don't have the closeness you can have in a very small parish."[43]

But the liturgy was on nearly everyone's list of what they loved most about the Community. The liturgy committees met at members' houses on weeknights. They selected a theme for their assigned Sunday, chose Scripture readings, and picked musical selections. The celebrant priest was always present—it might be Kuhn, or it could be one of the guest priests whose visits he encouraged—and a member of the musicians' committee always attended to suggest music and ensure that the committee's selections did not exceed the musicians' capabilities. The committee would help design a dialogue homily for the priest and congregation. Sometimes they planned skits.[44]

Eugene Breyer was music director from 1973 until his retirement on May 9, 1982. "Typically we had electric keyboard, drums, several guitars, mandolin, two flutes," he said. "Especially early on, we did a lot of popular stuff that seemed to carry the right message for a particular liturgy—Simon and Garfunkel." Breyer had veto power over music selections, but he overruled the liturgy committees only once. One of the committees had chosen a gospel arrangement by a local composer, James Moore. Breyer and his musicians tried to get the song to sound right, but they knew something wasn't working. Breyer went to see Moore for advice. "After spending about an hour and a half with him, I said, 'You know what? I think you may need to be black.' And he said, 'You know what? You may be right.'"[45]

With the dialogic homilies that required audience participation, the liturgy committees that needed members, and the masses that lasted about an hour and a half, the Community of Hope was unusually demanding of its members. They wrote new prayers. They solicited new music. Like gay Unitarians, and like the progressive Jews and Southern Baptists we will meet, folk Catholics did not seek to escape responsibility; their new projects inevitably ate up more time and energy than they had spent on religion before. Members of the Community helped plan the liturgy, write the bulletin, track the finances, and fill leadership positions. Except for Kuhn and his successors, there were no administrators—no church secretary, no accountant. When it came time to find new buildings in which to meet, the volunteer leaders conducted the search. Lay members staffed the adult and children's classes. Although they could not always agree what, besides liturgy, they wanted from the Community—a February 1970 survey shows that forty-three were interested in a "discussion group, based on tapes or movies"; twenty-eight wanted a "social action group"; and twenty-two wanted "Socials: dances and parties"— they willingly gave time.[46] They were fleeing tradition, not commitment.

That may be one reason why the archdiocese continued to sanction the Community of Hope. The archdiocese could not, after all, argue with success. At a time when numerous books and articles bemoaned falling attendance at masses, a 1971 report by Kuhn showed an average of 628 people attending Mass at the Community every weekend, with 551 taking communion. When in 1973 Kuhn wanted permission to celebrate three spring masses outside, permission was granted so long as "the liturgical prescriptions will be fulfilled and due reverence for the Blessed Sacrament maintained."

Occasionally, Kuhn wrote letters reassuring the archbishop that he and his congregants were not assaulting tradition, just massaging it a little. In 1972, for example, after an unspecified incident, Kuhn wrote to Archbishop Leibold, "I was dismayed and rather put out to learn of the lack of sensitivity to liturgical propriety which happened at St. Francis Seminary. Members called me and I advised them to return to what is approved and admonished them that if they wished to build community there was no visible way to do this except within the framework of the Church and the proper guidelines." The same day, he wrote in a separate letter, "I've learned that it's not only possible but highly desirable to remain within the liturgical guidelines and still have a participative and sound liturgy. There is no need to feed cookies to the pre-schoolers or use leavened bread at the Liturgy."[47] Kuhn probably believed what he was saying, but there is no doubt that it was what the archbishop wanted to hear, and a succession of archbishops—Alter, Leibold, Joseph Bernardin (who later became archbishop of Chicago), Daniel Pilarczyk—let the Community be, even offered help when needed.[48]

When conflict arose, it was not with the archbishop but with the Franciscans in whose home the Community met. In August 1972 the Franciscan Provincial Board announced that "in order to meet the needs of the Formation House and St. Anthony's Friary, it would be necessary for the Community of Hope to establish itself in a new place or places by November 1, 1972." Ron Hilvers explained: "Sometimes we clashed with them, because they are a quiet people who had become accustomed to living out there in the woods. The Community of Hope was noisy, and we would meet with Father Ulmer in the evenings. And we were voted out by the Franciscans who lived there. Their House chapter finally said, 'They've gotta go.'"[49]

In November the Community began to meet at its new home, Our Lady of Presentation Church, on Westwood-Northern Boulevard in Cincinnati. But a year later, in the fall of 1973, the Community was again looking for a new home. "At Presentation Church," Kuhn wrote in 1977, "we were cramped for space and time and lost many of the high school group and even others who felt the pinch of time and space." They considered buying an old building, "the former Girls' Town property," but the development company that owned it failed to submit a proposal on time, and so on October 19,

1973, the Community voted, by a two-to-one margin, to accept the offer made by the Rev. James Shappelle of St. Leo's Church.[50]

Ron Hilvers, who as lay coordinator in 1973 was in charge of finding new quarters, said the Community left Presentation for St. Leo's "because the pastor invited us to come down there. There was more room. It had better parking and it was being underused. It's in a German neighborhood that had had eight hundred families and was down to about fifty families, mostly Appalachian black. A very poor neighborhood, and we helped with rent and utility bills. It was beneficial, but there were some problems. They were territorial too, and didn't like to see these newcomers with electric piano and drums."[51]

Alternative religious space sometimes must be physical if it is to be spiritual: the gay Unitarians wanted their one hundred square feet of office space. The folk Catholics found that though they worshiped the same God, they could not do so in the Franciscans' space. It would be interesting to know just how loud the Community of Hope was on Sunday mornings: were they really too loud, or was it just the fact of their "electric piano and drums," or perhaps the crying babies crawling around, that made them unacceptable to the Franciscans? Their music was, after all, a culture, and within the Catholic Church, these new sounds struck some as the ultimate counterculture.

Both Kuhn's historical memorandum of 1977 and a planning memo of 1973 suggest that, around the time of the move to St. Leo's, there was concern about falling numbers. Could the Community have been past its prime at so young an age? The memorandum says that average Mass attendance in 1970 had been 460, but in 1971 it was 370, then fell to 285 the next year, then 235. However, archdiocesan records show that the number of "souls" affiliated with the Community had grown from 784 in 1971 to 910 in 1972. This means that the sclerosis that afflicted large, traditional parishes had already set in: bigger numbers but lower rates of participation.[52]

Under such circumstances, moving to a new building might be a tonic to reinvigorate the membership. The Community initially found the bucolic friary an escape, a flight into a freer physical and religious space, a freedom they embraced by holding outdoor masses. "If suddenly on a lovely Sunday morning in May you saw hundreds of balloons—red, blue, yellow, green—floating skyward above St. Anthony Friary in Cincinnati, Ohio, you probably wondered what the sons of St. Francis were up to," an anonymous member wrote in an early history of the Community. "The balloons were freed as a climax to the outdoor Pentecost liturgy, May 30, 1971."[53] The outdoor mass would become something of a Community tradition. The character of the Community, its members knew, was shaped by the space that held it, and the outdoors was its own space. The subsequent moves—into the old churches, churches that looked like churches and were in urban neighborhoods—had to affect how people felt about the Community. It became less heterodox, and less of a statement. Their Catholic family began to feel a little less unusual, and more catholic.

In 1972 or 1973, when the Community was at Presentation Church, it prepared a "Talents and Resources Directory." The document is a real period piece, recalling that brief moment when food and day-care cooperatives flourished, encounter sessions replaced traditional therapy, and free "universities without walls" were started in large cities. The idea was to deprofessionalize Americans' lives, to integrate their vocations and their avocations. People could call on their own spiritual gifts and make a go of it without religious professionals. Since everyone had talents, if you had enough generous friends, your needs could be met without turning to the consumerist Yellow Pages.

In the Talents and Resources Directory, you could find babysitting or pet sitting or financial planning, all provided by fellow Community of Hope worshipers. For knitting, call Joanne Byrne. If you need a beautician, call Evelyn Ducker (but only after 6:00 P.M., she says). Suzanne Davidson is a reading specialist, Kent Slaughter works

In the years after Vatican II, outdoors masses, like this one in Pennsylvania, became popular among liturgically liberal Catholics. Photograph by Charles Blahusch, *The Catholic Witness,* ca. 1971.

with the mentally retarded, and Jeri Lynne Riesenberg can help you with adoption or foster care. Dottie Hilvers is a nurse.[54]

The directory is an artifact of a small community dedicated to forging real friendships among people who prayed the same liturgy. It was Catholicism made softer, less Gothic—but, again, with more demands on people's time. It looked different, but made no new theological claims. In all the written and oral histories of the Community of Hope, there is no evidence that people chose it for political reasons. "There wasn't a lot of political activity in the Community of Hope," said Ron Hilvers. "One time a radical feminist, I would describe her, took over the microphone, and she monopolized it, basically dressed down the priest for being part of a male-dominated clergy. It became obnoxious. I always suspected she was invited by someone to come in." Eugene Breyer, the music director, said, "Politically I would say we tended toward the liberal, although that's not really much of an issue and that's not universally true."[55]

There is no evidence, for example, that the Community had positions on woman priests or the birth control pill. They just wanted an innovative Mass, and they wanted friends who dug new music and a more relaxed mood. They wanted a place where kids could sit on the floor and parents could wear jeans as guitars played. But they still confessed sins and took communion. This was a counterculture, but not a political one. It was a counterculture in a strictly religious sense, and religious in a very specific way, aesthetic and musical, not doctrinal. The religious lives these Catholics wanted simply could not fit into the traditional parishes. But that did not mean they had to move out of their neighborhoods or quit their jobs. Nor did it mean they wanted to flee Catholicism. By allowing them their own parish, the archbishop gave them religious lives that were distinct, yet still Catholic.

That the Community had no political goals helps explain why, in the end, it faded away gently. Folk music and the new liturgy seemed very radical to William F. Buckley and Garry Wills; the guitars might as well have been playing "Taps." Yet the Community of Hope, founded to promote such abominations, shrank drastically after its first few years. It lasted until 1989, but it never regained the vigor of the early 1970s, when as many as ten liturgy committees planned the Sunday masses, ten musicians played on Sundays, and the music service often featured new songs by Joe Wise, Eric Sylvester, and Ed Gutfreund. In 1974 Kuhn wrote to his flock, "Perhaps after six years we can say the honeymoon is over."[56] Helen Buswinka, a Community member, wrote in 1976 that "by 1974, the number of people involved in the Community had dwindled."[57] A 1982 newspaper article said that "about 150 persons worship regularly" at the Community of Hope; in 1989 the Community had shrunk to about 80 people, and the archdiocese, faced with a shortage of priests, reassigned its pastor, the Rev. Ted Kosse, to another church.[58]

The Community had gotten so small because it was no longer so different. Yes, it had become less intimate and more rote—but, more important, the rest of the Catholic Church had become more intimate and less rote. "Community of Hope no longer considered outlandish," read a *Cincinnati Post* subheadline in 1978. "Earlier, there was a lot of resistance," Ron Hilvers told the paper. "Anymore, we have people calling us or visiting us for ideas in worship." In 1989 the *Enquirer* reported on the Community's closing: "[Ann] Fox, 46, of Bridgetown and the chairperson of the parish council, said the community's decline in membership . . . could be a sign that the parish churches now offer what people have sought in the community. 'The community has perhaps fulfilled its mission.'"[59]

It is hard to quantify how deeply folk music and worship permeated the Catholic Mass. But both liberal and conservative Catholics talk about guitar masses as if they are now everywhere. And we do have some hard evidence. In 1976, for example, F.E.L. Publications, a prominent publisher of Catholic folk music, sued Chicago's Archbishop John Cody and ninety-seven of his parishes for copyright infringement. Although F.E.L. had offered to sell individual sheets of music at two and a half cents each, or to license churches to reproduce anything they wanted for one hundred dollars a year, illegally photocopied sheets and hymnals continued to appear. F.E.L. estimated its annual losses at three million dollars, and it filed suit for two million; in 1978 F.E.L. won. That was a lot of money, especially by mid-seventies standards, and it suggests that if nearly a hundred Chicago parishes were using F.E.L.'s folk music, thousands of parishes across the country were, too.[60]

According to one observer, by 1978 folk music had "invaded" Catholic churches everywhere. The National Association of Pastoral Musicians, founded in 1976, immediately became a thriving home for music directors, choirs, hand-bell choirs, organists, guitarists, and Catholic musicians of all kinds. While it did not focus specifically on folk music, the association was populated by folkies, and its members were Vatican II enthusiasts and liturgical liberals. Catholics nostalgic for the old days loathed the group, but by 1980 it was sponsoring twelve regional conventions, in Philadelphia, Miami, San Antonio, Dubuque, Baton Rouge, San Francisco, and elsewhere. Musical experimentation was, in other words, an accomplished fact. It was an international phenomenon, celebrated in every country that had Catholics. Regretted, too, by mourners from the common to the famous: in England by Auberon Waugh, son of the novelist Evelyn Waugh; in the United States by Patrick Buchanan; in Australia by Hutton Gibson, leader of the Australian Alliance for Catholic Tradition (and father of movie star Mel Gibson).[61]

During the molestation scandals of 2002, the *Boston Globe* ran a story about one priest's struggle to comfort his parishioners. The priest, the Rev. Bernard McLaughlin, considered himself "a conservative turned moderate," not a liberal. Yet his Mass might have been transported from Cincinnati, circa 1970: "The breeze that blew across the parking lot at St. Gerard Majella Church on a recent Sunday carried with it the smell of sizzling hot dogs and hamburgers, the occasional cry of a baby, and the soulful sounds of teenage girls singing contemporary hymns. The Rev. Bernard McLaughlin, his portly frame cloaked in emerald green, stepped up to the mike set up for the parish's outdoor Mass and barbecue."[62]

The folk Catholics were on a mission. "Missions" are religious, and this religious quest was for newer music, less formality, and more warmth. In the years after Vatican II, the Roman Catholic Church responded to demand by changing its supply. Once Vatican II gave priests the latitude to permit changes in the liturgy, the popular liturgies were going to find homes, in the churches and the diocesan cathedrals where at first Simon and Garfunkel and Peter, Paul and Mary were feared. The Community's battle was won before it began; they had only to sit out the Vatican II culture wars for ten years or so—though, in the end, the Community lasted twenty—and when all the pyxes and fronds had been swung in disgust, the liturgy would be "updated," in the spirit of *aggiornamento.*

The Catholic Church looks different today. It reacted to the counterculture by providing a place for the aesthetics of the late 1960s, but without liberalizing in any other sense. Any political changes resulted from the perestroika ushered in by the new, more liberal feel of the church—and that feel was created by the new Mass. The countercultural legacy in the Catholic Church is primarily aesthetic, and the leadership did not contest these aesthetic changes. Though Catholics had had the most standardized liturgy of any American religion, a Mass fashioned by Rome, they became famous for guitar masses. But it was the Catholic Church whose official stands on other matters changed the least: abortion would not be approved, or birth control. Women never became priests. Because Vatican II had given the folkies permission, aesthetic changes were almost entirely decoupled from politics. In the Catholic Church, the hierarchy retained its tight, conservative control on what Catholics were supposed to believe, while the iconography of liberalism—the sandals, guitars, and hugging—seized the day, easily.

THREE

Jews and Communal Worship

American Jews have long had a special affinity, or at least toleration, for countercultures. Twentieth-century America's most notorious counterculture was the Communist Party, which, though moribund by the 1960s, had offered a self-sustaining, alternative world to disaffected anticapitalists, many of them Jews, during the Great Depression. "The Party" provided them with friends, summer camps, a network of professional services—communists wanted a politically sympathetic doctor, dentist, or insurance salesman—and a whole culture, marked by books to read, language to use, and ideas to adopt. Jews had participated in the criminal underworld, another counterculture. Consider Arnold Rothstein, the gambler who fixed the 1919 "Black Sox" World Series, or Bugsy Siegel, who helped build Las Vegas into a gambling mecca. Jews were important, too, in bohemian and avant-garde artistic circles: Gertrude Stein the modernist writer (abroad in Paris, of course), Clement Greenberg the art critic, Arnold Schoenberg the immigrant composer. From Hollywood to Tin Pan Alley, Jews showed a special affinity for African-American art forms, too.[1]

The majority of Jews were never so noteworthy, of course. But American Jews tended to be skeptical enough, to have enough critical distance from the assumptions of American life, to be at least suspicious of the status quo. As a minority culture, they were willing to support racial integration. They were generally urban dwellers, and urbanity correlates with liberalism; it also provides exposure to bohemian art and left-wing politics. Eastern European Jews had some history of labor activism and radical thought, and they were more likely to give a tolerant wink to their grandchildren's long hair or premarital cohabitation. Combine these factors with the concentration of Jews on college campuses, and the late 1960s yielded a good number of Jews off on an errand of self-discovery and societal critique. Some were famous—Bob Dylan, Allen Ginsberg, the guru Baba Ram Dass—but most were not. And in the Nixon years, many anonymous left-wing and hippie Jews came together in the *havurah*.

A havurah (the plural is havurot) is a small community of Jews who have decided to study, worship, or celebrate religious rituals together. About 1960, synagogue rabbis, eager to create small communities within their large congregations, began to form havurot, groups of ten or twenty families, within the synagogue membership. The havurah members would meet during the week, away from the rabbi. They would share Shabbat (the Hebrew sabbath) dinners, celebrate milestones like Bar Mitzvah ceremonies and weddings, and pray together. They might study or do volunteer work. By the 1970s these havurot had become common, resembling the small house Bible study groups organized within Protestant megachurches, making the impersonal more personal.

By the late 1960s, however, Jews dissatisfied with the institutional feel of their religion began to leave synagogues altogether, dropping out to form unaffiliated havurot—not within synagogues, but against them.[2] The countercultural havurah, as we will call it, could center around a study group, a coffee shop, or a communal living house. Havurat Shalom in Somerville, Massachusetts, the New York Havurah in New York City, and Fabrangen in Washington, D.C. were all countercultural havurot, a species that existed from 1968 to 1975, before winding down toward ignominy. Like the synagogue havurot, these groups would often just pray, celebrate the Sabbath and holidays, and do charitable work. Sometimes, though, they would picket, smoke dope, gaze at stars, and procure draft deferments.

Few Jews, probably no more than a couple thousand, ever joined countercultural havurot. It was not a profound experience for all of them; many alumni drifted back toward irreligion, or toward a rather undemanding affiliation with a large synagogue, the kind of institution they had held their parents blameworthy for joining (and then rarely attending). For many, being a hippie or a political leftist was the main idea, and Judaism gave extra bite, adding the teeth of ethnic flavor. But it is also true that an extraordinary number of havurah alumni became influential rabbis, professors, fund-raisers, and community activists. The spokespeople of Judaism in 2002 were the young *haverim* of 1972. We examine countercultural havurot, then, not because they peopled Judaism with thousands of learned, spiritually alive activists, but rather because they were central to a Jewish counterculture more influential than its small numbers would suggest.

In the early twentieth century, Rabbi Mordecai Kaplan started the Jewish renewal movement called Reconstructionism, which held that Judaism was best understood as a "civilization." It was more than a religion and more than an ethnicity: it was a nation of people, with their own folkways, and it would survive only if Jews lived, prayed, ate, played sports, and sang together. They had to integrate their entire lives, not just pray the *Shachrit* service every morning.[3]

Reconstructionism advanced in small brigades, study groups that formed to read Kaplan's 1934 magnum opus, *Judaism as a Civilization*.[4] When Kaplan visited Cleveland in 1935, he learned that several groups had already convened to study the book. Throughout the 1930s and 1940s Reconstructionists founded discussion groups that resembled the small, voluntary societies known later as havurot. Kaplan encouraged such endeavors, and in 1943 he and his protégé (and later son-in-law) Ira Eisenstein created the institution of the Reconstructionist Fellowship, a title they hoped interested groups would take on. Their members, Eisenstein wrote, "must undertake to seek in Judaism the means of spiritual growth, by cultivating habits of Jewish worship, study, and action"—a goal of 1960s havurot, too. "They must, finally, undertake to seek the maximum of fellowship and collaboration with other Jews." By 1948 these book clubs had yielded four fellowships, and there were forty-one study groups working toward certification as fellowships, in places as diverse as Alexandria, Virginia; Oakland, California; and Orlando, Florida.[5]

After World War II, Jews, many of them returning from war, got college degrees, moved to the suburbs, and joined the hundreds of

new synagogues being built there. Most of these synagogues affiliated with either the Conservative or Reform movements, and few
officially identified with Reconstructionism; in the 1950s the few
new Reconstructionist fellowships tended to be offshoots of Conservative synagogues whose rabbis had studied with Kaplan at Jewish
Theological Seminary. In 1955 Kaplan and Eisenstein established an
umbrella organization—a fellowship of fellowships, we might say—
to unite the groups.[6]

In 1960 Jakob J. Petuchowski wrote an article in the *Reconstructionist*, Kaplan's house magazine, diagnosing what he saw as the ail-
ments of the Jewish people: alienation, lack of learning, indifference
to tradition, and so forth. American Jews, having left behind the bigotry of old Europe, which had forced them to huddle together, were
living in the United States, with its smooth road of assimilation.
They faced constant temptation to abandon the tribe. The freedom
of the suburbs was deadly. Reform Judaism, which had proposed to
solve the dilemma by ignoring religious restrictions and embracing
American living, had failed. Reform Judaism, Petuchowski writes,
"originally envisaged a Jewish piety without a Jewish environment."
But "what, in point of fact, has come about is the Jewish environment without the Jewish piety."[7]

While the Jew neither could nor would return to olden days, he
could strive to recapture the feeling of Judaism not as a legal system
but as a "people which had committed itself to the Torah as its constitution. The ideal set-up for this kind of life, would, of course, be the
corporate life." One possible construction of the corporate life, Petuchowski suggests, might be borrowed from the first-century Pharisees, who sometimes joined in *habhurot*, "brotherhoods." Members
agreed to bind themselves to more stringent standards of observance
of the dietary and purity laws. While Reconstructionists like Petuchowski did not recommend obsessive observance of purity laws,
Petuchowski does propose that modern intimate brotherhoods,
modeled on the Pharisees', could begin anew or be started within

existing congregations. The heart of Petuchowski's vision was intentionality: one would join a habhurah not because one needed, in Eisenhower-era America, to affiliate with a congregation, but because one wanted to undertake willingly the observance of rituals in a like-minded community. A year later, in the same magazine, Jacob Neusner writes that in the years after the Alexandrian conquest (330 B.C.E.), many Pharisees joined havurot to cope with dislocation and assimilation—issues facing contemporary American Jews, too.[8]

We can see how this rhetoric would later prove so appealing in the late 1960s. The dissatisfaction with bourgeois society, the hunger for authentic community, the willingness to seek spirituality through rituals and communal living, the resistance to anything institutional—the Reconstructionist rabbis were already, years before the hippies, damning the dominant culture and wondering aloud how to find an alternative. Rather vaguely, Neusner suggests that the havurah could resemble Masonic lodges or service societies; he also notes that Rabbi Shamai Kantor of Toronto had already experimented with synagogue-based havurot, each based on a small number of members who have coherent interests. A Chicago study group founded by Eisenstein in 1955 began to describe itself as a havurah. The havurah was a central theme of the third annual conference of the Reconstructionist Federation, held in 1962 in Skokie, Illinois. In 1963 "ten Reconstructionist havurot were reported to exist; a Vice President for Havurot was among the new officers elected for the Reconstructionist Foundation." The next year, Ira Eisenstein went to Washington, D.C., to speak with some Jews interested in starting a havurah there.[9]

Mordecai Kaplan, a professor at the Conservative movement's Jewish Theological Seminary, had always envisioned Reconstructionism as a movement within other branches of Judaism. But Ira Eisenstein, his spiritual heir, was committed to building a separate branch, and in 1968 the Reconstructionist Rabbinical College opened outside Philadelphia, its propaganda boasting that "the idea of *havurah,* which we sought to publicize some nine years ago . . . has apparently caught on."[10]

One place it had caught on winningly was southern California. In September 1961 three Whittier couples, influenced by the *Reconstructionist* writings of Jakob Petuchowski, Jacob Neusner, and Ira Eisenstein, declared themselves a havurah. Dissatisfied with their synagogue rabbi's traditionalism, they covenanted to study, celebrate life's milestones and holidays, and worship on the Sabbath together, "enriching our lives with the cultural heritage of Judaism." Soon, a group of twenty-five was meeting twice a month. At the same time, an influential experiment was beginning in the Los Angeles suburbs. In summer 1970 Rabbi Harold Schulweis assumed the pulpit of Congregation Valley Beth Shalom of Encino, California. Before his arrival, some members had assembled a havurah, and early in his stewardship Schulweis went on a retreat with the members. Schulweis, a follower of Mordecai Kaplan who was aware of the havurah in Whittier, was impressed by the haverim and decided to take their experiment further. In his first Rosh Hashanah sermon at his new synagogue, in September 1970, Schulweis proposed organizing havurot within the congregation. The idea took hold, and by 1973, some thirty havurot operated under the auspices of Valley Beth Shalom. By 1975 some five hundred havurot had a combined membership of ten to fifteen thousand Californians.[11]

This expansion did not happen by word of mouth alone. Harold Schulweis evangelized for his cause, speaking and writing prolifically. "The synagogue must be HAVURIZED"—the capitals are his— "divided into groups of families, into clusters of congregational families who pledge to celebrate Jewish life, to learn together, to grow Jewishly together." Schulweis did not invent the synagogue havurah—it seems that the Toronto rabbi mentioned in Neusner's article may have, and beginning in 1963 havurot had begun to spread through Colorado—but he preached its good news at an auspicious time, to receptive ears. He convinced people that it could work.[12]

Havurot spread about the United States. The simple idea that Judaism works best in small groups is one of the religion's oldest ideas: in traditional Judaism, the quorum for prayer is ten Jewish adult males (all but the Orthodox will now accept women in the *minyan*). Yet in the 1950s Jews, when they bothered to attend services, practiced an institutional religion devoid of meaning and spirit—so the charge went. The havurah represented an alternative path. In 1972 Jacob Neusner collected seminal articles about havurot in *Contemporary Judaic Fellowship in Theory and Practice,* which was widely read by rabbis and students interested in Jewish renewal.[13] That book introduced them to the idea of the havurah (and to the word itself), and it also married in one volume the intellectual aspect of havurah, emphasized by Kaplan and the Reconstructionists, with an alternative version being practiced by innovative young adults. That newer, Aquarian version could be mystically introspective or fiercely activist.

"Our Hebrew school students," Harold Schulweis wrote in 1974, "are not unlike so many of their older brethren of the beat generation, the hippie generation, the generation flirting with Zen Buddhism, with Meher Baba, with the Jews for Jesus. . . . Often they are there because they are children of a pressurized middle class . . . and [because of] the terrible strain to get into a college of great status. The street and the campus missionaries enter into the vacuum of that spiritual anomie, pick up our children in VW vans, bring them to a commune, feed them, bathe them, embrace them. I recall pointing out [to one such youngster], 'You know, they only want your soul.' And he replied, 'I don't care if they want my soul, at least they want *my* soul.'"[14]

While Jews may have left in disproportionate numbers, most apostates were Christian, and religious leaders from all traditions worried about how to keep young people from straying.[15] Yet for all the elders' worries, many countercultural Jews had no intention of forsaking their people; they wished to combine their politics, their style, and their Judaism into a new, Jewish counterculture.

Grandchildren of the immigrant proletariat, these idealists may have received cursory religious educations in Hebrew school or at a Jewish summer camp. A high school visit to Israel, with an eye-opening trip to a praiseworthy kibbutz, solidified in them a *Yiddishkayt*—Jewishness—that would have been nurtured in a predominantly Jewish neighborhood, where Mom and Dad had Jewish friends and where Jewish playmates abounded. During the Kennedy years, Jews whose parents had been teachers or small businessmen began seeing that they could rise to positions of influence in this country. As the decade wore on, Jews' moderate liberalism, which encouraged people to work within the system for civil rights and a just foreign policy, was tested by three events: the war in Vietnam; the Six-Day War of 1967, which underscored the fragility, and then the strength, of the state of Israel; and the shift within the civil rights movement from integration to black separatism.[16]

Everybody saw the body bags arriving from Vietnam, everybody knew of the My Lai massacre. But people drew different conclusions. Some decided that the United States must fight harder, while Jews tended to take a more pacifist position. Within the antiwar ranks, however, we would be hard-pressed to find a "Jewish" position. When Jews turned against the war in Vietnam, their reasons were much the same as those of other Americans. Five of every six Yeshiva University students voted to join a nationwide student moratorium in 1970 to protest both the killing of four Kent State University students by National Guardsmen and President Nixon's decision to expand the war in Cambodia. The vote called for permitting students to withdraw from classes three weeks early for either a letter grade or a "pass." The Jewish Peace Fellowship ran an advertisement in the Jewish student press, rhetorically asking, "Can a Jew be a Conscientious Objector?"[17] These actions resembled those of secular and Christian groups opposed to the war.

If the Vietnam War did not have an unusual effect on Jews, the Six-Day War and the changing character of the civil rights movement did, both helping to fashion a *Jewish* counterculture. After the Six-Day War, in which Israel soundly defeated its Arab neighbors in 1967, a self-consciously Jewish student movement arose, comprising loosely connected groups organized around support for Israel, Soviet Jewry, and Jewish studies, and protests against institutional Jewry.

Young Jews, some of them products of the Conservative movement's Hebrew-speaking Ramah camps, noticed that Jewish artists were winning acclaim for writing about Jews—poor Jews, striving Jews, suffering Jews, unmistakably Jewish Jews. They read Philip Roth and Elie Wiesel, and to a lesser degree Bernard Malamud, Saul Bellow, and Isaac Bashevis Singer, who all received tremendous acclaim in the years after the war; Bellow and Singer each received the Nobel Prize for Literature. Jewish students read intellectual quarterlies filled with learned and blustering essays by Jews. They noticed that being Jewish did not seem to inhibit these artists' success. The essayist Edward Hoagland wrote a witty essay in which he argued that had he been a Jew, rather than a pale-skinned Nordic type, he might have received more attention. Its droll title: "On Not Being a Jew."[18]

It is not coincidental that Bill Novak, an early member and chronicler of the Jewish counterculture, and a seminal member of the New York Havurah, paid close attention to what we might call the Philip Roth Question. Roth's fictions—most notably *Goodbye, Columbus* (1959) and *Portnoy's Complaint* (1969)—struck some readers as anti-Semitic, others as magnificent, and still others as both.[19] His depiction of the overbearing Jewish mother driving her poor son Alexander Portnoy to neurotic fits of fornication with a piece of liver struck a painful chord with many American Jews, who saw it as sexist and demeaning toward the Jewish woman, or as an unfortunately accurate depiction of the Jewish son.

Novak's two favorite topics, the Jewish counterculture and the Philip Roth Question, were linked. Both the Jewish counterculture and the novels of Philip Roth signaled a discomfort with the American project of assimilation. The Jews, so the critique went, had tried desperately to live the American dream: in a sense, invisibility had been the goal. Jews might practice politics, but except when supporting the state of Israel, they must practice a disinterested politics of republican virtue (see Herbert Lehman, the Depression-era governor of New York), or the politics of civic boosterism (so perfected by the half-Jewish Fiorello La Guardia, mayor of New York City during the Depression and World War II). Leftist Jewish politicos like Morris Hillquit, the Socialist candidate for mayor of New York in 1917 and 1933, had in principle eschewed ethnic identity in favor of class consciousness (even as they depended heavily on Jewish voters). Jews might own a newspaper, but, like the Ochs and Sulzberger families' *New York Times,* that paper must take pains not to seem "Jewish."[20]

When countercultural Jews organized as Jews to press Jewish causes—emigration rights for Soviet Jewry, support for the state of Israel, Jewish studies curricula in universities—they were ignoring a code of inhibition that their suburban parents had felt keenly. Throughout the 1950s even the Nazis' murder of six million Jews during World War II was little discussed in the United States (at least as compared with the enormous industry of Holocaust scholarship, literature, art, and films produced from the 1970s on). For many Jews in the United States—and in Israel, eagerly perpetuating its mythology of the new, stronger, self-sufficient *sabra*—the Holocaust was a source of such sorrow, even shame, that leaving history quietly behind and becoming fully American took on special urgency.

For Jews who had become rather secular, joining a synagogue was all of a sudden preferable, in the 1950s, to having no institutional affiliation—which was what queer folk like atheists and communists did. Belonging to a synagogue was not quite as American as belonging to an Episcopal church, but it was more American than raising one's children with no religion at all. But to some young Jews, using Judaism as an assimilationist shield came to seem wrong, one more example of how American society blanched ethnic flavor and enforced codes of homogenous opinion.

The Jewish counterculture was political, but it aimed to be cultural, too. These "New Jews" argued questions of politics and literature, in campus Hillel dining rooms, in countercultural synagogues, and in havurot. (Hillel is the national organization of campus Jewish groups, named for an early Jewish rabbi.)[21] Above all, they wrote. "The first seedling in what has come to be a near-forest of distinctively Jewish papers was planted in the fertile soil of Berkeley, Calif., when students of the Radical Jewish Union published *The Jewish Radical* in 1969," said the *New York Times* in 1971, on the occasion of a three-day Jewish student press summit in New York City. The *Times* estimated that the Jewish student press comprised thirty-six newspapers with a combined circulation of three hundred thousand. This number is too high, of course, reflecting the combined populations of all the campuses with Jewish newspapers; most free newspapers left outside college dining halls go unread. But the papers were read by a certain segment of campus intelligentsia, and they were vehicles for the transmission of certain important tropes.

For example, "The papers, which frequently express revulsion at Jewish assimilation, have given currency to a figure called 'Uncle Jake,' a kind of Jewish Uncle Tom who is so busy serving other people's causes that he neglects the cause of his own people."[22] Though the character of Uncle Jake soon died out, he was a popular caricature in the Nixon years, an epithet used to describe any older Jew busy serving the uptight, reactionary synagogues and philanthropies. His toadyish specter was familiar to thousands of Jews, reading scores of publications. At Columbia there was *Response*. In Boston, *Genesis 2*, "a tri-weekly newspaper distributed free on campuses in the Boston area . . . had 15,000 readers and a reputation for sophisticated and critical articles, especially those on Israel and the Palestinians." The Jewish Student Press Service syndicated these periodicals' articles, so that Albuquerque's *Out of the Desert* might reprint copy from Minneapolis's *Hakahal* ("The Congregation") or Milwaukee's *Echad* ("One"). Starting in big cities and major college towns, the

Jewish student press grew by 1975 to have outposts in some unlikely spots, like El Paso, Texas, and Norman, Oklahoma.[23]

Through major journals like *Response* and periodic conferences of the North American Jewish Students Network, the Jewish counterculture coalesced in the late 1960s into a discernible movement. Young Jews peopled the counterculture at large, of course. But for some, countercultural identity had a distinctly Jewish cast. The Jewish counterculture differed from secular countercultural Jews—and Gentiles—by seeing a place for their traditional religion, however radically altered; they identified as Jews, and they usually embraced Zionism, which was rejected by much of the left.[24]

The Jewish counterculture had a political program. With the civil rights agenda largely achieved, Jews turned to peace. In fall 1969 the National Jewish Organizing Project convened to articulate a Jewish position against the war in Vietnam. Joining the national moratorium movement, the Jews appropriated the august American fast-day tradition—older than Abraham Lincoln, going back to the days of John Winthrop—and proclaimed December 12, 1969, a fast day. This symbol resonated, too, with the Jewish commandment to fast on Yom Kippur, the annual day of atonement.[25]

A year later, on November 15, 1970, at the peace rally on the Mall in Washington, D.C., Jewish groups marched under two banners. One, the Jewish Organizing Project, was "a loose coalition of groups organizing within the Jewish community on racism, the grape boycott, the war, and other general issues." The other, the Jewish Liberation Project, was a radical Zionist group "fighting against assimilation of the Jews as a group into a corrupt American society."[26] Despite their proclaimed differences, the two groups were more alike than not; they shared the youth counterculture's sense of a "corrupt American society."

But with a Jewish twist. While they disliked the establishment in general, and shared the counterculture's antipathy to politicians and their warmongering, they had in the "Jewish establishment" a more proximate, specific enemy. An early *Response* article laments an "American Judaism so dominated by... 'executive directors,'" who were robbing the tradition of meaning. The problem, the writer argues, was particularly acute on campuses, where fundraising for Jewish charities mattered more than spiritual or intellectual renewal. As early as 1967, Alan Mintz, a founder of *Response* and later coeditor of *The New Jews,* a popular essay collection, published in *Response*'s first issue a critique of United Synagogue Youth. And, as Bill Novak wrote, "the fact that Mintz was national president of that organization is entirely typical of those within the [Jewish counterculture]. It is perhaps entirely ironic that so many were involved—and turned off—by Hebrew schools and Jewish youth groups."[27]

Or not so ironic; perhaps we could have guessed that the young Jews would turn, Oedipus-like, on the organizations that had nurtured them. In November 1969, the young rabbi Hillel Levine, a graduate student at Harvard, led about two hundred students picketing the annual convention of the Council of Jewish Federations and Welfare Funds, in Boston. Wearing the one suit he owned, Levine forced himself onto the meeting's agenda and gave a speech attacking the spending priorities of the Council. Campus Hillels and student projects were woefully underfunded, he said. His speech was covered by *Newsweek* and the *New York Times,* and Levine successfully embarrassed the Council into making $40,000 available for student activities not sponsored by Hillel. Six months later, there was a sit-in, civil rights–style, at the convention of the New York Federation of Jewish Philanthropies.[28]

Countercultural Jews rejected regnant authority in the United States. They rejected authority in the hierarchy of Jewish organizations. So it was only a logical next step to reject authority in the synagogue. The havurah proved the right vehicle for rebellion.

If Rabbi Arthur Green had not heard of the havurah, he would have invented it. A scholar of mysticism who himself looked somewhat mystical—bearded and serene, a Jewish Santa Claus with a soothing baritone—Green later wrote a biography of the Hasidic sage Nahman of Bratslav, was president of the Reconstructionist Rabbinical College, and taught at Brandeis University. But in 1968, not yet thirty years old, Green founded Havurat Shalom in Somerville, Massachusetts. Havurat Shalom, which proved extraordinarily influential among liberal, intellectual Jews, was not a Reconstructionist havurah. Green was after radical social and mystical experience, both of which were anathema to Kaplan's strict rationalism. Kaplan's kind of renewal was tamer than what Art Green had in mind.[29]

Green had come to the havurah idea through his friendships with countercultural figures, not through Reconstructionist theology. In the mid-1960s Green had met the radical Catholic priest Daniel Berrigan, himself quite alienated from the priesthood, and Berrigan had gotten Green interested in noninstitutional religious life. Green discussed the possibility of a Jewish communal experiment with his friend Alan Mintz, the Columbia student who had founded *Response*, but Green soon moved to Boston. In Boston, Green met Rabbi Albert Axelrad, director of Brandeis Hillel, who shared his worries about the alienation of Jewish youth. In 1967 they began to look for students, teachers, and an advisory committee, and in 1968 the Havurat Shalom Community Seminary began, with twelve students.[30]

Green may, then, have crystallized his conception of the havurah with the advice of Rabbi Axelrad, who surely had seen the seminal articles by Jakob Petuchowski and Jacob Neusner in the *Reconstructionist*, required reading for any progressive rabbi. But it seems that Green and Axelrad knew nothing of the extant havurot in California and Colorado. That ignorance was liberating, as Green and his followers built a havurah following only their instincts, some limited learning, and the swirling energy of a college town in the late sixties.

Havurat Shalom began as a seminary. The earliest faculty included Zalman Schachter, later a renowned Jewish mystical exhorter, and Michael Fishbane, later a professor of Hebrew Bible at the University of Chicago. James Kugel, later an Old Testament scholar at Harvard; Jim Sleeper, later a columnist for the *New York Daily News* and author of books about race and national identity; Barry Holtz, later a professor at Jewish Theological Seminary; and Gershon Hundert, later a professor at McGill University, all taught or studied at Havurat Shalom. Students could take classes on subjects like Martin Buber's *I and Thou;* the biblical, legal, and *aggadic* (nonlegal) sources relating to the harvest festival Sukkoth; *davening* (prayer) techniques; Talmud; and Jewish mysticism.[31]

As a residential seminary, based first in Cambridge but soon moving to Somerville, Havurat Shalom (sometimes spelled Chavurat Shalom) offered a Jewish way to be separate from the denomination-controlled rabbinic schools; at the same time, it offered its members a communal way to infuse their lives with Judaism. More valuable, as a state-recognized educational institution, Havurat Shalom offered the possibility of 4-D draft deferrals. Arthur Green downplayed this aspect of Havurat Shalom, wishing not to detract from its central missions; he was "quick to point out that only half the students have availed themselves of the 4-D's."[32] But in the late 1960s, avoiding the draft was part of the appeal of all seminaries, Jewish and Christian.

Havurat Shalom never ordained any rabbis. It did, however, become well known in the counterculture of greater Boston. As late as 1973 Jewish high school students and college dropouts were drawn to the havurah's patina of cool and its intense spirituality.[33] "We thought of spirituality and political revolution as two different poles of attraction," Green later said. "There were people who thought all this neo-Hasidic talk pointless if we weren't there on the barricades. I thought the barricades had to be grounded in something spiritual."[34]

Unlike Havurat Shalom, the New York Havurah, founded in 1969, never became a residential community, and so it drew a somewhat different crowd. It began in Brewster, New York, in spring 1969, at the Brewster Conference, a gathering of left-leaning Jewish groups like Jews for Urban Justice in Washington, D.C.; the House of Love and Prayer in San Francisco; and the *Response* magazine collective. Afterward, some of the participants began to meet to plan a possible community of countercultural Jews. The meetings stopped after a few weeks, but the members knew of Havurat Shalom—some had been part of it—and the idea of a New York community arose again later that year when area Jews gathered to support the draft resister Burton Weiss. Fleeing federal authorities, Weiss had claimed sanctuary at the Jewish Theological Seminary, and in the hours before he was arrested and led away, several hundred young Jews gathered around him, as one observer wrote, "in meditation, study, song and fellowship. . . . Many of the participants felt a bond of common purpose and common spirituality, and some were anxious to pursue the idea further. Shortly afterwards, in Rabbi Eugene Weiner's apartment overlooking Central Park, the Havurah in New York City was born," with seven founders.[35]

The New York Havurah (again, sometimes spelled Chavurah) always had an apartment on the Upper West Side, and at times one of the haverim lived in it; but learning and discussion, not group living, animated this collective. The group met for the first time in September 1969 in Nyack, New York, to plan a curriculum. At its start, the New York Havurah benefited from connections made over many years in Ramah camps, the Ivy League, and Havurat Shalom. Gershon Hundert and William Novak were both alumni of Havurat Shalom in Massachusetts. Alan Mintz, another founder, had known Jim Sleeper in Mador, the Ramah counselor-in-training program, and they had founded *Response* when Sleeper was at Yale and Mintz at Columbia. Martha Ackelsberg had been a Ramah camper and counselor-in-training, and she had been a close friend of Paula Hyman's at Radcliffe. And so forth.[36] The connections will seem familiar when we examine the Southern Baptist Convention, whose liberal wing could not have functioned without blood and school ties.

Like folk Catholics, countercultural Jews loved the outdoors, which functioned as an implicit rejection of the institutional synagogue. The New York Havurah prays in Nyack, New York, on the harvest festival Shavuot. Photograph by Bill Aron.

In the havurah's first year, a pattern was established: study groups would start if there was sufficient interest in a given topic; if the class thrived, it continued, and if it languished, it died. According to Martha Ackelsberg, later a professor at Smith College, there were usually two or three courses being taught at a time, on topics like creation stories of different religions, the history of the havurah idea, the history of Jewish community, and women in Judaism. And while class participation could be sporadic, the havurah's social life was vibrant. Members had regular Thursday evening dinners, weekly Shabbat services, and monthly retreats in the country. The New York Havurah exemplified Bill Novak's assertion that there was "no binding ideology in the *chavurot*"—in Somerville or New York—"so much as an understanding that only in small, friendly, compatible groups can people begin to learn and grow."[37]

The groups had to be "small" and "friendly" to foster intimacy and affection; we might pause to examine what Novak meant by "compatible." The New York Havurah admitted new members only after interviews designed to assess the applicants' politics, commitment, and intelligence. Only the liberal, dedicated, and smart need apply. The havurah did not permit itself to grow beyond twenty-five members, and it was accused of fostering "isolation," a charge that today would be rendered as "elitism." Founding member Bill Novak defended that characterization, saying that the Havurah demanded a "unique kind of commitment." As part of a community of intellectuals, the members had a stake in keeping the level of discussion high. In 1970 virtually all the members had strong interests in Jewish learning; of the nineteen members, one was a Jewish Theological Seminary dropout, two had been rejected by the seminary, two were current rabbinical students there, and one was a graduate. One was getting a Ph.D. in Jewish studies at Columbia and another a Ph.D. in political science at Princeton. Other members studied or had studied at the Jewish Institute of Religion.[38]

"Compatible" meant something more. Alumni of the New York Havurah and Havurat Shalom spoke of wanting a new—or rather very old—approach to Judaism, one that did not slot religion into Friday evenings. These Jews wanted, like the Community of Hope's Catholics, to "integrate" their lives. "We hated the *Goodbye, Columbus* Jewish community we'd come from," Jim Sleeper later said. "The suburban temples and the Bar Mitzvah parties." According to Martha Ackelsberg, "The idea was to try to overcome what we perceived as the fragmentation of our lives, so the fact that we socialized with one another in addition [to praying and studying] was a big part of it." Here is Alan Mintz: "Politics was a very important visionary mode at the time, but it had to do with a larger vision of life, affective forms of expression, and our relationships to institutions. The New York Havurah was deeply influenced by the countercultural question of how a life is to be lived." That is what Arthur Green

The New York Havurah—men, women, and children together—
celebrates Simchat Torah, the completion of the annual cycle of Torah
reading. Photograph by Bill Aron.

meant when he said, "The barricades had to be grounded in something spiritual," and what Ackelsberg meant when she said, "We were
looking for something that was more intimate, more spiritual, I
guess. . . . We wanted to know each other, be part of each other's
lives, and that was a part for us of relating to God."[39]

While the New York haverim were generally more political than
their Somerville peers, they did not use the havurah as a vehicle for
activism. Rather, the New York Havurah supplemented the members' other activism. While Bill Novak deemed this absence of political activity in the Havurah its "single outstanding failure," another
observer, Gerald Serotta, took a more sanguine view: the "New York
Havurah changed self-definition to virtually exclude self-conscious
groupwide political involvement," but its members "formed the
active nuclei for activities as diverse as Breira [a peace organization],

Ezrat Nashim [an organization of Jewish feminists that began as a class in the New York Havurah] and the Jewish Feminist Organization, *Response*, Projects Ezra and Dorot (working with elderly Jews)... and Tzedakah [charity] collectives." But these efforts did not "emanate from the Havurah qua Havurah."[40]

If politics was out, Jewish life was in. But what kind of Jewish life? Was it Judaism, a faith tradition, or Jewishness, a cultural affinity? When Jacob Neusner, the early herald of the havurot, met with Havurat Shalom in summer 1970, he was told, "You take for granted a commitment to Judaism. But we do not. WE are here to listen for the new voices of God." Neusner deplored this heresy, but perhaps not with the scorn he might have heaped on David Sperling of the New York Havurah, who referred to prayer this way: "I get positively high on *tefillot*."[41]

The third eastern, urban havurah founded at the turn of the decade was in Washington, D.C. Fabrangen (in Yiddish, "coming-together" or "gathering") emerged from Jews for Urban Justice, a coalition of Jewish leftists begun in 1969. That year Jews for Urban Justice sponsored an early "Freedom Seder," one of the first of the now-common leftist versions of the Passover meal. The *Jews for Urban Justice Newsletter* reported that "there was a huge diversity of people at the seder. In addition to students, non-students, hippies, black militants, there were many young professionals and white middle class suburbanites. Also, a group of orthodox Yeshiva students walked several miles from their suburban neighborhoods through the ghetto (yarmulke and all) to attend." Sounding like the New Yorker high on tefillot, the writer concluded, "The contrast of the old and the young, the religious and the non-religious, was really beautiful!"[42]

Jews for Urban Justice, if it was to thrive, needed a permanent home. Groups or clubs ensure their survival by moving from members' living rooms, mailing lists, and phone trees into actual rooms with walls; it's a sign not just of financial viability—"We can now afford our own quarters"—but also of spiritual vitality. The members of the New York Havurah could have met in living rooms indefinitely, but somehow they knew that the group would have petered out. Having an apartment of their own, to decorate and make special, to drop by any time, embedded in rocks and drywall the group's commitment and sense of purpose. This is a main reason that gay Unitarians wanted an office at headquarters. Jews for Urban Justice had regular programming, including seminars at members' houses on women's liberation, racism, and Jewish learning. It had to give that programming a home.

In 1971 their newsletter, by then called the *Jewish Urban Guerilla,* announced, "The Fabrangen is opening Monday, February 8 at 2158 Florida Ave. NW. It is a community house near Dupont Circle which shall work towards making a Jewish counter-culture. The life-style will be communitarian. We'll be doing draft, drug and personal counseling, so come if you need or want it. There will be a coffee house in the evenings with occasional folk singing, poetry reading, and any other stuff you might want to see it do; where anybody can come and rap, relate, read and do your thing, do anything. There will be an art workshop, and we hope to start film and writing workshops as well. Relevant, unstructured and free shabbas services will be held every week. Free courses relating to politics, alternative life styles, Judaism and their relation to one another shall be given."[43]

That April, the *Jewish Urban Guerilla* reported that the Fabrangen had opened on Valentine's Day with a rousing party. The rabbi, troubadour, and Jewish folk hero Shlomo Carlebach had performed in a "joyous Hassidic-style celebration." The calendar listed events scheduled for almost every night, sometimes two a night: on Thursday, "Photography workshop and Jewish music jam session"; on Friday, "Shabbat: Communal dinner and Tefilot"; on Saturday, Torah study; and on Monday, "Coffeehouse . . . A representative of Gay Liberation will be there to rap with us." The seminar on Marxism, Anarchism, and Judaism was on Tuesday. Hebrew and silkscreening were taught on Thursday.[44]

A 1975 issue of *Network,* published by the Jewish Students Movement, estimated that in the United States there were about sixty independent havurot and *batim* ("houses," literally, referring to Jewish campus houses).[45] Because each group needed ten members for a prayer quorum, and because they tended to consider numbers over twenty-five too large, we might guess at twenty members each. That would mean 1,200 young people were involved in countercultural havurot by the mid-1970s. It was a small number, far smaller than the many thousands who had joined synagogue havurot; but the countercultural havurot's alumni were to become the intellectual leadership of late-twentieth-century Judaism.

Because countercultural haverim in the East opposed hierarchy and looked askance at organization, each havurah had its own character. The haverim in Somerville had the strongest commitment to living communally, while those in New York eschewed rabbis and charted their own course of study. In Washington, singing and the arts mattered most. ("Why a *Jewish* Urban Coffeehouse?" one article in the *Jewish Urban Guerilla* urgently asked.) Regardless of their differences, the haverim in different states often knew each other, and certainly knew of one another. In 1973 they held the first of several semiannual havurah retreats at the Weiss Farm in New Jersey, and the group that met became known as NACHAS, a Yiddish word (usually spelled *naches*) meaning pride and pleasure, and an acronym for the North American Chavurot and Assorted Simchas.[46]

Still, it is remarkable how isolated groups, each comprising only one or two dozen members, could see themselves as part of an entity called the "Jewish counterculture." What gave them this sense of unity? Their shared religion, for one, and the far-flung Jewish student press. Opposition to the Vietnam War and support for the Israelis in the Six-Day War contributed to the Jewish counterculture's identity, separate from the counterculture at large. "It made people realize how Jewish they were, how much they cared," Arthur Green said. "People came out of the woodwork at the thought of another Holocaust." Green's wife, Kathy, noted that "there was disillusionment with . . . Christian friends over Israel," and it is true that many liberal Christians, and especially black Christians, sympathized with the Arabs and began to view Israel as an imperialist "white" power oppressing a colonized, Third World, "minority" people. This divide, this sense of abandonment, was what made many Jews realize, as Alan Mintz put it, "that in the end my fate was with the Borscht Belt Jew, not with some non-Jewish counterculturalist."[47]

But it was the ethnocentricity of black power that, while telling the white liberal to mind his own business, ironically catalyzed the Jewish counterculture more than any rabbi could. In 1969 the *Other Stand,* a Jewish student newspaper at McGill University in Montreal, editorialized that in "an era when Jewish radicals support other popular particularistic movements (blacks, French-Canadians), it is time for them to recognize and support their own particularism." At the same time, an article in the *Flame,* a Jewish newspaper at the City College of New York, applauded the view expressed by one speaker at a forum that "Jews who are Zionists have no trouble understanding black separatist philosophy while American Jews who are not Zionists cannot understand it."[48] Sometime between the death of Malcolm X in 1965 and the Black Panther Eldridge Cleaver's quixotic run for president in 1968, the philosophy of Black Power had become more than famous; it was now influential. Integrationism had been the rallying cry of progressive Jews during and just after the Kennedy years, but ethnic separatism was now the regnant, hip alternative.

Both the Six-Day War and the 1968 conflict between the heavily Jewish teachers' union and black community activists over school control in the Ocean Hill–Brownsville section of Brooklyn had led Jews to question the efficacy of an interracial leftist coalition, yet it was the rhetoric of black separatism that permitted Jewish ethnocentrism. Only the most politically engaged Jews would pay attention to the school-board politics of Brooklyn, but all Jews with countercultural tendencies would have noticed, and often admired, the style and posturing of the Black Panthers and their allies.

The black separatists had a political *and* a cultural message. A politically minded Jew might write, as one did, that "the Black Panthers may or may not be the equivalent of the Irgun (the Jewish terrorists who drove the British out of Palestine) but surely the equivalent is there." The Jew more inclined toward cultural semiotics might understand this quotation, from Bill Novak in 1970: "In effect, the black said to the Jew: 'You have a culture, so dig it. You have a language; speak it. . . . And finally, you have a people, work with it!' For most Jews, however, the message was still hidden. For many it came out during . . . the Six Day War."[49]

"We felt that push from the blacks at the same time we felt that push from Israel," Arthur Green said. "They sent us that message, the blacks. They wanted to do it on their own, and we began to feel that about ourselves." Blacks from James Baldwin to Eldridge Cleaver were drawn to Jews in a way that they were never drawn to Poles or Greeks; on the other hand, because Jews had been so involved with civil rights, radical blacks were eager to distance themselves from Jewish patronage, and Jews eagerly read black separatism as a text relevant to the Jewish struggle. As the blacks ridiculed their Uncle Toms, young Jewish writers castigated Uncle Jake. Jews even appropriated black literary allusions, one writer warning that the Jew, "not today's black, is the invisible man; he, like yesterday's Negro, wanders in a no man's land." In a wonderfully suggestive reclamation of the Italian word once used to denote Jewish ethnic enclaves, he concluded, "Ghetto Jew, you better do some fast thinking."[50]

Not all Jews took such direct cultural license from black separatism, but "Black is Beautiful" was an infectious creed. "Jewish is beautiful," a Long Island woman wrote, "as is Black, Puerto Rican, Chinese, Greek, Polish, and Spanish." In declarations of ethnic pride, one could hear the echoes of black separatist rhetoric. Getting back to one's roots was in. In the inaugural issue of *Brooklyn Bridge,* the editors wrote, "We are coming home. To Brooklyn. . . . We are coming home to Brooklyn to live, to love, to begin building a new world, and to be Jewish. . . . Our oppression as Jews is only one of the ways in which we are oppressed. The ruling class in America oppresses all people." Assimilation was out, and Jewish newspapers railed against identification with the deracinated WASP.[51]

In 1970 countercultural Jews were excited by the appearance of a "small group of delinquent youth of Jerusalem" who took the name the "Jerusalem Black Panthers." The Jerusalem Black Panthers had the chutzpah to use the name Panther, the most evocative artifact black separatists had produced. According to press reports, the Jerusalem Black Panthers were Sephardic Jews from Middle Eastern or North African countries; in Israel, Sephardic Jews have been poorer cousins to the European, or Ashkenazic, Jews. Protesting against economic inequality in Israel, the Jerusalem Black Panthers appealed to some American Jews because they were not European, and so presented another challenge to the assimilationist ideal.[52]

Black Panthers paid Jews the compliment of attention, but that attention was not always benevolent: when the Black Panthers published a position paper calling Israel an imperialist aggressor, Jews could not ignore the cognitive dissonance. When the Panther Eldridge Cleaver attacked Zionism, Berkeley's leftist Jews were flummoxed. "We have regarded Eldridge Cleaver as a friend and teacher. We think his anti-Zionist and anti-Israel positions, large [sic] corresponding to his stay in Algiers, are dead wrong," an editorial in the Jewish Radical read. The hopeful writers tried to find common ground: "The parallel between the Jews at the time of the coming of Theodor Herzl and the present situation of black people in America is fascinating." Jewish liberals decided that if a homeland for the Jews had once seemed both desirable and unattainable, they could say the same for American blacks' dreams of autonomy in 1970. Albert Axelrad, the Brandeis rabbi whose counsel was instrumental in the founding of Havurat Shalom, insisted that Jews support the Panthers. Some Panthers may be anti-Semites, he admitted, but that should not blind American Jews to disparate views within an organization that spoke for an "exploited 'colony' class." Rather than attacking the Panthers, Jews, "still an alien people, a tolerated stranger in a wasp-dominated society," should forbear.[53]

In the early 1970s, as oppression of Soviet Jews became the signal issue of Jewish liberation, and certainly with the 1973 Yom Kippur War in Israel, tolerance for black anti-Zionism became more difficult. "We will march with our brothers of the left," one "Radical Credo" declared, "but when they call for the death of Israel, when they acquiesce in plans for the liquidation of the Jewish state, we then have no choice but to fight them." By that point, however, black separatist rhetoric had become an unmistakable marker of righteous anger and authentic protest. In 1977 a Philadelphia Jewish student newspaper headline announced how young Jews saw themselves: "The Student as Nigger."[54]

Haverim like Martha Ackelsberg, Jim Sleeper, and Paula Hyman had strong Jewish backgrounds; in camps, in Hebrew school, and in conversations with proudly Jewish parents, they had learned to cherish their Judaism. Such Jewishly learned Jews did not need black power to generate ethnic pride—they had been raised with it. But for hundreds of countercultural Jews who founded publications like *Brooklyn Bridge,* black power was a necessary model. "My sense," Martha Ackelsberg said in 2000, "is that the people for whom this sort of ethnic identity thing was most powerful were those people who came from somewhat more assimilated backgrounds, or at least where they had not had solid Jewish education. . . . It was like, all of a sudden, 'Oh my God, I have an ethnicity, I have a community, I have something I can claim just like they do!'"[55] The educated haverim in Somerville and New York were trying to revitalize a tradition they'd been raised in, while assimilated Jews were trying to engage a tradition they had ignored.

And black separatism inspired other movements, too. Havurot, which could, of course, be seen as a species of Jewish separatist groups, proliferated alongside Jewish feminist groups. Sometimes Jewish feminists found each other through havurot, as with Ezrat Nashim, which grew out the New York Havurah.[56] Martha Ackelsberg and Paula Hyman, who with their spouses were members of the New York Havurah, were also members of a feminist consciousness-raising group, and the issues discussed in that group sensitized them to gendered roles and language in the havurah.

"For me," Ackelsberg said,

> the incident that got this class and ultimately Ezrat Nashim started was one Shabbat morning a bunch of us were davening together . . . and we had just finished doing *Nishmat,* a prayer that talks about "The breath of all living things shall praise you," and it goes through and it lists all the living creatures and all the different parts of the body, my bones, my breath—which I have always loved. And after we finished saying this, Alan Mintz said, "I have always loved this, how it talks about all of these dimensions of the self awakening and filling up," . . . and then he said, "At the moment of ejaculation . . . "
>
> And at the moment he said it I didn't have a conscious reaction to it, but I know that sometime thereafter, ten minutes, twenty minutes, a half hour, I found myself in another room, just kind of wandering around, and Dina Rosenfeld, who was also there . . . she also wanders into the room. And we started talking and realized that we had both, at this moment that felt like intense connection, felt profoundly excluded by the way he had articulated his experience.[57]

For some Jews, then, a feminist consciousness came with their experience of Judaism in the havurah. For others, prior feminist

While celebrating Sukkot in rural Connecticut, a man and a woman wrap themselves in a *tallit,* or prayer shawl, traditionally worn only by men. Photograph by Bill Aron.

commitments made havurah Judaism the only viable alternative to the traditional synagogue. Havurah newsletters would plug feminist causes, and articles written to oppose assimilation would attack the WASP beauty myth in feminist terms, disparaging hair bleaching and nose jobs.[58]

We should not make the historian's error of forgetting change over short periods of time. Nineteen sixty-nine was not 1974, and one will find far more attention to feminism in the Jewish counter-cultural community as time went on. Ezrat Nashim was founded in 1971, *Ms.* magazine in 1972. The full confluence of ethnic particularism and feminism, both unleashed by the example of black separatism, occurred from 1971 to 1975, when havurot began arising on college campuses and in college towns.

In spring 1971 Jewish students at the University of Pennsylvania moved into their "Coed Kosher Commune." The previous semester, several students had placed an advertisement in the *Daily Pennsylvanian* inviting others to join them in a "creative experience in Jewish living." "The idea first began to take shape at a meeting at the Penn Hillel Foundation last December [1970]. Though over 20 students attended the initial meeting, all but five had decided not to join by the beginning of the second semester"—and for most of the reluctant, the reason was their parents' opposition to co-ed living. Sometime at the end of March or beginning of April, the five haverim moved into Talmidai Aharon ("students of Aaron"), the objective of which, according to freshman Rachel Abramson, was "to create a total Jewish environment, something that only having our own house will enable us to do."[59]

The following September, *Hayom,* the Jewish student newspaper in Philadelphia, reported on Makom ("place"), a Jewish coffeehouse probably not unlike the "Jewish urban coffeehouse" opened by Fabrangen in Washington. The reporter describes a place where Marxists and Nietzscheans discussed "the synthesis of religion and ecology" and where "Bob Dylan is better known as Zimmerman." Mitch Smith, who frequented Makom, said that it was "essentially an attitude about ourselves as young Jews, and about our community. What we are saying is that there is a Jewish community which finds religion, politics, culture and social camaraderie not to be incompatible." This was the same "integration" that the New York Havurah discussed, an alternative to the perceived fragmentation of their elders' lives.[60]

The students of Makom were saying something else, too. They were saying not just that there was a community of people who happened to be Jews, but also that there was a *Jewish* community. The 1950s, beatnik, coffeehouse tradition had derived much of its cachet from its integrationist character: blacks would hang with Jews and Catholics, wannabe-Coltranes with ersatz-Ginsbergs, and maybe an Italian like Ferlinghetti would drop by. It was the scene that had nurtured Dylan—Zimmerman—in Greenwich Village in the early 1960s, but it was a scene whose catholicity had abated. Coffeehouse

In 1966, on his way to go shopping at Fred Segal in Los Angeles, Bob Dylan, *né* Zimmerman, models his kinky "Jew-fro" hair, which young, ethnically proud Jews adored. Photograph by Lisa Law.

Jews were trying to revive the old scene, but with a kosher twist.

In October 1971 Jewish women at Penn "liberated" Penn Hillel, instigating a confrontation over a *mechitza,* the curtain separating men from women, at a Simchat Torah party. (Simchat Torah is the celebration of the annual cycle of Torah reading.) The women had the mechitza taken down but were denied the privilege of touching the Torah. In spring 1973 the Philadelphia Union of Jewish Students hosted its first conference, where students from Penn, Temple, Villanova, Swarthmore, and several other schools congregated to discuss Soviet Jewry, the Jerusalem Black Panthers, and Jews in poverty.

And the movement toward communal living and coffeehouse culture accelerated. In 1973 there were Jewish communes at Columbia, the University of North Carolina at Chapel Hill, and the University of California at Los Angeles. By the next year, a Jewish collegian could join the Bayit in Carrboro, North Carolina; Kibbutz Langdon in Madison, Wisconsin; Hebrew House in Ann Arbor, Michigan; Havurat Hamidbar in Albuquerque, New Mexico; Havurat Aviv in Cleveland; the Havurah at Carleton College in Northfield, Minnesota; the Havurah at Cornell University; or the Jewish Co-op at the University of California at Santa Cruz.[61]

Another national gathering of haverim was held in Madison, Wisconsin, in March 1974. By that time there was a national havurah newsletter, *Kesher,* and, as we have seen, scores of campus havurot. Yet these communities had short life expectancies. One founder of the Columbia Bayit, Jon Groner, moved out and published a cynical account of his three terms in the house. "Who would ever have imagined," he writes, "that residents of this sort of Jewish community would be so suspicious of 'outsiders,' non-residents in the building?" The same year, Jacob Neusner, an early proponent of havurot, predicted that solipsism would be their downfall. Almost ten years later, an editorial in the *Reconstructionist* wondered whether "there are some dangers in the *havurah* which ought to be avoided: they tend to isolate small groups from the larger community." One critic noted that the havurot tended to be run by young people without careers or the responsibility of families; in order for a havurah to last, new members would have to replace those forced to abandon the groups for other obligations.[62] While some havurot met that challenge over the short term, almost no countercultural havurot lasted more than ten years.[63]

Havurot were, after all, countercultures: they existed apart from the society, in order to offer a model incompatible with the society. To Jon Groner's befuddlement "that residents of this sort of Jewish community would be so suspicious of 'outsiders,'" we might answer that small, close-knit, alternative communities, founded by young adults with strong critiques of mainstream America, would have to be suspicious of outsiders. If anyone can join, then the experiment becomes diluted. If the New York Havurah had admitted dullards, could it have maintained its intellectual character? Could a kosher house admit a resident with a taste for bacon? Countercultures are more, not less, exclusive than the culture at large. The Communist Party had more stringent membership standards than the United States.

The havurah appealed to young Jews, got them to join, and held them at least for a time; something about it was appealing over and above other possibilities. Personal fulfillment and the resolution of psychic conflict may be sought down many avenues: drugs, psychotherapy, New Age religions. What, during the 1960s and 1970s, made the havurah compelling?

The havurah appealed to Jews still grounded, however tenuously, in their tradition. In some ways, Mordecai Kaplan's Reconstructionism may have been a more influential philosophy in the years before it became a denomination. From 1920 to 1945 approximately 25 percent of all students at the Jewish Theological Seminary—the seminary for Conservative rabbis—identified as followers of Reconstructionism.[64] From Harold Schulweis (class of 1950) to Arthur Green (class of 1967), a generation of rabbis was impressed by Kaplan's thought. Many of them subscribed to the *Reconstructionist,* where in 1960 and 1961 they would have read about havurot. When countercultural Jews looked for leadership, it was to such rabbis that they turned. And such rabbis founded havurot.

Schulweis and Green were avatars of two principal kinds of havurah. Schulweis popularized the synagogue havurah, while Green, almost simultaneously, started the independent, residential Havurat Shalom outside Boston. Although establishmentarian rabbis did not always approve of the rebellious, left-wing, or mystical nature of some independent havurot, they rarely condemned them.

The greater risk, they knew, was that Jews would turn against religion or discover Eastern or New Age movements. It was the fear expressed in a 1973 article by a Jewish sociologist: "Cambridge, Massachusetts. In crowded Harvard Square, a few miles away from Somerville, six girls pass, beating tambourines and chanting '*hare krishna*.' Two young women sell incense sticks and one fellow stands with a sign: 'philosopher available.' We have come to expect the Cambridge scene. We have come to lament—and accept—that young people, a disproportionate number of them Jews, go questing after every off-beat movement."[65]

The synagogue havurot existed mostly for families, unlikely to drop out and join a counterculture. For younger Jews, the more countercultural havurot, the ones more influenced by Green and his ilk, had an ethnic particularism that made them sexy and current. As Jews imbibed the rhetoric of black separatism—and tensely watched Israel fight two wars for its existence—they began to focus their liberationist impulses on themselves. The havurah, after all, was separatist and nationalist in nature. It was a study and worship group, or residential community, that existed for one nation of people.

Unitarians reacted to countercultural movements in ways dictated not by theology but by their religious cultures; Catholics were following a template from Rome. Unitarians had a culture of tolerance, a culture that historically was countercultural, while Catholics, being Catholic, obeyed church dictates. Jews, too, experienced the counterculture in ways dictated by their religion, and that religion was, as Mordecai Kaplan had accurately explained, a vision of nationhood. While Unitarians and Catholics had to stay within their churches in order to maintain a sense of affiliation with the religion, Jews had no such worries. Jews are Jews because of descent; they don't have to be under a synagogue roof, in communion with other Jews, or in good standing with a religious hierarch. They were always freer to experiment outside the established religious bodies. Kaplan had encouraged small fellowships in the 1930s and 1940s, other

Reconstructionists had continued the trend after the war, and countercultural Jews like Arthur Green started havurot in the late 1960s. Jews could be profoundly, traditionally Jewish while rebuking Jewish institutions.

And Jews who sought to live apart from Gentiles, unaffiliated with a synagogue, in a house with a kosher kitchen, amid Jewish music, and with friends nearby for a prayer quorum were a counterculture. Influenced by the same countercultural movements that had seeped into Unitarian discourse—black liberation, feminism, pacifism—Jews reacted differently. They had grown up in the same American culture, but they had a religious tradition that offered more possibilities for dissent. They also had liberal parents and, sometimes, socialist grandparents. So a feminist Jew who opposed the war in Vietnam would be unlikely to fit in comfortably at the nearby synagogue, but if there was a local havurah, she might well join. A religiously learned and liberal Jew from an Ivy League campus might feel less traditional than the campus rabbi, less secular than the New Left politicos, and more Jewish than the preppies over at the *Animal House* fraternity—so he would head to the havurah. Havurah Jews were free-thinking Jews. By the 1990s former haverim filled the ranks of the Jewish professoriate and intelligentsia, and Jewish feminism, nurtured in so many havurot, had helped produce hundreds of female rabbis.[66]

The Jewish culture had never relied on bureaucracies, which don't flourish well on the run or in the desert. So when young Jews decided to rebel, they didn't have to slay their parents, or even argue with them. They just had to stop going to synagogue.

FOUR

Episcopalians and Feminism

I n 1529 King Henry VIII of England, famously eager for a
divorce, severed ties with the Roman Catholic Church, and he
severed his subjects' ties, too. The Church of England became
the state church. A reformation had existed in England for two hundred years, and many of Henry's subjects embraced his repudiation
of the popes; others bitterly resisted, and despite the sacking of
monasteries and the burning of Roman relics, England was never
free of Catholics. But the Church of England became the norm
throughout the empire. Today it goes by different names in different
countries—in Kenya, for example, it is the Anglican Church of
Kenya, in Spain it is the Spanish Reformed Episcopal Church—but
the Church of England remains one communion. That is, whether
one is worshiping in an Episcopal church in the United States or in a
chapel of the Church of South India, the rites and prayers will be rec-
ognizable, and the priest's so-called ABCs—the powers to absolve of
sins, bless the sinner, and consecrate the bread and wine of the
Eucharist—are the same.

But the separate national branches of the Anglican communion
are self-governing. They have a summit every ten years at the Lambeth Conference in England, but that occasional show of unity cannot mask stark differences within the communion. The African
churches, for example, are more conservative than the American
churches on sexual matters, like the ordination of homosexuals, and
they are more faithful to the 1928 version of the Book of Common
Prayer, the standard liturgical text that American Episcopalians have
replaced with the revised version written in 1979. They have different procedures for choosing bishops and raising up priests. They use
different music, and they pray in a wide variety of languages.

The Church of England was brought to America by the king's
subjects in the seventeenth century, held its first convention in 1785
in Philadelphia, and consecrated its first bishop here in 1789, the
year that it was organized as the Protestant Episcopal Church in the
United States of America. In 1967 it began calling itself, simply, the

Episcopal Church. Because of its English heritage and the wealth of its early adherents, the Episcopal Church has been a house of privilege, or at least has been seen that way. In the South, Episcopalians stand above Baptists and Methodists in the social hierarchy, however faintly, even today. In New York the Cathedral of St. John the Divine on Amsterdam Avenue remains a fashionable place for society misses to marry their millionaire beaux. The National Cathedral, in Washington, D.C., is where President Bush presided over prayers in the aftermath of the World Trade Center's destruction. St. Alban's School, for boys, and the National Cathedral School, for girls, enroll the children of Washington gentry and politicians; Al Gore attended the former and his daughters the latter. In New England the Congregational churches are older, and have the best claim to being the Standing Order, but local Episcopal churches often have more money and, of course, Anglophilic hauteur. Two of New England's richest and most prestigious boarding schools, St. Paul's and Groton, affiliate with the Episcopal Church. President Franklin D. Roosevelt attended Groton. So did the novelist Louis Auchincloss, whose classic *The Rector of Justin* is based on his experiences there. In our country's centers of power, from Greenwich, Connecticut, to Winnetka, Illinois, the Episcopal parish priest has historically had social prerogative and prominence. The people who make the important decisions have belonged to his church and asked for his advice.[1]

Or hers. For in the United States, women may be Episcopal priests. The General Convention approved the ordination of woman priests in 1976, two years after a renegade ceremony that ordained women without the blessing of the church hierarchy. From the time ordination became an issue, about 1970, to the final change in canons in 1976, advocates on both sides of the debate antagonized each other with nasty rhetoric. Unpleasantly misogynist language was used, and all manner of stereotypes. Some angry men—and women—invoked the language of witchcraft, heresy, and menstrual impurity in their arguments against female ordination. The proponents of female ordination responded with New Age clichés, the language of biblical prophecy, and the precedent of blacks' civil rights.

The Episcopal Church, which remained united during the Civil War as Baptists, Methodists, and Presbyterians fell into schism, stayed whole through this crisis, too. But the struggle for female ordination left scars. The scars are still visible, revealing a denomination that was at once elite and demotic, highbrow and quite progressive. They tell the story of a wealthy, mostly white church that somehow came to talk about its women in the language of liberation theology and anti-imperialist struggles. Today, the Episcopal Church allows women to serve as priests, ritual stand-ins for Christ. It is a dramatic symbolic shift that has changed the content, the entire feel, of Episcopal worship. A small group of women used the language of feminism and identity politics to win a right that eluded Catholic women even after Vatican II.

The Episcopal Church differs from other mainline American churches in three ways. First, it is more sacramental, with some "high" churches celebrating a Mass with incense and bells, one that would look familiar to Catholics; second, it is in communion with churches in Europe and throughout the world, and so it has an "Old World" feel; and, finally, it is more visibly hierarchical than most Protestant denominations are. Deacons serve under priests who are under bishops, with a presiding bishop over all the bishops.

While those differences are real, the Episcopal Church has always fit snugly into the mad jigsaw puzzle of Protestant denominations. In the nineteenth and early twentieth centuries, Episcopal women, like other Protestant women, joined church benevolent and reform societies. The first Episcopal women's benevolent society was organized in 1823, and others followed. In 1871 Episcopal women's groups amalgamated into the Women's Auxiliary to the Board of Missions, antecedent to the Episcopal Church Women. The Daughters of the King emerged in 1885, and the Girls Friendly Society, similar to the Girl Scouts, in 1877.

In 1864 Episcopal women resurrected the early Christian office of deaconess (the word is from the Greek *diakonia,* servant). The deaconess revival, which also occurred in the Lutheran, Presbyterian, and Methodist churches, gave women an office to practice pastoral care, teaching, and counseling, although in the Episcopal Church, deaconesses did not have the male deacons' privilege to read the Gospel during the service. At the same time, a few Episcopal women joined religious orders, similar to Catholics'. In the twentieth century, Episcopal women were often lay professional workers in churches, church schools, and missions.[2]

Episcopal women thus had some of the pastoral opportunities that other Protestant women had. But scores of women from other Protestant denominations—Methodist, Baptist, and Congregational—were preaching, and some, like the Pentecostal Aimee Semple McPherson, the Shaker Ann Lee, the Seventh-Day Adventist Ellen Gould White, and the Christian Scientist Mary Baker Eddy, had founded their own denominations.[3] The first sign that an Episcopal woman might exercise high leadership came in 1944, when Bishop R. C. Hall of Hong Kong, citing the shortage of priests in wartime, ordained Florence Li Tim Oi as a priest. But when English bishops objected, she agreed not to function as a priest.

In 1964 James Pike, the notoriously liberal bishop of California—who was to die of exposure and dehydration in 1969 after wandering into the Jordanian desert with only his wife, an Avis map, and two bottles of Coca-Cola—recognized Phyllis Edwards, a deaconess, as a deacon. (This was also the year that the General Convention dropped the requirement of celibacy for deaconesses.) Horrifying many fellow Episcopalians, he conferred on her a New Testament and a stole, the historic signs of the male diaconate. In 1970 the General Convention, meeting in Houston, agreed to seat women in the House of Deputies, one-half of the church's bicameral governing body; at the same time, the General Convention agreed that, as Pike had argued, deaconesses were part of the diaconate. The church began to refer to them as deacons. This was an important symbolic concession; the male version of the word had more status. But by that point few women wanted to be deaconesses; there were only thirty active in the United States. Episcopal women could be nuns, and some continued to be. But for the majority of Episcopal women with a call to holy orders, it was clear that priesthood, rather than equal status in the diaconate, was the goal.[4] The next year, the Rt. Rev. Gilbert Baker, bishop of Hong Kong, ordained two female deacons, Jane Hwang and Joyce Bennett, to the priesthood. This time, no outcry from England nullified the ordinations, and Hwang and Bennett became the first women accepted in the Anglican priesthood.

The Episcopal Church did not seem poised for a women's rights insurgency. The clergy had its share of politically progressive members, those who might favor an expanded welfare state or support the United Nations, but they had not been known for, say, antiwar activism. The leadership of the ecumenical group Clergy and Laymen Concerned About Vietnam included the Presbyterian William Sloane Coffin, the Congregationalist John Bennett, the Catholic Robert Drinan, and the Jew Abraham Joshua Heschel—but no famous Episcopalian. Some Episcopal priests had worked for civil rights in the early 1960s, and there was an active Episcopal Peace Fellowship, but Episcopalians did not have the Social Gospel reputation of, say, Quakers or Unitarians.[5]

Yet the Episcopal Church was gingerly dipping its toe into the countercultural waters of the late 1960s. In 1968, for example, the Rev. Richard York, an Episcopal priest, presided over a wedding in Berkeley, California, that included a "psychedelic blaze of lighting" and a recording of "Today," by Jefferson Airplane, a rock group known for its lyrics about drug use. Present were two hundred hippies and eleven dogs that "barked enthusiastically." The same year, a conference of church schools meeting in Alexandria, Virginia, chose drug use as its annual topic.[6]

At the same time, folk music, and the kind of people who enjoy folk music, were becoming common features of Episcopal worship. In 1968 a group called the Mind Garage played its *Electric Mass*, with rock-and-roll versions of the Kyrie and the Gloria, at St. Mark's-in-the-Bouwerie, a New York City church; the crowd included "many worshippers as long haired and colorfully dressed as the musicians." Also that year a mixed group of Catholic, Episcopal, and Lutheran young people in La Grange, Illinois, wrote a folk Mass that used Van Morrison's "Gloria" for the Gloria and included folk standards like "Michael, Row Your Boat Ashore" and "Kumbaya." The next year, the Rev. Ian and Caroline Mitchell, a well-known married singing duo, released their album *Songs of Protest and Love* on the Friends of the English Liturgy label. The album included "The Jazz Rock Mass" and "Kill I Never Will." In 1971 more than seven thousand people crowded into the Cathedral of St. John the Divine to honor the third anniversary of the rock musical *Hair*. The celebration featured the premiere of the *Mass in F* by Galt MacDermot, composer of *Hair*. Alla Bozarth-Campbell, later to become one of the renegade women ordained against the wishes of the bishops, was married that year in a ceremony that included the Beatles' folkish ballad "Here Comes the Sun." In 1973 Anne Phillips, one-half of the husband-wife jingle team that wrote Pepsi's advertisement "The Taste that Beats the Others Cold," debuted *A Spark of Faith*, a "rock cantata," at St. Paul's Church in Montvale, New Jersey. Scott Muni, the legendary rock deejay of WNEW in New York, narrated the cantata, which was directed by Bhen Lanzarone, musical director of *Grease*.[7]

Like new music, the rights revolution penetrated the Episcopal Church, as minority groups vied for attention. In Washington, D.C., more than four hundred people attended a homosexual-themed worship service at the Church of St. Stephen's and the Incarnation, where in 1975 four dissident woman deacons were to be ordained. Women, of course, were not a minority, like gays or blacks, but rather a majority, and the plight of numerous women who wanted to be priests was quite unhappy. Women had for some time been studying at divinity schools: Episcopal Theological School in Cambridge, Massachusetts, which became Episcopal Divinity School in 1974, first admitted women in 1958, as did Berkeley Divinity School in New Haven, Connecticut, in 1971; General Theological Seminary in New York City had been enrolling women in classes since the 1950s. Women had been serving as deaconesses, and they constituted the majority of Episcopal churchgoers on any given Sunday. In 1970 the World Council of Churches reported that seventy-two of its member churches had opened full ordination to women, and Episcopal women, as part of a worldwide church, one that seemed to be updating its image in so many ways, felt their disability keenly.[8]

The trends in women's ordination abroad coincided with the new prominence of women's liberation in the United States. Highly educated, devout Episcopal women, many of them veterans of the civil rights movement, began to believe that tradition was choking, not sustaining, their church. Some felt a call to the priesthood, while other women, and men, wanted to support those who heard a call. As they learned about feminism, they adopted its arguments, symbols, and language. To fight their battle for ordination, some militant women became an advance guard of civil disobedience; others kept their faith in proper channels.

"Proper channels" would have been fruitless if all Episcopalians had been like the journalist Louis Cassels, who in 1971 wrote an imaginary interview with King Solomon on the subject of women's ordination:

Q. Where is the woman's place?
A. The wisest women build up their homes. (Prov. 14:1)
Q. What does a foolish woman do?
A. She raises her voice in public places. (Prov. 1:20)
Q. What kind of woman gets involved in these protest movements?

A. A woman never contented to stay at home, lying in wait at every corner, now on the street, now in the public squares. (Prov. 7:11–12)[9]

Cassels is one kind of ordination opponent: the one who finds it *unseemly* for women to want to be priests, and who cannot help mocking their daft ideas. Few Episcopalians shared Cassels's stridency. Most opponents of ordination simply believed that the tradition could not bend in this way, that God did not wish it.

But for the first time, an important group publicly supported female ordination. In 1970 the Triennial Convention of the Episcopal Church Women, the women's auxiliary to the General Convention, voted 222 to 45 that the church should permit women to be ordained. Coming just as the General Convention first seated women and elevated deaconesses to the status of deacon, the Church Women's stand suggested that the next frontier would be ordination. Emily Hewitt and Suzanne Hiatt, who would become two of the first woman priests, argued in their 1973 book *Women Priests: Yes or No?* that the existence of woman deacons—as well as woman acolytes, vestry members, and wardens—made the restriction on woman priests a silly anachronism. If women could be deacons, surely they could be priests. The diaconate had always functioned for men as a "pre-priesthood": future priests were first ordained as deacons and then, with occasional exceptions, became priests six months later. If that was the actual function of the diaconate for men, why could it not function that way for women too?[10]

At a 1971 special meeting the House of Bishops, which, along with the House of Deputies, governs the Episcopal Church, carried a motion endorsing "the principle of the Ordination of Women to the Priesthood and the Ordination and Consecration of Women to the Episcopate," or office of bishop.[11] So by 1971 the largest organization of Episcopal women and the collected body of Episcopal bishops both supported women's ordination.

It was not clear, though, what the bishops were going to *do* about it; they had resolved only to form a committee to study the question further. Fifty women calling themselves the Episcopal Women's Caucus signed an angry letter to Presiding Bishop John E. Hines, condemning the bishops for this feckless move. The women refused to serve on his committee, calling more study "negative action" that would only confirm the rightness of what they already knew to be right. The Caucus, the first group formed to address women's issues in the church, not merely to serve as an auxiliary, had gathered in October 1971 in Alexandria, Virginia, organized by Suzanne Hiatt and Nancy Hatch Wittig to respond to the bishops' meeting. The letter they sent may have been partly responsible for the bishops' greater boldness in 1972, when they again affirmed ordination in principle and also instructed the Committee on Canons to put the resolution on the agenda for the upcoming 1973 General Convention in Louisville, Kentucky.[12]

In June 1973, in preparation for the General Convention, the Caucus and another group, Priests for the Ministry of the Church, combined to form the National Committee of Episcopal Clergy and Laity for the Ordination of Women to the Priesthood. The movement appeared to be growing. But the bishops' report, prepared by the committee that the women had opposed, did not make a favorable recommendation: it merely insisted that the question of ordination be "met head-on" in Louisville.[13] On this much, it was becoming clear, the women were right: committees rarely get much done.

The progressives on the committee, like Paul Moore, bishop of New York, had fought the conservatives to a draw, but no better. The House of Bishops had twice affirmed the principle of women's ordination, so it seemed they would do so at future conventions, too— that wasn't the problem. Rather, a more aggressive stand from the bishops might sway the House of Deputies, the more conservative half of the Episcopal legislature (it plays House of Representatives to the bishops' Senate), but the bishops were not willing to be more forceful on behalf of the women.

As the women feared, a change was not about to come. To pass a change in canon law, both houses must support the change. The House of Bishops votes by simple majority rule. But the House of Deputies votes according to a complicated system enacted in 1901. Each diocese sends a delegation of two priests and two laymen. Each order, clerical and lay, from each diocese gets a vote. If the two representatives of, say, the New York clerical order vote yes, their single vote is a yes; if the two vote no, their single vote is counted as a no; but if they split, their single vote is also cast as a no. Thus are each order's votes tallied, and both orders must pass a resolution for the entire House of Deputies to have passed it. A majority of deputies can vote yes but still lose the vote.

That is what happened at the General Convention in Louisville. On October 4, 1973, on the proposal to change canon law to permit women to be ordained as priests, the clerics voted 50 yes, 43 no, and 20 divided; the laymen voted 49 yes, 37 no, and 26 divided. The nos and divideds combined, then, outnumbered the yeses.[14] Women were not to be priests, at least not for the next three years.

The issue was not settled, not for women who heard a call to the priesthood. That December 15, five woman deacons—Carol Anderson, Emily Hewitt, Carter Heyward, Barbara Schlachter, and Julia Sibley—arrived at the ordination ceremony of five male deacons at the Cathedral of St. John the Divine. As the Rt. Rev. Paul Moore laid his hands on the male ordinands, the five women presented themselves for ordination, too. They believed that Moore, a well-known civil rights liberal and outspoken proponent of female ordination, would accept this chance to act against the will of the General Convention. They hoped that he would ignore the canons of the church he had sworn to serve, and that he would ordain the first female priests in America.

Bishop Moore stood close to seven feet tall in his miter. He looked like what he was, a rich son of the American establishment, someone who

This plaque at the Cathedral of St. John the Divine, in New York City, dramatizes the issue of women's ordination by showing Bishop Paul Moore's hands symbolically tied behind his back. Reprinted with the permission of Farrar, Straus and Giroux.

had no choice but to honor the God who had treated him so well. He had studied at St. Paul's School, where he had rowed for the crew team, and at Yale College, where he had been a member of Wolf's Head, a prestigious senior society. His ancestors included the founder of Bankers Trust Corporation. From 1964 to 1990 Moore served on the Yale Corporation, the university's governing board, rising to senior fellow before he retired. But the female activists of his diocese hoped that his liberal sensibility, and his patrician's sense of noblesse oblige, would defeat his sense of establishmentarian duty.

Moore had learned to mistrust the establishment. In 1951 he had traveled south to Florida with Walter White, executive secretary of the National Association for the Advancement of Colored People, Roy Wilkins, and Thurgood Marshall to monitor the second trial of two of the four young black men accused of raping a white girl in Groveland, Florida. But while Moore and the others were there, before the trial was to begin, Sheriff Willis McCall had shot the defendants, killing one; he had alleged that they were trying to escape from custody. "That really radicalized me," Moore said in 2002, in his summer house in Stonington, Connecticut, on Long Island Sound. "You know I fought for freedom in the Marine Corps, and I love my country. I had been [a priest] in Jersey City, and we'd run into a lot of bad stuff there, police brutality, but nothing like this." When asked if his liberal views on race disposed him to support women's ordination, he said, "I think so, don't you? If you're liberal on one thing, you're likely to be liberal on another, unless there's a very strong reason you wouldn't."[15]

Moore was indeed a friend to blacks, and in 1977 he was to ordain Ellen Barrett, the first openly gay or lesbian priest. But on that 1973 day in the Cathedral of St. John the Divine, in the last tortured year of the Nixon presidency, he refused to ordain the women, prompting Carter Heyward to read a statement she had prepared for just such a refusal:

My sisters and brothers, there is an impediment because of which we should not proceed. There are 10 deacons here today.... Yet five of us have been told by the Episcopal Church that we cannot be ordained today because—and only because—we are women....

To sin is human, a condition in which all of us participate. To perpetuate willfully this sin—this intentional brokenness, this prolonged injustice, this exclusion of women throughout history—is a condition we find intolerable....

We are also aware of the uncomfortable position in which our pastor and friend, Bishop Paul Moore, finds himself. There are precedents in church history for this uncomfortable position. James himself was no stranger to the snarls of Pharisaic law. Paul, we cannot spare you the discomfort of your position.[16]

Placed in an uncomfortable position, Moore did not act as the women wished. But Heyward and the other women had put Moore, and the Episcopal Church, on notice. If proper channels would not work, the women would become more assertive.

Heyward's speech, while sounding an activist tone, was also quite Episcopal in its content. The discussion of Christian notions of sin, the references to James and the Pharisees in the New Testament—Unitarians would never use biblical language, and Catholics would be more likely to appeal to the Thomist or Augustinian traditions, or to find precedent in papal writings. Heyward alludes to the feminist cause—"this exclusion of women throughout history"—but wants to state the women's case in terms of continued allegiance to the Episcopal tradition. Heyward's actions, at this point in the ordination movement, were not explicitly countercultural; they appealed to tradition even as they sought to reform it. But the image of women circling the pulpit like scavenger birds, eager to get at the choice meat of the priesthood—that is how opponents of ordination saw the five women.

On February 9, 1974, the Episcopal Women's Caucus met at Betty Mosley's apartment in New York City. The action at St. John the Divine had garnered publicity, and the Caucus was hopeful about the 1976 General Convention. But the women disagreed about how to proceed. Some favored more direct emphasis on ordination, spoke in more feminist terms, and wanted to recruit laywomen in a grassroots movement. Others saw ordination as an important issue but also believed that the Caucus should be maximally inclusive, serving woman deacons and Episcopal laywomen uninterested in ordination. The next fall, the women favoring a broader mission would form the National Coalition for the Ordination of Women to the Priesthood and Episcopacy, the "Coalition," as a more moderate answer to the Caucus.[17] Put crudely, the Caucus would serve the feminists, the Coalition, the ladies.

The two organizations planned to work in tandem. The Coalition would lobby the House of Deputies for support at the 1976 convention, where ordination would be put to another vote; the Caucus would concentrate on building grassroots support and raising consciousness. And they were united by a common challenge, the one issued on July 29, 1974, when eleven women were ordained at Philadelphia's Church of the Advocate. They were ordained by Daniel Corrigan, Edward Welles II, and Robert DeWitt, all retired bishops of the Episcopal Church; a fourth bishop, Antonio Ramos of Costa Rica, was also present. The "Philadelphia Eleven" thrust the ordination battle into the national news and ensured that the two years leading up to the next General Convention would be contentious. Episcopalians, who prided themselves on being compromisers, would have to choose sides.

Bishop DeWitt, Suzanne Hiatt, and the Rev. Edward Harris had all met the previous June to discuss the possibility of an irregular ordination. Harris had delivered a sermon arguing that women ought to be ordained, and six weeks earlier a group of Pennsylvanians had heard Daniel Stevick, a professor at Episcopal Theological School (later Episcopal Divinity School), discuss the possibilities and dangers of such an ordination. Once the idea had been floated, and Hiatt and DeWitt had committed to it, more women and bishops expressed interest. Hiatt got Emily Hewitt to commit, and Hewitt solicited Betty Bone Schiess, a friend from their work in the Episcopal Peace Fellowship. On July 10, twenty-one people attended a meeting to plan the irregular ordination.[18] On July 20 the three ordaining bishops sent a letter to the Caucus and others, announcing their plans for July 29. "There is a ruling factor which does require this action on our part," they wrote. "It is our obedience to the Lordship of Christ, our response to the sovereignty of His Spirit for the Church."[19] Once again, the feminist cause was inscribed in appeals to church tradition.

Of the eleven women to be ordained, several were already well known in Episcopal and feminist circles. Jeannette Piccard, born in 1895, was among the world's greatest aviators, male or female. In 1934 she and her husband Jean had piloted a balloon to 57,579 feet, a world record for highest altitude achieved by human beings. Jeannette Piccard held a Ph.D. in education and had been a consultant to NASA. But her first career ambition, at age eleven, had been to be a priest. At Bryn Mawr College, M. Cary Thomas, the president, had asked Piccard what she wanted to be, and when Piccard—then Jeannette Rildon—had answered that she wanted to be a priest, Thomas had said, "If you study philosophy and the humanities, when you graduate in 1918, by then the General Seminary in New York will be open to women." Which, of course, proved untrue, although sixty years later Piccard had not lost her calling.[20]

Suzanne Hiatt, too, had as a young child wanted to be a priest.

I thought it would be fun to march up and down that aisle, talking to people, being helpful to people. But as a child I put it out of my head and thought about other things girls

could do, none of which sounded like much fun. I was baptized at age 11, because my parents had never got around to
it in Hartford, where we lived before Minneapolis. So [my
brother] John and I were baptized with all these infants.
John at 14 was acutely embarrassed, but I, at 11, thought it
was fun, and I was moved by it.

We went home and had a party—being Episcopalians,
we had a drink. I went out on a neighbor's swing and thought,
"Wheeeee! Now I'm a member of the church, now I'm a
Christian. Now we'll see who gets to walk down the aisles."

In her high-school years, Hiatt lapsed into "a late-adolescent panthe-
ism," but after attending Wellesley, transferring to Harvard, graduat-
ing, and working for the Girl Scouts and the Episcopal Church's
American Indian mission efforts, she heard the call again. One day
she walked into St Giles' Cathedral in Edinburgh, Scotland, "frankly
to get warm. It was a medieval cathedral. It had the beautiful painted
statues. It was empty, and it was a workday. I wandered around, and
then sat down on a radiator. I thought, 'What am I going to do with
my life?' And a voice said, 'You're going to be a priest. It's what you've
always been called to do.' And I thought, 'No, this is a Presbyterian
church.' And the voice said, 'That's true, but you're called to be a
priest.' That's what you'd say is a true call to the priesthood."[21]

As a teenager, Isabelle Carter Heyward (who went by her middle
name) had been chair of the Youth Commission of the Diocese of
North Carolina and had led a fight against the racial segregation of a
church camp. Katrina Welles Swanson was the daughter of Edward
Welles, the retired Missouri bishop who took part in the 1974
women's ordination. Betty Bone Schiess had marched for civil rights
in the South. And so forth: the eleven women united, across diverse
interests, by their liberal politics and a deep connection to the Episcopal Church.[22]

The ordination was scheduled for the symbolically freighted day of the Feast of St. Mary and St. Martha. Hundreds of women and men drove or flew to Philadelphia to watch. If they were hoping for drama, they were pleased. When the Rt. Rev. Corrigan asked whether anyone objected to the ordination, a man called out, "Right Reverend, Sir!" and five priests proceeded to the chancel to read statements of opposition. "The proceedings here enacted are unlawful and schismatical, constituting a grave injury to the peace of Christ's church," said the Rev. Canon Charles H. Osborn, executive director of the American Church Union, a conservative Episcopal group. When another priest accused the women of "offer[ing] up the smell and sound and sight of perversion," the audience jeered. The ordinations proceeded, and afterward the women gave communion, horrifying the conservatives present.[23] But that day, across the country, more than sixty services were held in solidarity with the Philadelphia Eleven.[24]

At first, panic. Within two days, Katrina Swanson's bishop in Missouri instructed her not to wear priestly vestments or exercise any sacramental ministry. On August 2 the Caucus's steering committee, which comprised several women who would soon break away into the moderate Coalition, sent a letter to its members promising that the Caucus "was involved neither in the decision nor in the planning of the July 29 ordination and no Caucus funds" were used to support the ordinands. Presiding Bishop John Allison announced a special meeting of the House of Bishops in Chicago for August 14–15.

Called away from their vacations—August is the traditional month off for clergy—to meet at a hotel next to O'Hare Airport, the bishops were irked and exasperated. They passed a resolution that the three ordaining bishops were "wrong" and "in violation of the collegiality of the House of Bishops."

In response, Charles Willie, vice president of the House of Deputies and its highest-ranking black member, resigned his post to protest the bishops' "blatant exercise of male arrogance." In the midst of chaos, the new female priests, or would-be priests, began honing their skills—and simultaneously committing acts of

churchly disobedience. On October 27 Alison Cheek, Carter Heyward, and Jeannette Piccard, three of the Philadelphia Eleven, celebrated the Eucharist at James Chapel of Union Theological Seminary in New York City. The same three also celebrated uptown at
Riverside Church. On September 20 Heyward and Suzanne Hiatt
celebrated Mass in Oberlin, Ohio, and on November 10, Cheek celebrated Mass at St. Stephen's and the Incarnation in Washington,
D.C.[25] Celebrating communion, the most sacred act reserved to the
priesthood, was a statement carefully chosen to affront the men who
would deny them their office. Celebrating communion would also
vanquish any ambiguity about the women's intentions or the
strength of their commitment. They meant to be priests.

In October, the bishops met again, in Oaxtepec, Mexico. They
again declared the Philadelphia ordinations invalid, but they also reit-
erated their support of the ordination of women "in principle," by a
vote of 97 to 35, with 6 abstaining. The last time they had voted on the
principle, in 1972, the yeas had won 74 to 61, with 5 abstaining; so it
appeared that the Philadelphia ordinations, while upsetting the bishops, did not cause them to change their minds about the principle at
hand. In fact, many bishops, perhaps fearing schism if the matter was
not resolved soon, were converted to the women's cause.[26]

In both the radical Caucus and the moderate Coalition, some
admired what the Philadelphia Eleven had done; others thought it
harmed the cause. Women's Ordination Now—WON (a nice inver-
sion of NOW, the feminist National Organization for Women)—was
founded in early 1975 explicitly to show solidarity with the Philadelphia Eleven. WON became the most vocal, and least compromising,
of the three Episcopal women's groups. "An exploding band of
Christians have linked together under the WON umbrella to challenge oppression in OUR church and to demand change," an early
publication stated.[27] Now the activist Caucus had been outflanked
by the more radical WON, and all three groups would press on to the
Minneapolis convention.

The strident dialogue on the women's side was met with equal vehemence from the conservatives. Frederick Wolf, bishop of Maine, wrote to the Philadelphia Eleven, "Iveson Noland [bishop of Louisiana] would not have died in that plane crash if you had not done what you did in Philadelphia." He was referring to Noland's death en route to a meeting in New York City to discuss female ordination. The same month that Wolf's letter was made public, four more women, as if to rebuke Wolf, were irregularly ordained at the Church of St. Stephen and the Incarnation by the Rev. George W. Barrett, former bishop of Rochester, New York. The bishops met again in late September, and once again they rebuked the ordinands. About the same time, dioceses in Pennsylvania, Ohio, and Washington, D.C., were debating whether to take disciplinary action against the priests who permitted irregularly ordained women, like the omnipresent Alison Cheek and Carter Heyward, to celebrate Mass in their parishes.[28]

A war of symbols was emerging between the new priests and their supporters on the one side and the traditionalists on the other. Women would be ordained, then male bishops would condemn them. The women would celebrate Mass, then aggrieved members of the parish would insist that someone be punished. As the skirmishes continued, the women began to feel strained, and they often took out their frustration on one another. Members of the Coalition believed that WON, the new, more militant group, was alienating potential supporters; the women of WON believed that they were authentic, while Coalition members were sellouts. Carter Heyward, by now a leader of WON, dismissed the Coalition as "wheeling 'n dealing on behalf of a 'cause' that is already won." For Heyward, her ordination was valid, and it was up to the recalcitrant conservatives to see the light, accept the truth, and move on; for the Coalition, canons still had to be changed, and so one must take care not to alienate potential allies.[29]

From the summer of 1975 until the summer of 1976, the Coalition continued to poll the deputies to gauge the level of support for ordination; they concentrated on persuading those deputies who were undecided, or whose decisions seemed soft. Heyward, Hiatt, Cheek, and the rest of the Philadelphia Eleven and Washington Four continued to speak and preach and celebrate communion, serving the wine and bread of the Eucharist, insisting that their ordinations were valid no matter what the General Convention said.

But their easy certainty escaped most Episcopalians. The typical layperson wanted official resolution, and resolution could only come with a change in the canons. If the canon change lost again, as it had in 1973, the fight would continue, with fifteen women regarding themselves as priests and several hundred other activists wringing their hands until 1979, when they would try again. By deciding that they were priests, the fifteen irregular ordinands had posed a question that would puzzle the church until it gave them the answer they wanted.

In September 1976 the General Convention met in Minneapolis, where the winsomely named McWON—the Minnesota Committee for Women's Ordination Now—coordinated a final lobbying effort. They staffed a booth at the convention, and they sponsored a prayer service also attended by Catholic women who favored female ordination in their church.[30] The bishops, everyone knew, would again vote for ordination; the deputies, it seemed, might finally agree. On Wednesday, September 15, the House of Bishops voted, as expected, to change Title III, Canon 9, Section 1 to make the canons for the admission of candidates to the diaconate, priesthood, and episcopacy "equally applicable to men and women." The vote was 95 for and 61 against, with 2 abstentions.[31] The next day, September 16, 1976, the House of Deputies voted to concur. The vote was 60 for, 38 against, and 16 divided in the clerical order, and 57 for, 37 against, and 12 divided in the lay order. Women would be priests.

Were the first Episcopal woman priests, then, the "irregular" ordinands of Philadelphia and Washington?[32] Or were the first female priests just around the corner, in 1977, after the canon change took effect? That is, was it the letter or the spirit of the priesthood that mattered? And had these women shown the proper spirit anyway?

As it turned out, the church accepted their ordinations without reordaining them. But that did not resolve people's conflicting emotions about the first fifteen. Were they courageous pioneers or radical, self-aggrandizing pests? How one answered that question—and how one felt about the new Episcopal Church—depended, in turn, on how one felt about feminism.

The feminist movement has not, in the twentieth century, been comfortable with religion. In Catholic countries, like Franco's Spain and de Gaulle's France, the church has been a conserver of tradition, an opponent of everything from modernist art to lenient divorce laws. Elsewhere, Catholic and conservative Protestant opposition to abortion has placed churches at odds with feminism. Before 1973, when the abortion issue became central, American feminists mostly ignored religion. A major exception, as we have seen, was Jewish feminism, which saw religious commitment and women's rights as inextricable. But the more typical feminist attitude toward religion can be seen in Betty Friedan's *The Feminine Mystique*, the best-seller published in 1963. She mentions religion only once, disparagingly, several hundred pages into the book, curtly noting that Catholicism and Judaism make women captive to domestic roles.[33]

Episcopal women never articulated an "Episcopal feminism" analogous to Jewish feminism, but there were feminists who remained Episcopalians and Episcopalians who became feminists. Either they saw the two commitments as mutually reinforcing, or they saw them in an uncomfortable, but surmountable, tension.[34] The tension would be familiar to countercultural Jews, who experienced the same anger toward institutions that had nurtured them. But while Jews could leave the institutions without abandoning their religion, Episcopal feminists had to stay and fight.

For women who wanted to be priests, or at least wanted the

right to be, the hostile and condescending responses they got pushed them to consider feminism. Even if they had not thought in feminist terms, they could be perceived in *anti*-feminist terms, and so they could not ignore the issue. "When women claim to have priestly vocations," Emily Hewitt and Suzanne Hiatt wrote in 1973, "many are offended and decide that the claimants are confused, blasphemously mistaken, or deliberately using the priesthood to further the aims of the women's liberation movement."[35]

Soon after the Philadelphia ordinations, Philip McNairy, the pro-ordination bishop of Minnesota, wrote to David E. Richards, of the church's Office of Pastoral Development, "The activities of the militant fringe of the Eleven are successfully alienating people who were once pro-women's ordination. . . . As I think of someone who could do this job of consciousness raising I believe you ought to consider Alla Bozarth-Campbell. This girl is low key, even though she feels as strongly as do some of the others about the need to be recognized as a priest. . . . She is brilliant, well educated, makes a superb impression in parishes where she has preached, taught, conducted quiet days, or served in some capacity. She might not want to be separated from husband and home, and she does have some commitments in Minnesota." It was not just men who preferred their activists suitably feminine. In 1976, the ordination fight almost won, a woman in Abilene, Texas, wrote to her priest to suggest that Helen Havens be invited to speak. "[Helen] will allay many apprehensions, and do much to offset the strident, militant, disagreeable images that many people seem to have," Jane Wolf wrote to the Rev. William W. Eastburn. "Helen makes a very low-key impression."[36]

The words used to describe the activists, and the preference for "low-key" women, could have awakened even an apolitical woman to the implications of her language. Attention to language was one of feminism's signal gifts. Certain words and terms moved from the secular feminist movement into the culture at large, and from there into the Caucus, the Coalition, and WON. A pamphlet about women in ministry was called "Our Ministry, Our Lives," a clear allusion to the 1973 feminist sexuality manual *Our Bodies, Ourselves*. Activists described lobbying efforts as "consciousness raising," a feminist term describing women's discovery of their bodies, their talents, and the oppression that had kept them ignorant. As we have seen, even male bishops like Philip McNairy spoke of "consciousness raising." Women began to speak of themselves as "sisters" (a term that, it so happens, already had a religious meaning for Episcopalians and Catholics).[37]

Even as women made the political point that they should be permitted to do anything men may do, they often used the language of feminine intuition and instinct against the more "male" notions of authority and rigor. One woman described taking communion from one of the Philadelphia Eleven: "No great bolt of thunder next, but such a sense of ease and naturalness, community and wholeness in receiving communion from a woman.... There was such joy. I wanted, in fact was greedy for, another Eucharist."[38]

For laywomen, this new language came unconsciously, as memes plucked from the air. But in seminaries, many women experienced obvious bigotry and began to search Christianity for patriarchal messages. In 1970 Betty White, a student at Episcopal Theological School in Cambridge, Massachusetts, wrote an open letter to her dean and faculty, describing indignities she had known: "In the dining room and by the single students we are treated as sex objects. We are not expected to make original or truly intelligent remarks in classes."[39] Her proposed solution, that female students be given extensive personal counseling and encouraged to take women's studies classes, was not adopted by the faculty; but in 1975 the school did hire two women to teach theology: Carter Heyward and Suzanne Hiatt, two of the Philadelphia Eleven.

Carter Heyward once wrote that Christianity's depiction of woman was a collection of demeaning stereotypes: "temptress, virginal mother, 'gateway to the devil,' 'misbegotten seed,' witch, saint: Everything but simply human."[40] While her description is not quite fair, and seems to ignore the Old Testament—was Ruth so one-dimensional? Naomi? Esther?—it does reflect a common hunger in the early 1970s for a feminist theological discourse. The years 1968 to 1974 saw the publication of several classic works of feminist theology. Mary Daly published *The Church and the Second Sex* in 1968 and *Beyond God the Father* in 1973; Letty Russell's *Human Liberation in a Feminist Perspective: A Theology* appeared in 1974; and Rosemary Radford Ruether's edited volume *Religion and Sexism* appeared in the same year. In 1971 Leonard Swidler wrote his influential article "Jesus Was a Feminist." Swidler contrasts the Jewish prayer thanking God for not making one a woman with Paul's Epistle to the Galatians, in which he writes that in Jesus "there is neither Jew nor Greek, there is neither slave nor free, there is neither male nor female." And while the Pharisees would not speak to women in public, Jesus strikes up a conversation with the Samaritan woman (John 4:5).[41]

This new discourse affected women's reading of the Bible much as nineteenth-century German higher criticism had affected male scholars': even people who didn't read the works inferred that they were now permitted to ask new questions of them. Episcopal feminists could now discuss, for example, Jesus' rejection of the blood taboo that had declared women unclean when menstruating. Feminists played with interpretation, asking about the significance of Jesus' female disciples, like Mary Magdalene, or the Canaanite woman in Matthew 15. "From this vantage point in history we are able to look back at Jesus and see him as a liberator of men in their relationships with women," wrote a male priest around 1973. Another priest recalled traveling in Israel and hearing an Indian priest preach about feminism. The Indian had described Paul as "the founder of women's lib."[42]

For some women, feminism was primary, the lens through which they saw their other commitments. Betty White wrote in 1970 that "to raise the issue of Women's Liberation within the Episcopal Church when everyone else is concerned with Cambodia and

STRIKES may seem out of place. It is not if you accept my assumption that Nixon's decision to go into Cambodia is just another symptom of the disease which affects the whole society." For White, feminism was instrumental, a mode to fight all injustices, whether committed by Nixon or by the Episcopal Church. "I myself see Women's Liberation as a powerful lever with which to force our sick society to become more humane."[43]

Carter Heyward—raised in North Carolina, one of the Philadelphia Eleven, a professor at Episcopal Divinity School, and late in life a member of an all-women's commune in rural North Carolina— described the priesthood as intrinsic to her identity, but she also saw it as a potential victory over the patriarchy. "I am a person," she wrote, "minister, deacon, student, priest, teacher, prophet, writer, fool and clown, and wise old woman. . . . I am a woman seeking, with my sisters, and some brothers, a priesthood that will be more than a male trophy, a priesthood that could, and will, be born out of nothing less than reformation." Suzanne Hiatt, like many others, focused on the concept of *sisterhood*, rather than the more politically freighted *feminism*. "Sisterhood is powerful," she wrote in 1971, "but it is slow in development and subject to harassment both subtle and overt. . . . Yet it is the cornerstone of any kind of sustained change in the commitment of the majority of Christians—*the female majority*."[44]

Heyward wanted to end priesthood's status as a "male trophy"; White wanted feminism to begin a deconstruction of all that ailed society; and Hiatt saw sisterhood as perfectly suited to Episcopal women's needs. In a 1985 address, Hiatt elaborated that perhaps the priesthood *needed* women—not for women's sake, but for the whole church's. "We entered the profession not to be ministers 'just like the men' but to bring women's gifts to the ministry," Hiatt said, "women's gifts of caring and making connections—something to balance men's gifts for abstractions and insistence on standards of excellence."[45] Equality feminism like Heyward's existed alongside the essentialist feminism described by Hiatt, according to which women have different but equally useful qualities. These different strands were a boon to the ordination movement: some Episcopalians who could not envision woman firefighters or soldiers could imagine that a nurturing, caring woman might actually make a fine priest.

Not everybody was persuaded, however. If some men belittled the idea of woman priests, some women were no kinder. In 1972 Mary Dona, an Episcopalian from San Francisco, speculated, "If the general run of women members of the church were to be polled you would find it a fact that at least 95% or maybe more are dead-set against making women priests." Another laywoman wrote an essay reminding feminists that "to iron a shirt, type a letter, plan a meeting or preach a sermon can equally be called ministry, if done with love and obedience to the spirit." A woman wrote to Carter Heyward, "All my life I have belonged to and loved the Episcopal Church. . . . Now it is being undermined by Women's Lib (so-called)."[46]

Even within the ordination movement, some saw feminists as detrimental. Mary Ann Peters complained in a letter to Helen Havens that while the Philadelphia Eleven might excite people on the coasts, they "raise anxiety levels in this part of the country," the Midwest. "The women's movement within the Church no longer needs screaming, protesting, button-wearing suffragettes who merely antagonize others within a seemingly Christian community."[47]

And for some women, including some who felt called to the priesthood, feminism was neither friend nor foe, but just a fellow traveler. They were Christians, and they preferred that label first. Merrill Bittner, one of the Philadelphia Eleven, protested that she was neither "bra-burning women's libber" nor "Super-woman, able to leap tall pulpits in a single bound," but just "a person who has discerned in her life a call to the priesthood." Nancy Hatch Wittig put the matter more bluntly: "I heard the Gospel long before I heard of the Women's Movement."[48]

Even ordination activists chary of feminist rhetoric benefited from the secular feminist movement. In the late 1960s the Episcopal

Church began to revisit its marriage canons, inspecting them for unfairness to women or divorced people, and seeking ways to make single Episcopalians feel more welcome. That attention, a direct result of secular feminists' criticisms of marriage, sensitized Episcopalians to gender issues. The National Organization for Women (NOW) slowly became interested in the Episcopal women's fight. Local chapters supported their efforts and invited Episcopal women to speak at NOW functions. (NOW needed new streams of membership, of course, and one may be skeptical of NOW's assurance, in a letter to the Coalition, that one of its goals was "the greater participation of women in religious life." Religion was rarely an issue that NOW wasted time on.)[49]

Just as the feminist movement aided Episcopal women, the women's ordination controversy fed members into the feminist movement. This is as one might expect: few people are drawn to abstract intellectual doctrines, but far more are piqued by seeing doctrine in action. We saw the same phenomenon in Unitarian churches, which got new members from feminist and gay groups that met in the churches. Alla Bozarth-Campbell, one Philadelphia ordinand, did not even join NOW until June 1974, a month before her ordination. She spent that month reading Mary Daly's *Beyond God the Father* and Simone de Beauvoir's *The Second Sex*. Those two books are now basic women's studies reading, but Bozarth-Campbell did not think to read them until well after she had become involved in the ordination fight; her Episcopal activism preceded, and drew her to, feminism.

Whereupon she became a feminist hero. The Philadelphia Eleven received scores of letters thanking them. Linda Van Vlack, a Skidmore student who saw Carter Heyward speak, wrote to her afterward. "You made me feel good about myself as a woman," she said, and she then described her own calling to be a Congregational minister. Suzanne Hiatt received an anonymous letter that began, "Dear Sue, I am being held captive by a male chauvinist. He let me out last night for one evening of consciousness raising and claims that is all that is in our contract. Liberate me. . . ."[50]

Liberate me. The anonymous writer of those words alludes to the genetic relation between women's liberation and its predecessor in the United States, civil rights. In American political discourse, slaves were "liberated"—think of William Lloyd Garrison's abolitionist newspaper *The Liberator*—and the woman writing to Hiatt fashions herself as enslaved: "I am being held captive by a male chauvinist." Episcopal feminism, like Unitarian gay rights and Jewish ethnic pride, reflected the example, tactics, and rhetoric of civil rights.

In the early days of Episcopal sisterhood, activists explicitly aligned themselves with blacks, positioning theirs as a similar cause. In April 1970 Episcopal feminists, including future Philadelphia Eleven ordinands like Emily Hewitt, Suzanne Hiatt, and Jeannette Piccard, and the black Episcopalian Pauli Murray, met at Graymoor, an ecumenical religious retreat in Garrison, New York. The statement they produced did not mince words: "The institutional Episcopal Church is racist, militaristic, and sexist; its basic influence on our lives is negative."[51] The signatories demanded that women be accepted on all parish committees, guilds, vestries, and councils, and in the priesthood, and that church seminaries move to a policy of open admission. These demands address questions of sex discrimination, of course, but the women began by accusing the church of being "racist"; the fight at hand was for women's rights, but the women interpreted their cause in terms of civil rights.

Many ordination activists had spent time in the black struggle, often in black neighborhoods. Carter Heyward wrote that her college summer working in the Henry Street Settlement House on New York's Lower East Side had forced her to think about her "black maid's exclusion from our dining room table," and then about her own exclusion from the sixth-grade baseball team, the eighth-grade sock hop, the church acolytes' group, and, finally, the possibility of ordination in the Episcopal Church.[52] After college, Suzanne Hiatt taught "in a ghetto school." Betty Bone Schiess lived in Algiers with her husband for several weeks. "When we came back to this country," she wrote, "we returned with the determination to do something about the plight of the Negro. We have taken part in many of the marches and demonstrations in the South . . . but I am even more committed to the cause for equality for women in the church." Ellen Barrett, the first out lesbian ordained, found Rosa Parks's language as suitable for feminism as for civil rights: "I remember Mrs. Rosa Parks' answer about why she sat down that day on that bus: 'I don't know, just tired I guess.' Yes, tired. . . . Tired of being second-class, good girl, virgin-whore, defective by nature. Tired of being told that the omnipotent God can't call me to the priesthood."[53]

At the same time, the Episcopal Church was reckoning with blacks' demands. James Foreman, head of the National Black Economic Development Conference, presented his "Black Manifesto" on April 26, 1969, and one of his demands was that the Episcopal Church pay a $60 million "share" of the $500 million it would cost to meet all his demands (which included a Southern land bank, four publishing and printing businesses for blacks, television stations in four cities, a United Black Appeal to establish cooperative businesses, a black university in the South, and so forth). The church did not pay $60 million, or any money at all, but church leaders and Episcopal magazines treated his demands seriously; two bishops even met with Foreman that July, despite his group's call to "resistance to domination by white Christian churches and Jewish synagogues." The magazines paid equally respectful attention to the Black Panthers, the Ocean Hill–Brownsville teachers' strike, and the case for reparations to the descendants of slaves.[54]

Most progressive Episcopalians would not, however, have been sympathetic to militancy or separatism, whether blacks' or women's. As ritualistic, Bible-reading Protestants, they learned from their theology that in Jesus all are one; even Episcopalians not as devout would, if raised in the church, favor metaphors of indivisibility and union. The Eucharist is an experience of communion; women agitating for the right to celebrate the Eucharist would have a constitutional aversion to all talk that divided people. In the Episcopal Church, white liberalism took forms other than separatism. For example, Bishop Robert L. DeWitt of Philadelphia began training Vaughan Booker, an imprisoned black murderer, for the Episcopal priesthood. Bringing a violent black man into the priesthood of the church—it was an unusual gesture that was the opposite of separatism. (Although women might have wondered why a man who had killed his wife could become a priest before they could.)[55]

Episcopalians entered into empathic relationships with black suffering. "I tremble at the idea that white women and black men will come in conflict," said Betty Bone Schiess. "It seems to me to be the black man and the white woman who have, indeed, suffered the greatest lack of self esteem with all its horrible consequences." Betty White called her compulsion to be a perfect seminary student her "Sen. Brooke complex," referring to the black Republican from Massachusetts; her point was that women, like blacks, must work twice as hard to get the same respect. Emily Hewitt and Suzanne Hiatt compared the treatment of women in the church to the old separate-but-equal doctrine. Pauli Murray, a black Episcopalian who had studied poetry with Langston Hughes, been an artist in residence at the MacDowell Colony, befriended Eleanor Roosevelt, attended Yale Law School, and taught at Brandeis, wondered if she needed to study traditional theology—"Or may there not be alternate routes which are equally valid? For example, the experience of being a Christian, a woman and a Negro in the United States and of being unwilling to forsake one's Christianity in the process of fighting for equality and humanhood?" Murray once wrote, "The problems of race discrimination and sex discrimination meet in me."[56]

The women's identification with blacks' struggle led them to appropriate blacks' language and symbols. Carter Heyward quotes from the Negro spiritual "O Mary Don't You Weep" in her book. A pro-ordination magazine, *Genesis III,* celebrates the Philadelphia Eleven for the courage they showed after having "been told 'wait' for too long"—an allusion to Martin Luther King's "Letter from Birmingham City Jail." In 1976 a pro-ordination activist at the convention suggested to Helen Havens "that a theme, much like 'I have a dream,'" be used in floor speeches. This spirit reached its perfection in 1978, when the Rev. Alla Bozarth-Campbell published these lines of poetry:

When they call me libber
I hear nigger.[57]

While civil rights lent a rich vocabulary to feminism, the antiwar movement rarely functioned in the language of women's rights. There were occasional exceptions. Carter Heyward wrote that Paul Moore's failure to understand the urgency of her cause was like her own reluctance, years earlier, to doubt the government's Vietnam policy, and the Rev. William Dois compared ordination activists to antiwar protesters at Kent State University in 1970 and at the 1968 Democratic National Convention in Chicago. Betty Bone Schiess said that she became an activist because of the civil rights movement, above all, but also because she was "just horrified by suddenly finding the Vietnam war raging in such a way" that she had to become politically active. Betty White compared sexism to the war in Cambodia.[58] Those comments were, however, unusual; feminist Episcopal activism was rarely allied, in the women's propaganda, with antiwar protest.

Today, gay rights is seen as an adjunct to feminism; in the early 1970s radical feminists sometimes discussed separating themselves from men, even the possibility that men were expendable. The title of Jill Johnston's 1973 book—a dense, stream-of-consciousness tract without much audience today—put the case rather starkly: *Lesbian Nation: The Feminist Solution.* But that language terrified most ordination activists, afraid that any signs of a subversive agenda would harm their ability to get the canons changed. One writer to the letters page of the *Living Church* said that for his priest he "would choose a woman with a history of emotional health, dedication to justice, and self-control, rather than a male homosexual, racist, or convicted murderer," and while his intentions were good, comparing women favorably to male homosexuals probably pleased neither the women nor the homosexuals.[59]

Homosexuals were finding no allies among the women. Whether in the moderate Coalition, the more broad-based Episcopal Women's Caucus, or the radical Women's Ordination Now, activist women hardly mentioned gay men or lesbians in their correspondence. True, feminism was omnipresent in the mid-1970s, while gay rights was still a boutique cause; but some Episcopalians knew of the Unitarians' wrestling with gay rights, and anyone deeply active in the feminist cause knew at least a few out-of-the-closet lesbians. Any active Episcopalian had surely heard of Integrity, a group for gay and lesbian Episcopalians. Yet the closeted lesbian Carter Heyward, writing to Suzanne Hiatt and others in 1976, reminded her "*to keep this issue separate from homosexuality*" (and the emphasis was hers). That June the Caucus refused to use a message of support, an unsolicited gesture of goodwill, sent by Integrity. "The Board is aware that you presented your resolution in good faith," Helen Havens wrote to the resolution's author. "All we can say is that we, after lengthy and painful discussion, decided it was not in the best interests of the Caucus to deliver the message at this time."[60]

Gay and lesbian Episcopalians saw the 1976 General Convention as a productive one for them. Integrity sponsored a panel in Minneapolis about homosexuality, and Integrity leaders said they were approached afterward by bishops and priests admitting their homosexuality.[61] Both the bishops and the deputies resolved that homosexual persons are equal before God and "are entitled to equal protections of the laws with all other citizens."[62] But there was no apparent alliance between feminists and homosexuals.

The convention's end, and the successful resolution of the

women's ordination question, signaled a rapprochement. An October 26, 1976, letter from an Integrity member to Helen Havens thanked the Caucus for a resolution it had just passed; it seems that the Caucus, its own battle won, now felt free to align itself with the gay men and lesbians. But the Rev. Ronald Wesner, Integrity's chairman, had written to Havens the week before to apologize for the fact that "one of the primary sources of anti-ordination sentiment is coming from closeted gays" and suggesting that perhaps "the best way of addressing it is not to speak of the women's issue at all, but rather working on the distress about being gay."[63]

So as the women came late to friendship with the homosexuals, the homosexuals had second thoughts about siding with the women. The closet impaired cooperation on both sides of the door. Closeted priests shied away from gay or feminist activism, fearful that any attention to sexuality would imperil their careers; even the vocal Carter Heyward did not come out until 1979, three years after the Episcopal Church began ordaining women. Women's ordination activists saw nothing to be gained by siding with the homosexuals—even though, according to the historian Heather Huyck, several more of the activists admitted to her confidentially that they were lesbians.[64]

Liberation begets liberation, however. Gay rights would enter the mainstream soon enough. In the 1980s numerous artists, politicians, ministers, and priests admitted their homosexuality. Their decision publicly to join a liberation movement was prompted, often, by the AIDS epidemic, but it was made far easier by the victories of feminism. Feminism, in turn, had capitalized on the successes of civil rights. Shulamith Firestone, whose *Dialectic of Sex* was a canonical feminist tract of the early 1970s, puts it well: "Just as the issue of slavery spurred on the radical feminism of the nineteenth century, so the issue of racism stimulated the new feminism: the analogy between racism and sexism had to be made eventually."[65] Her analysis accurately describes many of the ordination activists: women who had worked in the civil rights movement and been sensitized to racial injustice, now contemplating their own circumstances, as the homosexuals would soon contemplate theirs.

Finally, Episcopalians, like all Americans in the 1970s, lived in an age of compulsive introspection. Tom Wolfe, in calling the 1970s the Me Decade, was close to the mark. Religious folk were some of the worst offenders. Trying to infuse their spiritual lives with the vim their parents' church had lost, they tried primal scream therapy (see Alla Bozarth-Campbell's memoir), Erik Erikson's psychiatric theories (see Hewitt's and Hiatt's book), Gestalt therapy (see Carter Heyward's memoir), psychotherapy, and consciousness raising without end.[66] If Stephen Covey, Peter Drucker, or another management guru looked at the minutes of some 1970s meetings, he would be astounded by the time wasted in sharing, screaming, nurturing, supporting, and, of course, trying to make all decisions by consensus.

But what hampered the movement from an efficiency standpoint may have enhanced it in other ways. The search for personal growth led many presumably content women to reconsider their lot and raise their expectations. The analogical leap from blacks' rights to women's was not inevitable. Not all women made it. Those who did were products of a time—America in the 1950s and 1960s, the age of Martin Luther King—and then a place—America in the 1970s, with its therapeutic culture—that led them to different selves, and led some to the pulpit.[67]

Some women fighting for ordination wanted only to answer a call they heard from God. But other women and male allies were part of a wider movement to scramble people's linguistic and symbolic patterns. They sought new words and metaphors to describe experience; they believed that new descriptions would produce new perceptions and, ultimately, new beliefs. The shift from *Negro* to *black* to *Afro-American* to *person of color* to *African American* followed that principle; advocates of *African American* believe that a geographic origin in the descriptor connotes respect for an ethnic heritage, shifting attention away from a purely physical conception of the person. And they hope that the term *African American* will change people's attitudes toward African Americans, and even change African Americans' attitudes about themselves. They aim not necessarily for semantic precision—linguistic changes often yield less precise, and more euphemistic, results—but for a change in how we think.

Alla Bozarth-Campbell was described by her bishop as "low key," a suitably ladylike spokesman for her cause. But she came to exemplify a certain language of radical feminism. Her 1978 poetry collection *Gynergy*, though not particularly good, is an important bit of historical evidence:

> creating a sisterspace for humankind
> designing the future with our sign
> WOMEN ORIENTED WOMEN
> wow!

Consider these lines from "Rape Poem":

> What becomes of the sound
> one hand makes as it beats itself to death.

Or these, from "Discipline Means to Teach, Not to Break":

> but right on time
> with the moon's course,
> the ocean's blood.

However inept the verse, the linguistic creation of a "sisterspace," in which women may talk about "the ocean's blood" of menstruation, was a feminist project, a project that could succeed even if the Episcopal canons had never changed and *Roe v. Wade* had been decided differently.[68]

As Carter Heyward wrote in 1973, "[women's] power lies in our having been . . . not a symbol necessarily of 'femininity,' but rather a symbol of difference."[69] The signal change in the way an Episcopalian experienced his or her church after women's ordination was perceptual, not economic or even political. That is, we have no way of knowing whether woman priests helped give women greater income parity in the United States, or whether they affected people's feelings about the Equal Rights Amendment. But we can see that woman priests detached the church from what has been called its "Victorian nostalgia," a longing for the days of strong, male preachers.[70]

Some Episcopalians could not envision their church without the unalloyed, adamantine masculinity of its leadership. They bitterly rued the day when deaconesses had begun calling themselves deacons. They used arguments like this one, from a 1971 letter: "Lady kings are called queens, lady dukes are called duchesses, lady priests are called priestesses. Look in the dictionary." The Rev. Carroll Simcox, editor of the *Living Church,* made a practice of referring in print to woman priests as "priestesses." "[W]e shall follow the dictionary," he replied when a correspondent complained.[71]

Priestess, with its superstitious connotations, never caught on, even among opponents of ordination. But the two sides sallied about other matters. Would a woman priest be called Mother? Should the "Our Father" prayer be revised?[72] Feminists and ordination activists in the Episcopal Church knew that language can be hegemonic; it brings the most reluctant souls under its sway. When the conservative antifeminist Dorothy Faber ran a column under the headline "The Defiant Women: Doing Their Own Thing," she actually, in spite of herself, accorded the defiant women a victory: what better sign of liberals' success than conservatives' adopting drug-culture language like "doing their own *thing*"? Or a conservative woman's accusing the church of having an "obsessive desire to 'be with it'"?[73]

Activists paid attention to visual as well as linguistic symbols. One of the Philadelphia Eleven wrote that she had hoped for a twelfth woman at the ordination, to make an explicit visual allusion to Jesus' twelve apostles. A woman wrote to Carter Heyward, probably after a 1974 celebration of the Eucharist, "The fact, also, that you celebrated in your jeans, Carter, was very freeing for me."[74]

C. S. Lewis, the novelist and Anglican theologian, was right when he wrote that "many religions have had priestesses. But they are religions quite different in character from Christianity."[75] Some insisted that opening the priesthood to women was in the best tradition of the Episcopal Church, but others knew that the question went beyond theology. The question was also formal and aesthetic. Seeing a person in jeans celebrate the Eucharist *is* different from seeing a black-clad man in a priest's collar; people who are "with it" are different from people who are "au courant" or "cool"; and being ministered to by a woman is different from being ministered to by a man. That is not to say better or worse, only different.

To opponents of ordination, then, women presented several threats. First, there were the theological arguments. Many Christians believe in apostolic succession, the idea that Peter anointed his successors, who have anointed their successors, and thus the priesthood continues in an unbroken line back to Jesus Christ. The priest acts as a stand-in for Christ, and as the apostles and early priests were men, church tradition insists on a male priesthood. Others read the Bible as prescribing a male priesthood; a key passage for them is I Corinthians 14:34, which tells women to "keep silence in the churches." Another argument against woman priests posited that they would cause gender confusion. C. Kilmer Myers, a California bishop, argued that "initiative is, in itself, a male rather than female attribute," and a necessary one for priests; ergo, women ought not be priests. One creative soul argued that women were *too* loving to be priests: a parish priest "must learn to love all the members of the parish equally," he argued, and the "protective, subjective" instincts in women make it impossible for them to spread their love over a large flock.[76]

Suzanne Hiatt suggested that the priesthood seemed so feminine that men, to preserve their own machismo, needed it to be a boys' club: "What the priest does is, first of all he dresses up in a long dress and then, in giving Communion, he prepares a meal and then he does the dishes," she said in 1975. "But the men . . . have all these fears our culture builds into men about being effeminate." They react by assuring themselves, "I do this because I'm a priest, and everybody knows priests are always men."[77]

Even in an educated denomination like the Episcopal Church, most arguments turn neither on sophisticated biblical critiques nor on considered appeals to precedent. Rather, people fight over symbols and their meanings. Emily Hewitt and Suzanne Hiatt admitted that "women's voices do not ring with the authority and power we find so comforting in the familiar liturgy."[78] But woman priests came, like Jesus, to bring not peace but war. Their model of faith recalled his promise, in Matthew, to take away peace between a man and his father, between a daughter and her mother—to rend the old, reassuring, comfortable images and create new ones.

It would be too grandiose to say that the church "healed" after 1976. It healed after the English Civil War, it healed after the American Civil War, but in the late 1970s it just needed to lick its wounds. Most Episcopal churches did not have woman priests—most still do not—and the issue remained interesting but distant for many Episcopalians. In 1976 the House of Bishops voted to "regularize" the ordinations of the Philadelphia Eleven and the Washington Four; in other words, it tacitly accepted their ordinations and did not insist on reordaining them, a process the fifteen women would have found insulting.[79]

The feminization of the Episcopal clergy proceeded slowly and without much alarm. On January 1, 1977, Jacqueline Means, a forty-year-old mother of four and wife of an Indiana truck driver, became the first woman ordained according to the church's new canons. Two days later, Robert Spears, bishop of Rochester, presided over a cere-

Three years after her renegade ordination in Philadelphia, the Rev. Jeannette Piccard delivers the invocation to the Minnesota House of Representatives. Photograph by Jay Reilly, Minnesota Historical Society.

mony that formally recognized the priestly status of the Rev. Merrill Bittner, and similar celebrations were soon held about the country for other irregular ordinands. By 1998, twenty-five years later, there were 1,955 woman priests in the Episcopal Church, 13.8 percent of the total. The American delegation to the 1998 Lambeth Conference included eight female bishops.[80]

We are left with two difficult questions. The first is whether women wanted to be priests because they heard a calling or because they wanted to fulfill a feminist vision of equality. That is, how *feminist* a fight was this? The second question is how, once women began fighting for ordination, did they win?

Only the women themselves (and perhaps God) know the answer to the first question. But there is no reason to doubt the sincerity of women like Merrill Bittner, who told a 1985 gathering of clergy, "I, like you, have been called to this curious vocation of ordained ministry within the Body of Christ. I, like you, have passed through moments when I wish it were not so—for the demands of servanthood are great, and so often we do not feel equal or nearly adequate to the task before us."[81] In fact, there are two good reasons to believe her. First, the feminist movement did not have much respect for organized religion—many feminists despised religion—and so the first woman priests are unknown in wider feminist circles. If Bittner, Carter Heyward, Alison Palmer, or the others had been mainly committed to feminism rather than to their church, they would have chosen another cause. Most of them were feminists, but they also believed they were called to the priesthood. Second, Episcopalians are not like Unitarians: they do not all see political action woven into their religiosity. A Unitarian feminist believes she *must* make her church a more feminist place, while an Episcopalian could take communion on Sunday, save her activism for the rest of the week, and not worry that she was being religiously derelict. Furthermore, the Unitarian woman who became ordained would have ample opportunity to preach on feminist issues, while the Episcopal woman priest has, by the nature of her faith, a far more prescribed, ceremonial role. The Episcopal women who sought the priesthood, then, probably acted as much from a religious calling as from a political agenda.

But the women's fight was feminist in many ways. Feminism caused many Episcopalians to believe they could change their church—it rekindled a spirit of protest from the Protestant heritage. Feminism gave the women a vocabulary that enlarged their sense of the possible, and it gave them supportive role models from secular society.

That synergy between the ordination movement and the transformative symbolism of feminism in the United States helps answer our second question, of how the ordination movement succeeded. The bishops had by 1970 decided, as a theological matter, that women ought to be ordained. The House of Deputies moved slowly toward that position over the course of six years. One reason was surely the lobbying of the Coalition and the education efforts of the Caucus; these committees, even if they did not describe themselves in aggressively feminist terms, used a model of activism and consciousness-raising borrowed from the secular feminist movement, which itself had learned activism from the civil rights movement.

Another reason was the successful gambit of the Philadelphia Eleven and the Washington Four. We have seen that their bold acts did not lose deputies' votes; by threatening schism, the women made deputies more likely to vote for ordination. Once the women showed that they would go on practicing as priests whether the General Convention approved or not, some deputies may have realized that the best way to control this radical force was to accept it. This was not a cynical ploy to co-opt the women's activist spirit, to bring them "in house," so to speak. It was a realization that schism was in nobody's interests and that, ultimately, a Protestant tradition that had absorbed so many changes in five hundred years could countenance this one, too.[82]

Just as the Catholic hierarchy encouraged lay participation in the Mass, ensuring supervision of these masses, so too did the Episcopal Church preserve its power by permitting woman priests. But that power is now exercised in a very different church. Seeing women celebrate the same ritualistic, ceremonial Mass, hearing them intone the same words: this was a visual and aesthetic shift, and it changed the Episcopal Church more surely than the updated 1979 Book of Common Prayer did. The Episcopalians decided that this counter-culture—proposed by feminists and promising a whole new vision of the clergy, one couched in therapeutic terms, less austere and more demotic—was preferable to a prolonged internecine war.

FIVE

Southern Baptists and
Vietnam War Protest

With few exceptions, no American religion welcomed the counterculture. But most religious people—like the Jews, Episcopalians, and Catholics—made room for countercultural types, whether long-haired troubadours with guitars, radical nuns, or mystical New Age rabbis. The stories we have heard suggest that in almost any group, sympathetic elders, clergy, and laity will encourage new forms of liturgy, new settings for worship, new music, and new members. No matter how conservative their theology, denominations are flexible, and what cannot be achieved in church law can be achieved by cultural insinuation. As a result, the tropes of American counterculture—the music, language, clothes, and permissiveness—found their way into religions.

In the Southern Baptist Convention, the country's largest Protestant body, an unusual pattern emerged: the only ones speaking the language of the counterculture were evangelists trying to bring young people into the church. Young people who themselves looked like hippies or held radical political views either left the denomination or, in order to be taken seriously, cleaned up their act to please the church elders. While the old fretted about the counterculture, and even proselytized hippies outside the church, young Southern Baptists never embraced the counterculture. The ministers were answering a question that nobody in their church seemed to be asking.

There was, for a short while, a small group of liberal students who organized to demand that the convention take stands on the Vietnam War, civil rights, and poverty. But those students, who called themselves Baptist Students Concerned, made a conscious effort to be culturally acceptable, to look and sound as unthreatening as possible. They had short haircuts and dressed soberly, and they completely avoided certain issues, like the ordination of women (most Southern Baptist churches still do not hire woman pastors) and gay rights. Many were from families of preachers, elders, and church administrators, and they guessed that their political message would not be heard if they looked or sounded too oppositional. As a result, the countercultural markings worn by activists from other religions—the hip language, the music, the identification with the plight of the Negro, the appropriation of the term *nigger,* the long hair and more colorful attire—are absent from Baptist Students Concerned. Their political dissent was entirely decoupled from countercultural aesthetics.

This was true even as Baptist evangelists tried to reach out to young people with Christian coffee shops, and even as the church debated liberal theologians (and a *Playboy* editor!) about current morality. When Episcopal women or Catholic folkies found some priests on their side, they took license to keep pushing, remaking church culture. In the Southern Baptist Convention, even when elders encouraged the students in their activism, the students remained careful and respectful of church norms. If they had any countercultural tendencies, they were extremely timid about them. Their group soon disbanded, and the Southern Baptist Convention later embraced conservative politics and fundamentalist theology.

It seems, then, that there never was a Southern Baptist counterculture. There were politically liberal students who took pains not to be countercultural, and there were conservative preachers who painfully engaged the counterculture. Then, of course, there was the mass of Southern Baptists who wanted to ignore these questions, who wanted "the sixties" to be over as soon as possible. In the end, the conservative masses won. Feeling besieged by secular America, they turned inward and squeezed the last traces of dissent from a tradition born of dissent.

Jews have a tradition of argument, and, with Vatican II, Catholics invited argument in. Southern Baptists did the opposite. By looking at the question of the Vietnam War, we can see the extent to which Southern Baptists' intertwined regional, religious, and political loyalties enforced a homogeneity that precluded counterculture. Hippies and homosexuals had no place. Folk music and new worship styles were acceptable only as instruments of conversion.

There was slight room for political nonconformity, but only slight: pacifism bled into questions of draft-dodging, and political dissent began to appear antipatriotic. And patriotism, it seemed, was as much a requisite for Southern Baptism as was belief in Jesus Christ. Liberal students knew this logical chain, and they knew that even their mild activism would arouse fears. That knowledge informed antiwar activism in the church, dictating how it must look, sound, and feel. Anything that appeared to question the daily norms of Southern, Christian life would be dismissed as blasphemous. Among the religions discussed here, only Southern Baptists had this strict line. The line worked; nobody crossed it.

In 1968 Terry Nichols, a student at the University of North Carolina at Chapel Hill, began to organize meetings of area students who thought Southern Baptists should take a more active role in addressing poverty, the war, and racial inequality. He eventually built a network of twenty-five or thirty students from campuses like UNC, Wake Forest, North Carolina State, and Vanderbilt, and his meeting at the Southern Baptists' 1968 national convention drew more than one hundred liberal Baptists, eager to promote dissent within the denomination. Baptist Students Concerned got the attention of seminary professors, nationally prominent pastors, and the media, and they demonstrated that the Southern Baptist Convention had room, a little room, for diverse opinions about the Vietnam War.

Baptist Students Concerned was one of very few organizations of young, progressive Baptists. While the high school and college arms of other denominations were politically active—we have seen the clearest case with the Unitarians—the campus Baptist Student Unions remained quietist. There were exceptions: Oklahoma Baptist University, for example, had a small group of students opposed to the war. But the evidence supports the Rev. Jim Greene, the Baptist chaplain at Duke University, who saw "very little support for antiwar expressions." Greene, who became the Baptist Student Union state director for North Carolina in the school year 1968–1969 and was an adviser to Baptist Students Concerned, "felt pretty much alone during the Baptist Students Concerned days."[1]

Walker Knight, who edited *Home Missions* magazine, organ of the Southern Baptists' progressive Home Missions Board, agreed: "The antiwar sentiment among Southern Baptists was not widespread during the period of 1968–1975. I would estimate it at less than 10 percent of the members among Southern Baptists, and the majority of that 10 percent were among students." When on November 15, 1969, four students and two faculty from Southeastern Seminary in Wake Forest, North Carolina, participated in an antiwar march on Washington, they carried signs identifying themselves as "a minority of students" and "some faculty members" opposed to the war; the words *minority* and *some* were added at the insistence of fellow students.[2]

A group uniting liberal Baptist students from widely scattered campuses was likely to be based in North Carolina. The state had for years been home to progressive Southern Baptists. Pullen Memorial Baptist Church in Raleigh (whose pastor, the Rev. W. W. Finlator, was a pacifist and opponent of the death penalty), Binkely Memorial Baptist Church in Chapel Hill, and Watts Street Baptist Church in Durham were known for opposition to the war, or at least toleration of opposition. As early as 1966 the North Carolina Baptist Student Union sponsored a debate on the merits of the American position in Vietnam. W. W. Finlator spoke at the debate, and Lt. Marvin E. McGraw of Fort Bragg spoke on the topic "Why I Am a Professional Soldier"; Clarence Jordon of Georgia answered with "Why I Am a Pacifist." In 1968 the state convention directed its Division of Christian Life and Public Affairs to consider the matter of conscientious objection; the next year, the committee announced the development of a pamphlet, to be distributed to boys of draft age, on the history of Baptist conscientious objection.[3]

Unlike many of the students he recruited for Baptist Students

Concerned, Terry Nichols was not from this progressive milieu. He was not from a family of intellectual Baptist preachers or convention honchos. He was originally from a small town in Tennessee; when he turned fifteen, he, his parents, and his four brothers moved to Lexington, North Carolina, "a little furniture town between Charlotte and Greensboro," Nichols said in 2002. In Tennessee "we lived on a farm, but we drove every Sunday to Bellevue Baptist [in Memphis], where the pastor, R. G. Lee, had been president of the convention. He was very fundamentalist, so we were totally indoctrinated in a fundamentalist Baptist environment." As a freshman at the University of North Carolina at Chapel Hill, Nichols joined the Baptist Student Union and was exposed, for the first time, to ideas outside the insular fundamentalist realm.

Explaining the genesis of Baptist Students Concerned, Terry Nichols said, "The original idea lay in the experience that some of us at Chapel Hill in the Baptist Student Union had in reaction to two things that clearly seemed to be contradicting one another. One was . . . things happening in North Carolina dealing with poverty: the North Carolina Fund, which Governor Terry Sanford had started, and which led up to the formation of VISTA [Volunteers in Service to America]. And this was 1967 and we started seeing the underground press and a lot of stuff starting up on campus around the horror happening in Vietnam. . . . And eventually the primary media picked up on looking at the daily body counts, which were often inflated, we found out later, to make it look like we were winning the Vietnam struggle."

In late 1967 Nichols and some fellow Baptists from UNC went to a conference in Columbus, Ohio, sponsored by a branch of the Christian student movement, based in England. "And that was eye-opening, because we met people from all over the world, we saw underground films. Allen Ginsberg was there, and it was a really neat experience for this little Baptist boy growing up on a farm in Tennessee. . . . Something seemed to congeal in my thinking, that the religion I had come to know growing up as a child was really not showing us the world as it truly is."

Prodded by a sly campus minister, Nichols soon found himself becoming an activist: "The Baptist Student Union at Carolina was always trying to talk about current issues. We had dinner meetings every Friday night. There was a group of us that hung around the center; it was sort of our fraternity or sorority. I think Jack [Halsell, the Baptist chaplain] brought us the program for the upcoming Southern Baptist Convention. I think it was a pretty deft thing for him to do. And he simply said, 'Well, what do you think about this program at the SBC?'—which was the blandest tripe we had ever experienced, and it stood out in such sharp relief with what the world was dealing with. We kind of looked at each other, said, 'We need to have some reaction to this.' And I think Jack was instrumental in saying, 'Calm down, focus, be kind of rational about your response and how.'"

Nichols and the others decided that this convention program posed a kind of test. "It was sort of like, 'What are we going to do with all this stuff we've been learning? If we can't confront our own, then who are we?' We were just incensed that [the program] had not one single word to do with anything that mattered to the world. So we were going to do something. We were going to shake some trees. We didn't know what or how. I know Martin Luther King had been killed in April. We may have been talking a while before that, but his death, it just cemented us. . . . We had to respond to this inane lack of attention to anything that mattered in the world."[4]

From statewide student Baptist meetings, Terry Nichols knew Stuart Sprague at Duke and Roger Sharpe at North Carolina State. He began to recruit other students, too, working so hard that the efforts ruined his grades; he needed to complete summer school after the 1968 graduation to get his diploma. But he succeeded in recruiting "about 25" students who planned to attend the 1968 national convention in Houston, where they would demand that the

Members of Baptist Students Concerned speak at a press conference at the 1968 Southern Baptist Convention. The "SBC News Central" sign in the background indicates that the convention was agreeable enough to invite the students to use its space. Reprinted with the permission of the Southern Baptist Historical Library and Archives, Nashville, Tennessee.

church address poverty, racism, and the war. "He circulated the idea, and within several months students from a number of campuses were committed," writes Stuart Sprague, a founding member of Baptist Students Concerned, who later became a medical ethicist. "There were long strategy sessions in which we debated how to make our point. Some were for a more confrontational style, while others thought we ought to do more of an inside job. In the end traditionalism won out. We even checked with the Houston Police Department to be sure our plans were okay."[5]

In keeping with the nonconfrontational strategy, the members of Baptist Students Concerned got themselves elected convention messengers (as delegates are called) by their home churches. When the students arrived in Houston, they held a planning meeting that

The empty placards toward the end of the line suggest that silence regarding America's problems is not an acceptable option. Reprinted with the permission of the Southern Baptist Historical Library and Archives, Nashville, Tennessee.

drew about one hundred people, many of them students who had come on their own after reading about Baptist Students Concerned. When the convention began, they wore coats and ties and dresses. "In fact," Sprague writes, "the signs for our picket lines were mostly blank to minimize confrontation. The first sign in a series said, 'Will this be the relevant response of Southern Baptists to social issues in 1968?' About 10 blank white posters followed the first." Since only state conventions and official arms of the national convention were entitled to a booth, the North Carolina executive secretary signed for the students' booth in Houston. To their booth and picket signs the students added pamphlets, distributed through a "subversive plot," Sprague writes, tongue in cheek: Lelia Routh, the daughter of Southern Baptist Convention Executive Secretary Porter Routh, had the job of distributing the convention's daily bulletin from a ticket booth

The students are attired as conservatively as the middle-aged
messengers. Reprinted with the permission of the Southern Baptist
Historical Library and Archives, Nashville, Tennessee.

at the entrance, and she stuffed the students' antiwar pamphlets into
every bulletin.[6]

By the time the convention started in June, other Baptists were
becoming a little more politically aware. On April 8 Martin Luther King
Jr. had been assassinated, alerting even the most apolitical Southern
Baptists to the turmoil in the country; that knowledge, coupled with
the awareness that this group of possibly radical students from North
Carolina would be attending the convention in Houston, caused
church officials to fret. "There were also fears that Southern Baptist college students might be on the march," a Baptist minister later wrote.
"When word came that students at the University of North Carolina
had formed 'Baptist Students Concerned' to 'wake up' the SBC at
Houston to 'the vital issues,' many Southern Baptists braced themselves
for another takeover as had occurred at Columbia University."

It is ironic, even funny, that as Southern Baptist students worried about how to appear as nonconfrontational as possible, Southern Baptist administrators worried about how to defuse confrontation. In the Episcopal Church, of course, it worked in the opposite way: as the Philadelphia Eleven planned their explosive renegade ordination, the bishops were comfortably certain that the issue of women's ordination could wait until the next General Assembly. Word of the Philadelphia ordination took the bishops by surprise, and their emergency meeting at O'Hare Airport was hastily convened at the last second. But while Episcopal leaders were perhaps too smug about their religion's resiliency, certain that nothing could bring about radical change, Southern Baptists were very afraid.

Their fears prompted a meeting in Nashville that included James Sullivan and Clifton Allen of the Baptist Sunday School Board, along with Foy Valentine of the Christian Life Commission and convention President H. Franklin Paschall. Eager to blunt the force of the students' arguments, they decided that Allen and Valentine would write a statement to prove that the convention was not ignorant of the growing unrest in America. The thousand-word "Statement Concerning the Crisis in Our Nation" was sent to all the convention's agency executives, state executive secretaries, and state newspaper editors. By the eve of the convention, seventy-one people had signed. Valentine, the liberal head of the Christian Life Commission, told a *Newsweek* reporter, "Southern Baptist officialdom is moving away from its old racist origins. The culture here is finally being rejected in favor of Christ."[7]

Years later, the statement appears remarkably mild. For Baptist Students Concerned, however, getting the convention merely to recognize that something was afoot in America, and that Southern Baptists would do well to think about the change, was a victory. "Our nation is enveloped in a social and cultural revolution," the statement begins.

We are shocked by the potential for anarchy in a land dedicated to democracy and freedom. There are ominous sounds of hate and violence among men and of unbelief and rebellion toward God. These compel Christians to face the social situation and to examine themselves under the judgment of God.

We are an affluent society, abounding in wealth and luxury. Yet far too many of our people suffer from poverty. Many are hurt by circumstances from which they find it difficult to escape, injustice which they find most difficult to correct, or heartless exploitation which they find most difficult to resist. Many live in slum housing or ghettos of race or poverty or ignorance or bitterness that often generate both despair and defiance.[8]

The statement continues in that vein, calling finally for "Christian ventures" to further the "inherent dignity" of all individuals (a phrase that directly echoes, probably coincidentally, the Unitarians' "first principle" of "the inherent worth and dignity of every person"), demanding full human and legal rights for all, and repudiating racism, violence, and mob action. The statement makes no policy recommendations, instead urging "fellow Southern Baptists to join us in self-examination under the Spirit of God."

The Statement Concerning the Crisis in the Nation is written in boilerplate crisis-talk. Asking Southern Baptists to examine themselves under the Holy Spirit is like reminding Roman Catholics to go to communion: it is what they are *supposed* to do. Yet for Baptist Students Concerned, the resolution was cause for great excitement. The students lobbied for its passage; in fact, they agonized over whether to maintain their picket line outside the convention hall or go inside to cast their ballots. Eventually, they called Porter Routh, the executive secretary, for advice. Stuart Sprague remembered the incident well: "We were concerned—this shows how straight we were—that

that [resolution] pass, and would our presence make the Statement on Crisis go down to defeat, in reaction?" In other words, would the statement stand a better chance of passage if it did not appear to be on the wish list of agitating students? "So we called Routh"—whose number they had gotten from his daughter Lelia, their plant who stuffed literature in the daily convention bulletin—"and said we were debating whether to pull in the troops and let the delegates vote, and his answer was, 'You're Baptists, do what you have to do, I am not going to tell you.' So that was a freeing thing, to hear the leader of the convention tell us from Baptist principle to do what we wanted to do. So we did go back out there, and we voted, and the resolution passed."[9]

Walker Knight summed up why the statement may have been so important to Baptist Students Concerned: "My experience was that as a whole the denomination strongly resisted being informed on what they termed 'social issues.'" In part, this head-in-the-sand attitude derived from the same principle of individual conscience that Porter Routh had invoked in his conversation with Stuart Sprague. Historically, Baptists are strictly congregational—nothing the conventions do is binding on the member churches—and beyond that they prize the priesthood of the believer, in grand Reformation style: ultimately, a believer must follow God's will as he understands it. That formulation does not jibe particularly well with the stereotype of Southern Baptists as uniformly conservative, but it is an important theological strain in all Baptist traditions. As the conventions and churches have shied away from taking political stands, they have traditionally left those questions to individual consciences. The students' goal, then, was to force apolitical Baptists to reckon with American culture—to be, in other words, more cultural, not countercultural.

So the minor ripples made by Baptist Students Concerned in 1968 were impressive. They ignored the apolitical tradition. They talked with people on the sidewalks and at their booth—about race, poverty, and of course war. They picketed. They helped get a resolution passed. When Foy Valentine arranged a special panel session for students to address curious messengers, 250 messengers attended.[10] The felicitously named W. C. Fields, public relations director of the executive committee, ensured that the students' actions were covered. W. O. Thomason, interim director of the national Baptist Student Union, watched with interest and later invited some of the students to address all the heads of the Southern Baptist agencies the following spring.

The next year the Pastors' Conference, which always meets just before the convention, invited the students to come early to the New Orleans convention to attend their luncheon meeting, where the pastors would be discussing reparations for descendants of slaves (a topic briefly in vogue during the Black Power years, then not again until the late 1990s). Always a fairly conservative body, the Pastors' Conference seemed least likely to engage the students, who were pleasantly surprised. The students met, too, with the E. Y. Mullins Fellowship, a group of liberal religion professors that had just formed, inspired by the students' actions the previous year; their joint meeting at St. Charles Avenue Baptist Church drew more than one hundred people. At the convention, the students submitted resolutions, which the Committee on Resolutions refused to bring to a vote, calling for economic aid for black Americans and the reform of denominational Sunday school literature to make it more scholarly and less dogmatic. They also insisted, fruitlessly, that messengers from segregated churches not be seated and that all denominational boards and agencies be integrated.

Also in 1969, in New Orleans, Jim Lowder, a religion major at Duke and Baptist Students Concerned member, presented a resolution to encourage the denomination to write and publish a sex education curriculum—which it did, though the curriculum was withdrawn two years later. Stuart Sprague, Tom Graves (later the president of Baptist Theological Seminary at Richmond, founded in Virginia in 1991 as an alternative to fundamentalist seminaries), and several other student activists attended the 1970 convention in Denver, but with a lower profile, without the large meetings or dramatic speeches that had marked the previous two years.[11]

Despite their tidy image and willingness to play by the rules, the Baptist Students Concerned were to the political left of most of the convention, and they expected to encounter some enmity, or at least conspicuous glares. Some of the students had even dabbled in draft-dodging: Roger Sharpe had applied for conscientious objector status, though his application was never acted upon. (He was called for his physical but never drafted.) And Tom Graves had asked to see the CO application form but was told that as a seminary student he would receive a 4-D deferral anyway, so he was not permitted to apply for conscientious objector status.[12]

The students pursued other issues, but they were most identified with the antiwar cause, distasteful to most messengers. Yet instead of being derided or ignored, the students were given platforms to speak and invitations to other events. Tom Graves offers a possible explanation. Not a North Carolinian, he discovered Baptist Students Concerned by other means: "I was at Vanderbilt [University, in Nashville], and found out through Stuart Sprague's sister, a classmate. My involvement was one of intense interest; my father was dean of Southern Seminary [in Louisville], and my uncle was president of Golden Gate Seminary [in California], so I had a great deal personally at stake in the discussion of Baptist life." The family connections here are key: just as Lelia Routh, daughter of convention administrator Porter Routh, used her connections to get the students' message across, somewhat surreptitiously, Tom Graves's relations certainly helped insulate Baptist Students Concerned from criticism. And Graves had come to Baptist Students Concerned through his classmate Susan Sprague, Stuart's sister. The web of connectivity gets even more intricate: W. C. Fields, the public relations official who covered the students for Baptist Press, had been a college classmate of Stuart Sprague's mother.[13]

Even when the connections did not originate in bloodlines, they could run as thick. Jim Greene, the minister who advised the students, guessed that the North Carolina executive secretary was willing to sign for the students' booth in Houston because he considered Greene "one of his 'boys' in the ministry."[14] Despite being the largest Protestant denomination in the United States, the Southern Baptist Convention had a small, communal feel. Though times have changed—more Southern Baptists than ever live in urban areas, and these demographic shifts were instrumental in splitting the church into conservative and moderate wings in the 1970s—an unusually high percentage of Southern Baptists still come from small towns. The vast majority live in the South, with its neighborly ways, hospitality, and keen respect for kinship ties. Reading the transcripts of Southern Baptist state and national conventions, one gets the sense that although not all Southern Baptists knew each other, they acted as if they did.

In the late 1960s and early 1970s, the Southern Baptist respect for individual conscience combined with regional habits of friendliness to make Baptist Students Concerned feel welcome. Tom Graves remembered that "the access to the officers of the SBC, and the offices, particularly the offices in Nashville, was just amazing. I think it was H. Franklin Paschall who was president of the SBC at the time, and he was very agreeable to sitting down and talking to us," as was Porter Routh. Graves and Dan Aleshire, later the president of the accrediting agency for North American seminaries, were even placed on a national committee studying student ministry and got to travel the country at the Southern Baptist Convention's expense. "I was very much impressed with how seriously we were taken," Graves said, adding jokingly, "frankly a lot more seriously than I thought we should have been." Lelia Routh said that the man in charge of selling speeches, into which she stuffed antiwar propaganda, knew she was doing so and looked the other way.[15]

If Walker Knight was correct that as many as 10 percent of

Southern Baptist ministers held progressive views on civil rights, and if Stuart Sprague was correct that "the . . . leadership was always ahead of where the folks in the pew were," then maybe Sprague was also right that some Baptist elders liked watching students' expressing views that they themselves could not. Men like Walker Knight, Foy Valentine, and W. C. Fields "couldn't have said this stuff themselves in their own position, but if the kids wanted to make a ruckus, we could. All these folks were open and perhaps even in sympathy with the students." Walker Knight remembered a liberal pastor who said to him, "If I preach what I really believe, I am not as successful at growing a church."[16]

So the church elders were tolerant of, even pleased by, the passionate young students. The students were putting the Baptist heritage into practice: respect for the individual conscience, congregational independence, identification with the weak and marginal, and horror at war. But if Baptist Students Concerned were successful, "success" was defined in terms set by the convention at large. Victory meant having their concerns ratified by the powers that be, whether in the "Statement Concerning the Crisis in the Nation" or with invitations to speak before important men. At the root of their political dissent was an eagerness to reform a traditional model, and this meant, by necessity, an eagerness to please. This project was fundamentally different from, say, Carter Heyward's—she considered herself a priest even if the bishops would not recognize her as one. She wanted their recognition, probably more than she would admit; but that was not the main criterion for success. Like Jews who formed havurot outside traditional synagogues, or Catholics in an alternative parish, female Episcopal priests were willing to distance themselves from the tradition, if only in symbolic ways.

The Southern Baptist Convention, however, was a totalizing fact for Baptist Students Concerned. They were related to church leaders, they had grown up in the church, and they selected an agenda they could argue according to Baptist principles. Pacifism, for example, had been particularly strong in Baptism—stronger than in Judaism, or in Catholicism, with its just war tradition. But when Catholics or Jews agitated for peace, they created strong peace movements within their religious bodies. Baptist Students Concerned did not. Even after playing by all the rules—that is to say, dressing well, being polite, and eschewing counterculture—they never won many converts to the peace movement. For the antiwar movement was seen as a Trojan horse, one that might bring pagan counterculture into the church. For that reason, pacifist views, even if supported by Baptist history and theology, ultimately had to be brushed aside.

In its style, language, and music, and in the unfortunate bedfellows that came with it, antiwar protest—even more than abortion rights or welfare policy—signified a dangerous cultural alternative. To understand why, it is necessary to look back at Baptist history.

In July 1751 Isaac Backus, a Connecticut evangelist already disillusioned by the Congregationalists' liberalization of church membership rules, decided that they were wrong about something else, too. God, he concluded, did not command infant baptism. Drawing on theology he had been reading, Backus argued that infant baptism was done through false analogy with circumcision; once people realized the difference between the Old and New Covenants, the latter brought by Jesus, they would cease infant baptism, or paedobaptism. After a series of synods from 1751 to 1756, Backus emerged as the leader of the Separate Baptists, who combined the old suspicion of lax Congregationalist membership standards with a new hostility to paedobaptism. When Backus died in 1806, he was the most prominent Baptist cleric in New England, which had more than three hundred Baptist churches, comprising Separate Baptists, Freewill Baptists, and Old Baptists.[17]

With the exception of Thomas Jefferson, Isaac Backus also was the citizen of the early republic most identified with keeping the church disentangled from government. He stood in a line of Dissenters going back to England, which had nearly fifty Baptist churches in 1644, and to the New World divine Roger Williams, founder of Rhode Island Colony in 1636 and of the first Baptist church in America, in 1639. Williams articulated a vision of separationism that sought to protect the church from the state rather than the other way around. Always in the minority, Baptists had a pragmatic political reason to want government to stay out of their way; if for some reason they came in conflict with another religion, Baptists knew they would lose in the court of public opinion. But the desire for separation had a more philosophical grounding, too. Backus put it like this: "The church is presented as a *chaste virgin to Christ;* and to place her trust and love upon others, is *playing the harlot,* and so the way to destroy all religion (Hosea 2:5)."[18]

The Baptist reputation for independent thought, aversion to hierarchy, and indifference to state authority proved tremendously appealing in Virginia, then ruled by Church of England gentry. Baptist evangelists prayed with slaves, encouraged sabbatarianism, and opposed gambling and drinking; by the 1760s they had won enough converts to provoke harassment from the Anglican elite. What was the appeal of this new, ascetic religion? It was—ironically, given Baptists' later history—a counterculture. Baptists' tightly ordered lives offered a radical psychic escape from the society ruled by the loosely Anglican southern gentry. This new religious community supported poor people as they fought disease, debt, deprivation, and violence— the common lot of small farmers.[19] Much as people dissatisfied with contemporary life seek refuge in fundamentalist religion, or sometimes in authoritarian cults, many Virginia poor saw the strict Baptist life as an escape into a new community, rather than as an ordeal.

Slowly, however, as poor farmers grew into the middle class of the new republic, Baptism became a mainstream religion. Even though many early Baptists had been abolitionists, Southern Baptists, as typical southerners, came to support slavery. In the 1840s sectional disputes multiplied, and the Southern Baptists found themselves clashing with abolitionist Baptists from the North. In 1845 the Southern Baptist Convention met for the first time, in Augusta, Georgia, effecting a split from the northern churches. Its member churches were concentrated in the states that would, fifteen years later, constitute the Confederacy.[20]

Southern Baptists, like most, were captive to their economic interests; people will tithe 10 percent of their incomes, but ever since Jacob and Esau they have been protective of their birthrights, their houses and farms and slaves. But in their split from the North and support of slavery, Southern Baptists were not driven simply by avarice. Their theology took seriously Paul's admonishment in Ephesians 6:5: "Bondservants, be obedient to those who are your masters according to the flesh, with fear and trembling, in sincerity of heart, as to Christ." This literalist theology was of course convenient in the extreme. While northerners, less invested in chattel slavery, began to nurture biblical criticism and liberal interpretations of the Bible, southerners remained committed to the strict reading that supported their economic system. That a theology is convenient does not mean it is insincere, of course, and this theological difference was enough to divide a church.[21]

Southern Baptists were not totally apolitical; after the Civil War state conventions often encouraged legislatures to prohibit Sabbath-breaking and ban the sale of alcohol.[22] But as conservatives in the true sense of the word, people who disliked change, Southern Baptists generally avoided political questions. The status quo was better than anything that legislators or social reformers might dream up. And this cultural habit of deferring to Caesar on matters of the state helped Southern Baptists, and the South, reconcile all sorts of contradictions after the Civil War, like being simultaneously suspicious of the federal government and deeply patriotic, both secessionist and jingoistic.

As the more conservative Southern Baptist Convention grew—from 1.2 million members in 1876 to 3.6 million in 1925—the northern Baptist churches, now called the American Baptist Convention, stagnated.[23] As the years wore on, the characters of the two denominations diverged. While Southern Baptists were suspicious of modernism and the evolving practice of biblical criticism, scholars at northern Baptist schools like Brown, Bates, and the University of Chicago happily engaged new scholarly trends. While Baptists in the North were cautiously progressive on race relations, Southern Baptists remained indistinguishable from other southerners on the issue. Most important, while northern Baptists remained less influential cousins to Congregationalists and Episcopalians in the North, Southern Baptists were on their way to becoming the dominant religious tradition in the South.

This picture is painted too boldly, of course, ignoring all kinds of nuances, from dissenters within the Southern Baptist Convention, like the Landmark Baptist and Primitive Baptist movements, to the continued strength of American Baptists in pockets of the North. It has never been the case that all Southern Baptists are fundamentalists, nor that they have a consensus on any political issue, from abortion to prayer in schools. We may say only this: that the 1845 schism resulted in a vibrant southern denomination and a more anemic northern counterpart. In the South religion became inseparable from one's social, regional, and American identities; as the widest-spread southern religion, Southern Baptism became the best metonym for southernness itself.[24]

With temperance and sabbatarianism lost causes, politically speaking, the Southern Baptists entered a period of political inactivity. The convention continued to pass resolutions that pertained to the secular world, but most pastors worried more about saving their congregants' souls and winning new converts. In the late 1960s Southern Baptists could be remarkably complacent about current events. In a 1969 poll of the editors of thirty Southern Baptist state newspapers, the denomination's response to Hurricane Camille was voted the "Top SBC Story of 1969"; concern over the Vietnam War followed distantly in ninth place. Two years later, Golden Gate Baptist Theological Seminary in California hosted not a soldier, or a pacifist, or a community organizer, but *Peanuts* cartoonist Charles Schulz, who spoke on the topic "What is the theology behind the Great Pumpkin?"[25]

Southern Baptists quietly deferred to the government on most matters. But given their historical interest in the separation of church and state, it is not surprising that a few Southern Baptists would always be suspicious of national war efforts. Southern Baptists were chary of supporting the Mexican War of 1846–1848, which they ignored in their writings, generally seeing it as a political event outside their spiritual concerns. They supported the Civil War, of course. But in 1895 the convention adopted a resolution offered by J. J. Hall of Virginia supporting "arbitration instead of war ... [and] the establishment of an International Arbitration Court."[26] Many Southern Baptists opposed the Great War and encouraged American neutrality, right until the United States entered the war in 1917. After the war most Southern Baptists supported President Wilson's League of Nations, and in 1921 the convention expressed support for disarmament.[27]

This is not evidence that most Southern Baptists were pacifists; the national convention that passed these resolutions often comprised only a few hundred messengers, and they were the most active, and often most educated, clergy. But we can suppose that the messengers represented at least a strong minority of Baptists who opposed warmongering. The 1940 convention not only recognized the right to conscientious objection but also expressed the Southern Baptists' commitment to helping to register conscientious objectors with the denomination, helping them avoid conscription. After World War II the convention went on record against the peacetime draft. Perhaps most surprising, the 1952 convention voted to "reaffirm its confidence in the United Nations Organization as the most effective available political device for world peace"—a position it would be allergic to today.[28] The Southern Baptist record in the twentieth century shows approval for fighting, yes, but fighting against the Central Powers, the Axis, and the Communists, which is not a record to be ashamed of. Most Southern Baptists ultimately supported these wars as necessary and just, but Southern Baptists who decided that the United States did not belong in Vietnam had plenty of church history on their side.

In the late 1960s and early 1970s, the Southern Baptist Convention had pockets of liberalism. On the matter of abortion, for example, the church passed a resolution at its June 1971 convention, in St. Louis, that has become infamous. "Be it further resolved," the delegates voted, "that we call upon Southern Baptists to work for legislation that will allow the possibility of abortion under such conditions as rape, incest, clear evidence of severe fetal deformity, and carefully ascertained evidence of the likelihood of damage to the emotional, mental, and physical health of the mother."[29]

The day that the convention passed resolution number 4, which became known as the pro-abortion resolution, it also passed a resolution calling for better educational and vocational training in prisons; the next day, resolution number 7 urged President Richard M. Nixon to "continue our American withdrawal" from Vietnam. Without question, these stands put the messengers to the political left of most of the Baptists they represented—though not as far to the left as it might seen. Abortion was not yet the schismatic issue it would become after *Roe v. Wade,* and a slow withdrawal of ground troops from Vietnam, while turning operations over to South Vietnamese troops, was President Nixon's official policy.[30]

There is more evidence that, in certain years, the messengers to the national convention were more liberal than the men and women who had sent them. In 1969, in New Orleans, the convention adopted a resolution directing a church hospital there to cease discriminating on the basis of race in its admissions. Yet Southern Baptist churches throughout the South had resisted integration.[31] Going back to their earliest pro-slavery days, Southern Baptists had been as slow as any to accept higher status for nonwhites. When a Maryland church accepted Barbara Horton, a black college student, to membership, the news was surprising enough to merit a national press release.[32] In 1968 Emmanuel L. McCall became the first black ever to hold a professional staff position with the Southern Baptist Convention.[33]

While surprisingly progressive on matters like abortion, prisoners' rights, the environment, sexual education, and women's rights, the annual convention never did muster much indignation over the United States's involvement in Vietnam. A survey of messengers to the 1967 convention—half of them pastors, 10 percent women—found "hawkish" attitudes, with two-thirds agreeing that the United States should do "whatever is necessary" to win the war and an equal percentage saying that the United States should "increase its level of fighting." Two years later, the convention refused, on a close vote, to reaffirm its 1940 resolution in support of the right to conscientious objection.[34]

That refusal is telling. While there was no movement afoot to shame or rebuke conscientious objectors, the messengers did not want to give them further aid and comfort. Men who refused to fight might have Christian doctrine on their side, but their behavior was unseemly, culturally discordant. Southern Baptists were, for the most part, particularly hateful of communism; it was okay to be a conscientious objector in the fight against the Nazis, but not in the fight against the Vietcong. A survey of pastors in Florida and Louisiana found them divided between support for Richard Nixon and George Wallace in the presidential campaign but united in their support for the war. Communism was, after all, the philosophy of atheism and, in its earliest, Leninist incarnation, free love. And while isolationists during World War II had been, after Hitler's invasion of Russia, almost always conservative, pacifists during the Vietnam War were leftists. During the Nixon years, the Southern Baptist Convention was remarkably flexible in its positions on most issues, not yet beholden to any political agenda, but still deeply suspicious of dissent that seemed to challenge the regnant faith in America, its laws, and its culture. They hated dissent that seemed, in other words, countercultural.[35]

Pacifism in the 1960s was associated with the countercultural style. Liberal politics, like environmentalism and conscientious objection, was one thing—it did not necessarily subvert authority, God, or patriotism. Southerners had been integral to President Franklin D. Roosevelt's New Deal coalition; in the South, there had always been both isolationists and warriors, both social democrats and free marketeers. So liberalism could be brooked. But long hair worn by stoned children listening to obscene music—caricature or not, the image was threatening.

Southern Baptists almost never became hippies, long-hairs, rock music aficionados, or drug users. Ministers, deacons, parents, and the officials at Southern Baptist schools were sufficiently horrified at the first rumblings of countercultural activity that no person, young or old, with such eccentric inclinations would remain too involved with a Southern Baptist church, even one he or she had grown up in.

The fears started early. "Parents of some junior high school youths report some shock at the way these youngsters behave at some of their parties," reads a 1969 Christian Life Commission report on "Churches Seeking to Bridge the Generation Gap." "Smoking is very prevalent. Although some ash trays are provided, most cigarettes are thrown on the floor of asphalt-tiled recreation rooms, often without bothering to step on them to put them out. Although waste containers are provided, most paper cups for refreshments are thrown on the floor, often with some cola still in them." Meanwhile, "many couples kiss and embrace rather ardently."[36]

Teenagers had, of course, necked and smoked in times past. The report seems more concerned with what they *do* with their cigarettes than the simple fact of them. They throw their cigarettes on the floor, along with cups. And not just any floor, but the floor of an "asphalt-tile recreation room." The report's rhetoric focuses on the despoiling of suburban safety: children are not showing proper respect to the rec room. These themes of disrespect for middle-class aesthetics and incursion into middle-class space recur throughout Southern Baptist writings on the counterculture. After a pop music festival tore through Lewisville, Texas, leaving residents disquieted by open-air consumption of marijuana, LSD, and heroin, a Southern Baptist press agent wrote, with shock and sadness, "The town has lost its virginity."[37]

Hippies did not just disrespect or offend; like Hell's Angels and Yippies, they trespassed and violated. In order to protect their vision of a well-ordered society, Southern Baptists engaged in a turf war. In October 1968, when Georgetown (Kentucky) Baptist College revised its rules in order to permit dancing, the reaction came swiftly: a month later, the Kentucky Baptist Convention censured the college. Two years later, when Carson-Newman College in Jefferson City, Tennessee, decided to permit dancing on campus, the Tennessee Baptist Convention, after considering and rejecting compromise proposals, voted to ask the college's trustees to rescind the new, permissive rule. (Knoxville minister John Buell said that any man who says he can dance with a woman and keep his mind pure "is either less than a man, or a liar.") In 1971 a poll of Southern Baptists found that a majority was willing to restrict constitutional rights for the sake of order. Only 52 percent of adult Southern Baptists surveyed agreed that everyone should have the right to criticize the government even if such criticism might damage the national interest. (Among student leaders surveyed, however, free speech mattered much more, as only 26 percent agreed with the adults.)[38] Administrators condemned people, not just acts. Not content to ban dancing, Howard Payne College in Texas outlawed "young men and women who would create social unrest." "We will permit neither hippies nor other bizarre personalities to enroll," the new policy stated.[39]

While it could be fun to mock the administrators' high-handed bravado, it would not be useful, and it would not be fair. Even today it is difficult to separate strands of the counterculture, to tell the peaceful hippies from the angry Yippies from the Deadheads from the New Left politicos, and it was even more confusing for Southern Baptist elders whose norms were crumbling. Reductionism is a human necessity. It is how we make sense of things. We create categories, essentialize, simplify. It was quixotic to write rules for spotting hippies, but it was a way that private, Christian colleges could fortify the walls around their communities.

All denominations build walls, of course. A religious identity is only as strong as its sense of whom it excludes. But while most Catholic, Jewish, and Episcopal clergy tried to maintain tradition against countercultural threats, they were not as draconian. Catholic colleges, which could have banned protests, did not; when students at Boston College protested the decision not to rehire the radical feminist theologian Mary Daly, the administration caved, hiring her back with tenure. But Southern Baptist colleges frequently clamped down on protest, dancing, and long hair. Furthermore, there were liberal Catholic, Jewish, Episcopal, and Unitarian clergy and theologians who encouraged dissent, and who made room for a countercultural fringe. But in the Southern Baptist Convention, liberal clergy, like W. W. Finlator, were constantly in danger of losing their jobs, and their peers dismissed them as irrelevant or heretical. The Southern Baptist Convention did not have the racial or regional diversity of the other religions: Catholics who got involved in national organizations would meet Latino Catholics from the Southwest and black Catholics from Louisiana, but Southern Baptists were mostly white and southern, and that limited their political imagination.[40]

Baptists had particular theological constraints, too. For by their nature, Baptists are unusually watchful of their children's development. To be a Jew one needs only a Jewish mother; being baptized as an infant will suffice to be a Congregationalist, Episcopalian, Roman

Catholic, or Lutheran. Not so for Baptists. When committed Baptist parents have children, they watch the children's spiritual development with constant anticipation, waiting for the day they are born again in Jesus Christ. A religious Baptist can always tell you the age at which she became a Christian. So we would expect the appearance of rebelling youth to trouble Baptist parents in particular. To a Baptist committed to a conservative reading of the Bible, a child who turns her back on Jesus is truly outside the fold, and when she dies, she will stand outside the gates of heaven. For theological reasons, above all, Baptists could not be sanguine about counterculture.

As a result, the only counterculture to be found among Southern Baptists lay in their missionary efforts. Which is not so surprising, when we think about the nature of proselytism. When missionaries learn the native folkways of Vietnam or Togo, it is often not from cultural respect, but in order to get the natives to abandon those ways. Just because missionaries live like natives, that does not mean that a good Southern Baptist, back home in the United States, may properly live that way. That was the attitude Southern Baptists took toward counterculture: it was okay to talk or look that way—but only in order to win converts.

As early as 1968 the Baptist Press, the Southern Baptist wire service, began publicizing evangelists who proselytized hippies. Arthur Blessitt, the well-known "Sunset Strip evangelist" in Los Angeles, barged onto the dance floor of the Cellar, a psychedelic nightclub, and began preaching. "Let's talk about a 'trip' to Calvary," he said. "The ultimate trip, a trip that lasts, an eternal high with God." The response rate on that evening was nil, though, as the Baptist Press noted with some poignancy: "Blessitt was treated with respect and perhaps as many as 25 people out of the 100 or so present bowed their heads when he prayed." Southern Baptist missionaries in Park Slope, Brooklyn, founded the Catacombs, which functioned as both a coffeehouse (on Friday nights) and a "Christian discotheque complete with psychedelic lights, black walls and long-

haired entertainers" (on Saturdays). Sadly, "there have been no pro-
fessions of faith yet." Southern Baptists also founded coffeehouses in
New London, Connecticut; Worcester, Massachusetts; and Hampton
Beach, New Hampshire, among other cities.[41]

It is hard to say how many hippies responded to these hipster
evangelists. Many of the Christian juice bars and coffee houses were
ineffectual and closed quickly, but Blessitt's ministries—first among
the toughs of Elko, Nevada, then in "His Place," as his clubs in both
Los Angeles and Times Square were called—attracted scores of newspaper and magazine articles trumpeting his success. Blessitt "fed free
sandwiches and Kool-Aid to the Strip kids, preached once or twice
every night, and saw hundreds respond to Jesus Christ," according to
a 1971 book by a very impressed fellow minister. "'Toilet Services' followed many conversions as the kids crowded into the rest room to
flush their pills and powders down the toilet. It was a tearful, moving
experience as they destroyed the last of their drugs and turned for
peace to Jesus."[42] The Rev. Martin Rosen said that he had brought
hundreds to Jesus, too, through his Bar Shalom Hebrew Christian
Fellowship, which proselytized Jewish hippies and "street people."

Throughout the country, eager Southern Baptists, sensing that
savvier Christians were going where they feared to tread, tried to
reach out with groovy tunes, funky lights, and slang words. They
called for a "Jesus Revolution," beseeched young people to heed the
words of a cool, Christian "cat," and enlisted the teenage son of a
leading Texas Baptist to tell a youth convention how he "blew off of
LSD and turned on to Jesus." They countered Jets quarterback Joe
Namath's endorsements of free love with Steelers quarterback Terry
Bradshaw's Christian exhorting.[43] Taking stabs at the slang lingo,
pumping up the dreaded rock music, and calling on sports heroes to
plead their case: the Southern Baptists were keenly aware that in the
war for people's souls, culture was a key weapon. The trick was learning how to use it.

In their efforts to become hipper, Southern Baptists rolled with some shady characters. In 1970 the Christian Life Commission—again, a liberal arm of the church—sponsored a seminar in Atlanta on the theme "Toward an Authentic Morality for Modern Man." Anson Mount, manager of public affairs for *Playboy* magazine, delivered a speech titled "The Playboy Philosophy—Pro." After ensuring his audience's attention by telling them that "tens of thousands of ordained ministers read *Playboy* religiously (if you'll pardon the expression)," Mount defended the Playboy Clubs against the charge that they were "brothels without a second story": "Our answer to this charge is simply that we feel that man's natural interest in sex is perfectly valid as an aspect of entertainment, that it is entirely normal and proper for a man to enjoy seeing a sexually attractive girl whether she is walking down the street, dancing on a stage, or whether he views her picture on a printed page, or a movie screen, or whether she is wearing a bikini, a ballroom gown, or just fingernail polish."[44]

In "The Playboy Philosophy—Con," William M. Pinson Jr., an ethicist at Southwestern Baptist Theological Seminary in Forth Worth, challenged Mount's endorsement of the bunny way of life. Pinson railed against "what some see as a new religion: Hugh Hefner is the Prophet; *Playboy* is the Book; the 'Playboy Philosophy' is the Creed."[45] Many Southern Baptists regretted that their church would condescend to sponsor such a debate. But it was a sign of the times. With more than six million subscribers, *Playboy* was a leading enemy of the constant morality that Southern Baptists valued.

Situation ethics was another foe. A kissing cousin of the "Death of God" philosophy that had appeared earlier in the decade, similarly mistrustful of any claims to transcendent claims, situation ethics might best be identified by the Rev. William Sloane Coffin's beloved maxim, "Rules are a guidepost, not a hitching post." At the same conference in Atlanta, one ethicist suggested three defining principles of situation ethics: people are more important than things, love is the ultimate criterion for making ethical decisions, and "what love demands in any situation depends upon the situation."[46] In other words, strict guidelines like the Ten Commandments were passé; people should feel free to judge for themselves when to apply the rules.

As another speaker at the conference pointed out, situation ethics was not entirely new: had not Jesus said that the Sabbath was made for man, not man for the Sabbath? There were times when violating the Sabbath, telling a lie, or taking a life might be the most humane or just act; and Christianity had long recognized this conundrum. But the new situation ethics was often deployed to justify premarital sex, and it would be only another year before its underlying assumptions led the Southern Baptist messengers to approve abortion in many circumstances. Like sexual liberation, situation ethics was a thicket with many snares; Southern Baptists recognized, and made sincere efforts to avoid, the potential troubles presented by this new, influential movement.[47]

The Jesus Movement—or the Jesus Freaks, or the Jesus People, depending on who was talking—also vexed Southern Baptists. Some young hippies, frequently Jesus lookalikes, were being baptized in the name of the countercultural Jesus, the one who threw the money-changers from the Temple, said that the last shall be first, ate with the poor and the criminals, and, not incidentally, wore long hair and sandals. These hippies for Christ harnessed cultural power toward Christian ends, and journalists marveled at the movement's rapid rise and deep hold on its converts. "Look at those kids grooving on Jesus in Long Beach, Calif. Look at the tears running down the faces of those Oklahoma youngsters; those crowds jabbing in their 'one-way' fingers skyward in Tennessee and the hot, clasped hands of those teenagers in North Carolina." "A rock group plays. It is hard rock; but pure, unadulterated gospel in content." Writers were impressed to find religious enthusiasm outside the institutional church. *Time* magazine guessed, without evidence, that converts "number in the hundreds of thousands nationally, conceivably many more."[48]

But the Jesus Movement, with its neglect of theology and its aversion to established churches, generally evinced little interest from Southern Baptists. While it was well and good for young people to worship Jesus, it was not so propitious for them to *look* like Jesus. These teenagers and collegians did, after all, wear long hair and sandals; spotted on the street, they were archetypal hippies. And hippies looked and acted in ways that contested cultural authority, ways that the Southern Baptist Convention was unwilling to tolerate, especially in time of war.

By 1969, when President Nixon began to shrink the American presence in Vietnam, it had reached 540,000 military personnel. The number of American soldiers in Vietnam had grown steadily over the decade, and the mainline denominations had expressed concern for several years. Congregationalists, Presbyterians, Methodists, Catholics, and, of course, Friends, or Quakers, had all tracked the war in their respective periodicals, beginning about 1965. These liberal churches tried to build ecumenical concern. At one point, the National Council of Churches deliberately sought to bring Southern Baptists into the discussion: R. H. Edwin Espy, the council's general secretary, sent a telegram in late 1966 to the Rev. Clifton J. Allen of the Southern Baptists' Sunday School Board and publishing house, imploring Allen to write a letter to President Johnson encouraging a cease-fire. "I urgently request you take every emergency step in this Christmas season."[49] But there is no record of Allen's taking any steps.

Paradoxically, the Southern Baptist Convention was the denomination most engaged with Vietnam yet least interested in the political debate about it. At a time when most of the mainline congregations, uncomfortable with the appearance of cultural imperialism, were abandoning missionary efforts, the Southern Baptists were seeking converts with all due zeal. American troops in Vietnam meant, above all, more souls to tend and save in Vietnam. When Wayne Dehoney, the president of the Southern Baptist Convention, returned from a

1966 trip to Japan, he reported that the servicemen's principal need was for spiritual help. "The wounded have been coming into the hospitals in Japan in great numbers, and I have gone from bed to bed. . . . One boy desperately needed spiritual help. . . . The boy accidentally shot a South Vietnamese mother and child as he charged into a village to rout the Viet Cong. Guilt weighs heavily upon him."[50]

Southern Baptists described American military engagement in Vietnam with sympathy and charity, but rarely with any second thoughts about the war. Compared with the attitudes of other denominations, this was a difference of degree, not kind. In 1966 few Americans had reservations about the war; Southern Baptists just had even fewer. Southern Baptist literature of the time reports on a Marine sergeant's teaching Bible classes in the USO "between battles against the Viet Cong"; a Southern Baptist chaplain's having "to counsel his troops over the roar of jet engines"; and another Baptist chaplain's being awarded a silver star for bravery.[51]

With missionaries in Vietnam, Southern Baptists, at least in the early years of the conflict, saw the country mainly as the home of unfortunate pagans and lucky converts. They sent packages of food and clothes to Vietnamese villages. They sent books and donations to the Saigon Baptist Seminary, a training center for Vietnamese ministers. By 1970 Trinity Baptist Church in Saigon was offering English lessons and a Sunday morning Bible class for curious Vietnamese. A press release boasted of four new conversions to Christianity.[52]

The sustained attention to Vietnam may have sensitized some Southern Baptists to the complexity of the situation: the considerable corruption of the Nguyen Van Thieu regime in the South; the real support for the Viet Minh in the North and pockets of the South; and the deplorable toll in lives on both sides. Some Southern Baptists did believe, before most Americans thought to care, that little good would come from the war. The North Carolina Christian Life Commission called for a negotiated peace in 1966, the same year that William M. Dyal Jr. of the national Christian Life Commission lamented, "Vietnam is claiming more than one hundred lives a week, and only God knows how many Vietnamese. Two billion dollars of resources are spent on the war each month. Perhaps that is why Dostoevski once said that war is an idiot who splits a violin for firewood. . . . The angry, anguished voice of Vietnam fills our ears."[53]

Dyal recognized that his hearing may have been more acute than his fellow believers'. Even among Southern Baptists with reservations about the war, support ran high. In 1967 the annual meeting of the District of Columbia Baptist Convention resolved, "We declare to the world that we take no pleasure in the searing and blasting of human lives. . . . We call upon Americans individually and corporately to seek Divine forgiveness for our contributions to the world's evils and dilemmas." But "we support our nation and those allied with us in the heroic efforts to prevent aggression against South Vietnam."[54] Here we get a poignant glance at the dilemma faced by conservative, patriotic Christians at war with a communist power: one could admit the "searing and blasting" quality of warfare in all its ugliness and still consider the fight "heroic." One could regret the killing and insist that it continue.

The closer they got to the fighting, the more martial they became. Southern Baptist Convention president Wayne Dehoney supported American policy before he left for a 1966 visit to Vietnam, and he returned "even more convinced." Chaplains never expressed doubts. All three Southern Baptist missionaries in Vietnam supported American policy.[55] Some Baptist state newspapers did criticize the war, but their criticisms were few and halting, hardly indicative of major change in church opinion. "Let Congress make a decision," the *California Southern Baptist* editorialized, "let Thieu and Ky take the Vietnamese case to the U.N., and let the president tell the people exactly what is happening and where we are. Otherwise, let's get out, now." Chauncey R. Daley, a Southern Baptist eminence with a regular column in the Kentucky *Western Recorder*, insisted that conscientious objectors "be respected when they are sincere," but he had no truck with "draft dodgers, draft card burners, and ministers or others who encourage such behavior." The *Maryland Baptist* supported the war without reservation. As late as 1969 nearly a dozen Baptist state conventions passed resolutions supporting President Nixon's policies. Only the *Arkansas Baptist* favored withdrawal, saying, "Any commitment we may have had in this fight has been met a thousand times over."[56]

As we have observed, the annual convention of the Southern Baptist Convention, a four-day meeting at which messengers (the number varies from year to year; early in the century it was in the hundreds, but in the late 1960s the meeting drew about fifteen thousand messengers) assemble to pass resolutions and make policy for their denomination, is an imperfect but still useful bellwether for Southern Baptist opinion in general. About half of the messengers are ministers, who in Baptist polity are "called" by, and serve at the pleasure of, the congregations. All the messengers, clerical and lay, are elected by the congregations, which often pay to send them. If there is any bias at the convention, then, it is in favor of the larger, wealthier congregations, with healthier church coffers and richer individual members; poorer congregations are less likely to have change to spare for plane tickets and hotel fare. Those large congregations are often urban, and perhaps slightly more liberal than the laity as a whole. Even so, with regard to the Vietnam War the convention's stances were mostly hawkish. In 1967 the messengers met in Miami Beach and resolved that the "patriot's prosecution of defensive war" called for continued support of American policies "in pursuing a just peace in Vietnam." The messengers meeting in Houston in 1968, when Baptist Students Concerned appeared, struck a more pacific stance, pleading for "an immediate cease-fire" and lamenting the "awesome toll in human life and property." At the Denver convention, two years later, the resolution combined renewed support for President Nixon's policies with a plea to bring soldiers home "at the earliest possible time."[57]

After 1970, as President Nixon brought ground troops home and focused on air strikes, the conventions paid little mind to the war. In 1971 Georgia messenger Gilbert D. Gibson's proposed resolution reaffirming the right to conscientious objection died in committee before reaching a floor vote. That year, convention president W. A. Criswell, author of the famous fundamentalist tract *Why I Preach That the Bible Is Literally True,* gave a rousing speech to the convention's Pastors' Conference about a soldier whose life had been saved when the New Testament he carried in his pocket stopped a bullet; nobody could doubt that Criswell meant to support the war, not just Jesus.[58]

Despite some opposition to the war, the convention was supportive enough that Chauncey Daley—who condemned "draft dodgers, draft card burners, and ministers or others who encourage such behavior"—was considered fairly liberal. In such an environment, anyone deeply involved in countercultural protest—anyone who might have friends who were "draft dodgers" or "draft card burners"— would have left the Southern Baptist Convention. Those liberals who remained, like Baptist Students Concerned, were sufficiently committed to the premises of the convention that they were unlikely to effect real change. And when some of the students found that they could no longer suffer the Southern Baptist Convention, they did leave. In later years, Marie Moorefield became one of the first female Episcopal priests, Tom Graves became president of a Baptist seminary formed as an alternative to Southern Baptist schools, and Lelia Routh left the convention. In other words, the fruitful antagonism between culture and counterculture that had allowed for vigorous fights in the Episcopal Church, and had allowed for multiple worship styles in Catholicism and Judaism, did not exist in the Southern Baptist Convention.

The Nixon years tested American religion. From the late 1960s to the mid-1970s denominations had to figure out how much dissent they could tolerate. The Unitarians and Jews could tolerate a lot, and the Catholics made room for counterculture. The Episcopalians decided they would assimilate to their church a new conception of gender roles, even as it would revolutionize some people's experience of the Mass. The Southern Baptist Convention decided that it could not tolerate dissent. The Baptist Students Concerned surely knew this, and that is why they made sure to appear as unthreatening as possible. Even so, they were unable to tap the old well of Baptist pacifism; it had dried up. Even mild political dissent, informed by Baptist tradition, seemed to undermine the culture, and it could not be allowed to blossom.

A prescient observer could have predicted, looking at the students' negligible impact, that the denomination that in 1971 had passed a resolution approving of abortion rights would dedicate itself to the criminalization of abortion. The environment and prisoners' rights disappeared from its agenda. And in June 1985, at a bitterly fought convention in Dallas, the conservative Charles Stanley defeated the more moderate candidate Winfred Moore for the presidency of the convention; by 1988 Stanley had purged Southern Baptist agency and seminary boards of liberal trustees, completing a conservative takeover.[59] The same people who in large measure supported Jimmy Carter in 1976 enthusiastically supported Ronald Reagan in the 1980s. The convention's position on abortion swung abruptly, and with finality. The Southern Baptist Convention, which had for decades opposed prayer in schools and all other kinds of political entanglements, became, in all ways, a vigorous participant in the culture wars. This happened in response to the counterculture.[60]

What was so different about 1960s and 1970s counterculturalists, as against, say, World War I pacifists, was, first, that they were seen as challenging the ethics that governed everyday life—alcoholic and narcotic vices, sexual freedom—and, second, that they used linguistic and aesthetic cues to remind the people around them of their differences. Pacifists of earlier generations had not had their own

In 1995, near the end of his life, the fundamentalist fire-breather W. A. Criswell has lost none of his enthusiasm for the Word. Reprinted with the permission of the Southern Baptist Historical Library and Archives, Nashville, Tennessee.

lingo; but hippies did, talking about the "cool," the "hip," and the "groovy." They often wore long hair, and they danced, often to overtly sexual music performed by blacks (Jimi Hendrix), druggies (Jerry Garcia), and convicted criminals (Jim Morrison).

Southern Baptists did engage this counterculture, whether by debating the "Playboy philosophy" or trying to adopt the young people's language. But such encounters were on the Baptists' terms: they would go forth from their churches to proselytize the hippies, but they did not want the hippies coming into their churches. That is why the Baptist Students Concerned made a conscious effort to clean up their acts, like the Eugene McCarthy campaign workers who in 1968 "got clean for Gene."

Had matters turned out differently, the dissenting students might have recovered their denomination's respect for pacifism and antiwar critiques, but they did not. One reason why is the extreme congregationalism of the Southern Baptists, which, by allowing every church to go its own way, diffuses any grassroots efforts directed toward the national convention. (The genius of the takeover of the 1980s was that the conservatives changed the character of the denomination not through the churches but through the seminaries and national boards that control financial disbursements to missions and schools.) Students and young people, then, are uniquely disabled in a congregational denomination. It is simply too difficult to change people's minds church by church, and only elders have the clout to make the appointments that will matter over time.

But the main reason is that Southern Baptists correctly assessed the power of countercultural values and aesthetics, and they understood its threat to their organic way of life. For Southern Baptists, the "church" was, by the 1960s, a unified system of traditional values, patriotism, and cultural homogeneity. The other four religions we have observed lacked that kind of integrated ethos. Judaism did not necessarily imply a set of attitudes toward one's country. Catholicism certainly did not imply one model of culture: Italians, Germans, Irish, and Latinos each had their own Catholicism, with its own folkways. The guitar Mass did come to represent a counterculture, but it was not so obvious, in the early 1960s, that it would. Havurah Judaism and woman priests did profoundly change people's religious lives, but because there was room for argument about what kind of threat they would pose, there was also room for them to succeed. And, after all, had Jews not been forced to change their prayer venues throughout history? Had Unitarians not made a denominational virtue of changing? Jews, Episcopalians, Catholics, and Unitarians fought the counterculture to various degrees; only Southern Baptists, however, were fortified by a combination of theological, political, and regional identities, all of which were being threatened.

For Southern Baptists, cultural dissent has always been the work of outsiders determined to end a way of life. It has been, since before the Civil War, the job of southern religion to shield that way of life from attack. To give comfort to a conscientious objector—something the Southern Baptist Convention would do in certain times and places—was in the 1960s and 1970s likened to promoting rock and roll festivals. To protect the environment was to please crowds of tie-dye wearers. This counterculture was a rabid, pagan dog barking at the door of civilization—it could not be allowed to enter, no matter how much it pleaded. However incoherent the Southern Baptists' portrait of the counterculture, it stuck. And it was used, with great success, to quash the debate that Baptist Students Concerned wanted to begin, and to homogenize a denomination that prided itself on respect for individual conscience.

Conclusion

t is probable," Percy Bysshe Shelley wrote in his 1821 *Defence of Poetry,* "that the poetry of Moses, Job, David, Solomon, and Isaiah had produced a great effect upon the mind of Jesus and his disciples. The scattered fragments preserved to us by the biographers of this extraordinary person are all instinct with the most vivid poetry." Shelley was saying that religions are built of art. That is not to say that a given religion is untrue. Christianity, for example, could be entirely true—Jesus Christ could be the crucified, resurrected son of God—but still depend on the creative instincts of mankind for its propagation. And the Nixon-era counterculture was, if nothing else, a period of creativity, what Nietzsche would call a Dionysian irruption of music, poetry, and sexual experimentation into an Apollonian world of serenity and rectitude.[1] Somehow, Christians and Jews took new ideas, at odds with the dominant culture, and tried to change their religions. Did they succeed? And if so, how?

All five of our countercultural movements were indebted to the African-American struggle, in its two guises of civil rights and Black Power. First, civil rights was a political template. Gay Unitarians, Episcopal women, Jewish haverim, and Southern Baptist pacifists had all paid attention to the issue of civil rights, worked to promote civil rights, and developed their organizing skills in the fight for civil rights. They often met other activists through the civil rights movement, and because of the blacks' example they began to wonder about their own oppression. Even in the Southern Baptist Convention, which had often been hostile to integration, some ministers and students had been awakened from apolitical slumber by the civil rights movement; Baptists from the liberal student Terry Nichols to the conservative convention president H. Franklin Paschall were alarmed by King's assassination and what it would mean. All five of the movements we have examined owe a debt to the civil rights movement. They could not have happened without it. The counterculture itself could not have happened without it.

Even the Catholic folkies, who did not talk specifically of civil rights, depended on it. Could their songs have become important without the imprimatur lent by the civil rights movement? The popular Catholic folk composer Joe Wise was bankrolled by a black priest, and he incorporated Negro spiritual and blues influences into his music. Great folk singers like Bob Dylan and Joan Baez were known supporters of civil rights; they both sang at the 1963 March on Washington, and their political stances helped popularize their music. And the struggle for desegregation in the South helped folk music spread like kudzu. Those songs of freedom and justice now had an obvious focus, an urgent issue of freedom and justice.[2] Their music, of course, depended heavily on black folk singers like Leadbelly and white folk singers, like Woody Guthrie, whose left-wing politics achieved new respect in the age of civil rights. On reflection, then, it seems that the Catholic folk Mass, too, shares the civil rights lineage.

As Black Power became prominent in the late 1960s, its separatism, cool mien, and bodacious style influenced liberal whites. Jews believed that Black Power had a message for them: they decried the sell-out "Uncle Jake," they applauded the Jerusalem Black Panthers, and they talked about the "student as nigger." Alla Bozarth-Campbell, the Episcopal priest, compared the women's libber to a nigger, and the Unitarian James Stoll said that homosexuals were niggers, too. The Yippie Jerry Rubin promised to "send niggers and longhair scum invading white middle class homes, fucking on the living room floor, crashing on the chandeliers, spewing sperm on the Jesus pictures." This appropriation of stark, black imagery—ten years after the activist and comedian Dick Gregory had published *Nigger: An Autobiography* ("Whenever you hear the word 'nigger,'" Gregory said, "you'll know they're advertising my book") and thirty years before the Harvard law professor Randall Kennedy titillated the publishing world by titling his book *Nigger*—owed more to the Black Panthers and Malcolm X than to Martin Luther King Jr., who avoided using the word. Because mainstream American political cul-

Huey Newton, just freed in 1970, and other Black Panthers show their infectious swagger and sartorial style in front of the Alameda County Courthouse in Oakland, California. Photograph by Michelle Vignes.

ture would not tolerate the word, any appropriation of *nigger* was countercultural (and it later became a countercultural signifier among black youth).

"For us, the drama of the Black Panthers was their style," two sixties survivors wrote in the nineties, "the flashy malevolence of their berets and bandoliers and the dauntless tone of their rhetoric meant far more than their ten-point party platform. We thought peace and love were good ideas in 1967; but to be honest, what we really liked was the way we looked in flowing hippie caftans with wildflowers in our long hair."[3] That easy segue from Black Power style to hippie style, and the diminution of politics in favor of aesthetics, reminds us of Jerry Rubin's Yippie threats. It also reminds us of James Stoll's defense of gay rights as "a groove," and of the Episcopal woman's describing the "ease and naturalness" of taking communion from a fellow woman.

Between the political example of civil rights and the stylistic example of Black Power, it's clear that the African-American struggle was the precondition, the stylistic and political inspiration, for the counterculture's engagement with traditional religion.

None of our countercultural movements was as broadly influential as civil rights and Black Power were, but to varying degrees the other four movements crossed from one religion to another. Folk music, for example, is famous for its permeation of Catholic worship, but the guitar is now a common feature of Reform Judaism, too; Jews didn't argue about it nearly as much, just proudly claimed Bob Dylan as one of their own and flocked to worship in San Francisco and New York with the neomystical, guitar-playing Rabbi Shlomo Carlebach. Later, the guitar-based melodies of composers like Debbie Friedman became standard in the Reform liturgy. In the Episcopal Church, women's giving communion was the biggest formal change in the Mass. But the other formal changes we have discussed, like the folk music that Episcopalians had performed from the late 1960s on, prepared Episcopalians for the even bigger change to come. Unitarians embraced folk music, too. The Southern Baptist Convention eschewed any music that seemed related to rock and roll, but not for long. Guitars and folk melodies were soon heard in many Southern Baptist churches.

Feminism and gay rights had more circumscribed appeal. Feminism transformed the Episcopal Church, was an important strain in the Jewish havurah movement, and was allied with the gay rights cause in Unitarianism. But Catholic feminism existed more in the realm of abstruse theology than in the parishes; some Catholic sisters espoused a proto-feminism, but it was compromised by the fact that nuns, no matter how vocal, were still obedient to a male hierarchy. And so far as we can tell, no prominent Southern Baptist identified as a feminist, although Marie Moorefield, one of the Baptist Students Concerned, left for the Episcopal Church, where she became one of the Philadelphia Eleven—creating the irony that Southern

Baptist conservatism helped beget Episcopal feminism. Southern Baptists and Catholics were equally indifferent to gay rights, and feminist Episcopalians were uncomfortable making common cause with homosexuals. Even Jews, known for their liberal views, had a don't-ask, don't-tell policy for gay men and lesbians. Martha Ackelsberg, who divorced and became openly lesbian, described the environment at the New York Havurah: "When I began to think of myself as something other than heterosexual, which was also happening a little later than 1970, it did not feel like something I could discuss or talk about with other people at the havurah; for all of its questioning and openness, in some ways it was very traditionalist in its attitudes toward homosexuality."[4]

Finally, the anti-institutionalism we have identified among the Jews did not take root in other religions. Many Catholics ceased going to church, but of those who remained, there was no strong anticlerical movement (except among men who dropped out of seminary). In the Unitarian Church, ministers led their flocks toward gay rights, not the other way around. Southern Baptist peace activists dutifully sought their denomination's ear and approval, getting the former but not the latter. And Episcopal feminists did not consider their fight won until they had changed the canons of the church. Although an occasional activist like Carter Heyward said that she didn't care what the hierarchy decided, her view was in the distinct minority—and besides, she *did* care. Most Episcopalians, including most Episcopal feminists, wanted the approval of the church. In all four of these Christian traditions, there were of course people, on the political left and the right, who got disgusted and dropped out. But we do not see anti-institutional movements among those who remained.

We thus see that while civil rights was deeply influential on white countercultural movements in America, folk music was somewhat less influential, feminism less still, and gay rights hardly at all. They did not have the influential ubiquity of civil rights. This would change as years passed, of course. By the 1990s feminism had obviously transformed the American family and workplace. But in the late 1960s through the mid-1970s, its influence did not rival that of civil rights.

Finally, we get to the Vietnam War. The war riveted Americans from about 1967 to 1974; they could not ignore the deaths, the draft notices, and the dissolution of the Johnson presidency. But the war did not inspire other forms of countercultural activism the way that civil rights did. That is to say, feminists, gay rights activists, communalistic Jews, and folk-singing Catholics did not talk about their particular struggles in terms of the Vietnam War. One might move from feminist activism to gay rights activism, or from civil rights activism to Jewish ethnic particularism; but despite the perception that sixties consciousness *was* Vietnam consciousness, religious people did not seem to move back and forth as much between antiwar activism and other kinds of activism. The war was an issue unto itself.

There are some obvious reasons for this. First, the draft was not a personal concern for all Americans. Women did not have to worry about it, older men did not have to worry about it, and for many years, students did not have to worry about it. As later presidential candidates made clear, anyone with enough savvy or political connections stood a good chance of avoiding combat. Those who fought were more likely to be poor or nonwhite, so many members of the white counterculture figured the war as a political issue but not as a visceral one that could change their own lives. This is not to say they didn't feel passionately about the war. And millions of Americans, after all, knew boys who were in danger of being drafted—or, already drafted, were in danger of being killed. It is only to say that an Episcopal woman stood zero chance of fighting in Vietnam, but she was getting very close to having the right to be ordained; a gay Unitarian would also, if openly gay, have been able to stay out of Vietnam; and those who planned innovative Catholic Masses were often over the draft age. Relatively few Southern Baptists had misgivings about the war.

Doubting the government is, often, harder than doubting one's preachers. It was easier to be arrested for trying to integrate the interstate bus lines than to be arrested for draft resistance: being a nigger lover was better than being a traitor. Carter Heyward, the radical, lesbian Episcopal priest, admitted that she had had great difficulty turning against the government's Vietnam policy. And denominational assemblies, chary of appearing anti-American, sooner passed resolutions in favor of feminism or civil rights than against the war. For many Americans, even liberal ones, opposing the war was like saying that all the boys had died in vain.

Furthermore, the peace movement seemed to some like a form of "square" political engagement, akin to lobbying congressmen or trying to change university policy. For those attracted to the counterculture as a locus of freedom and personal development—what we might call a personal, rather than political, counterculture—foreign affairs could seem dreary. In the mid-1970s one alumna of a Catholic college wrote, "A visit to the campus that fall [1968] by Philip Berrigan came as something of a distraction. We were asked to turn our attention to Vietnam when another war was brewing closer to home, in our collective Catholic psyche."[5] Some people, of course, had energy enough for both a personal, religious dimension to their psyches and an activist, political dimension: Allen Ginsberg, for example, shared his Hare Krishna and then Buddhist spirituality with the world, even trying to use it to levitate the Pentagon and stop the war. But he was a full-time exhorter, spiritualist, mystic, rabble-rouser, poet, and shaman; he was unique. Most of us are mortals with limited time and energy, and if we serve on the liturgy committee, we probably do not have time to head the peace committee.

Vietnam-era pacifism, then, was not as central to other countercultures, or to "the counterculture" as a whole, as we have been led to believe. Although it left indelible marks on certain aspects of American life, like rock music and the journalism and literature of wartime, it did not reach across religious traditions, or across political subcultures, with the pervasive reach of civil rights, women's rights, or new musical styles.

What all our religious activists shared, then, was not a commitment to free love, feminism, or burnt draft cards. Rather, it was a creative engagement with the legacy of African-American struggle and a willingness to embrace countercultural language—"with it," "groove," "this is my thing"—and symbols and music. These aesthetic and formal cues were often derived from Black Power, as well as from feminism, the human potential movement, rock and roll, and folk music; they were far less indebted to the peace movement.[6]

Religious counterculturalists, like blacks, were not necessarily politically or economically radical (Black Power, for one, became quite capitalist). They were culturally radical. They wanted aesthetic and formal changes, and they got those. But they rarely sought or won changes in church polity or theology. In none of the five groups we have studied was there any change in how the religious organization was governed. The laity won no power. Bishops still run the Episcopal Church; the pope makes decisions for the Roman Catholic Church. Unitarian and Southern Baptist policies are still made at their assemblies, where Unitarian progressives always win and Southern Baptist conservatives always win. In Judaism, power is still diffuse, as it has been for two thousand years; but if we look, for example, at the governance of Jewish charities and the administration of Jewish denominational bodies and seminaries, we find no structural changes; power remains concentrated in the hands of the rich and properly credentialed. American religion responded to the counterculture by acceding to some of its demands, primarily the formal and aesthetic ones—what worship looked like and who performed it—without relinquishing much institutional power.

This does not mean that the formal and aesthetic victories didn't matter—in religion, few things matter more. "Counter-culture," Umberto Eco reminds us, "comes about when those who transform the culture in which they live become critically conscious of what they are doing and elaborate a theory of their deviation from the dominant model, *offering a model that is capable of sustaining itself.*" This model of counterculture could be theological or intellectual, but it need not be. Catholics wanted to change the sound, look, and feel of their Mass; Episcopalians wanted to change its gendered symbolism. In each case, theology mattered little. The Catholics already had permission from the Second Vatican Council, and the bishops of the Episcopal Church endorsed woman priesthood years before the laity did. What mattered was that Episcopal women moved from feeling excluded and frustrated to doing something about it: they envisioned a church in which women could do all that men could; in which the laity became accustomed to receiving communion from women; and in which tradition was forced to bow before innovation.

It would not have been countercultural, in other words, for Catholics to suggest that they might feel more comfortable if the priest faced the pews. But when that change became one aspect of a self-conscious, multifaceted project, a project meant to revolutionize the relationship between the hierarchy and the lowly believers, then it was countercultural. For Reform Jews, deciding that those with Jewish fathers but not Jewish mothers be considered Jewish was not countercultural. It was not "a theory of deviation from the dominant model" or an alternative to the normative Jewish culture. Rather, it was a liberal change in the rules. But it was countercultural when young Jews began dropping out of the synagogue altogether, rebuking the leading Jewish philanthropies, and making left-wing Passover seders.[7]

In general, then, the counterculture succeeded in American religion by winning aesthetic and formal, rather than institutional or theological, victories. It insinuated new models by providing new sounds and images: the guitar, the woman in a stole, the living room synagogue.

The Unitarians and the Southern Baptists appear to be special cases. In those two religions, protest worked differently. Gay rights, which would seem to be the most radical proposal of all in mid-1970s America, was endorsed by Unitarians over little opposition. And in the Southern Baptist Convention, a mild request for more dialogue about the Vietnam War was soon forgotten. Why?

Unitarians, unmoored from the Bible or any doctrine, had become a church of toleration. Every liberal movement imaginable has succeeded among Unitarians, quickly: civil rights, gay rights, feminism, transgender rights, paganism, extrasensory perception. The Unitarians even provided funds to their separatist black caucus. Within the context of the Unitarian Universalist Association, then, gay rights was not really countercultural at all. It made some people uncomfortable, but it was quickly accepted. The debates over ordaining homosexuals, debates that have rent other denominations, never occurred among Unitarians. It was simply assumed that no category of person was excluded from ordination.

The Southern Baptist Convention, though on the opposite end of the political and ideological spectra, was similarly captive to its culture. Although it had the strongest resources, theologically, for a defense of pacifism—it had been vocally pacifist for much of its history—this latest version of pacifism seemed to come from hippies and the left-wing American culture. Even though the pacifists within the denomination were clean-cut students, the Southern Baptist Convention was keenly on guard against counterculture. Truly radical antiwar activists had no place in the convention, and the liberal students left behind were respectfully heard, but quickly forgotten.

Unitarians and Southern Baptists had a lot else in common, too. They are both highly congregational, vesting almost no authority in the national body. Unlike Catholics, they call their own ministers. Unlike Catholics and Jews, they require no special classes for conversion. Unlike Episcopalians and Catholics, they belong to no international body. And, compared with Episcopalians, Catholics, and Jews, they have relatively little ritual. Finally, unlike the other three religions, Unitarians and Southern Baptists allowed little room for dissent. Unitarianism and Baptism were both founded to promote free-dom of conscience, but when dealing with dissent, they balked. Being an antigay Unitarian or a pacifist Southern Baptist meant feel-ing very alone. Unitarians had become stridently liberal, Southern Baptists staunchly conservative, and both groups rather deaf to other points of view.

If the Unitarians and Southern Baptists make an unusual grouping, the Catholics and Episcopalians make a more sensible pair. They are both hierarchical, highly ritualized, and deeply con-cerned with members of their international communion. They are also liberal in ways that belie their conservative reputations. Although Episcopalians are seen as patrician defenders of the status quo, their clergy eagerly endorsed the principle of women's ordina-tion. And although the Catholic hierarchy is seen as being more con-servative than its laity, it was the bishops who, through the Second Vatican Council, initiated liberal changes in the Mass and insisted that laypeople assume responsibility for realizing those changes. It is worth remembering that traditionalists directed their anger not at young flower children but at the cardinals and bishops who, they believed, had betrayed the tradition. The hierarchical polity of Catholics and Episcopalians had the effect of opening those churches up to change—while the congregational, localized polity of Southern Baptists and Unitarians ensured conformity.

Somewhat surprisingly, we must conclude that hierarchicalism can facilitate, rather than inhibit, change. Liberal Episcopal bishops presided over women's ordinations; liberal Catholic bishops permit-ted innovations in the Mass. In the Episcopal Church, the bishops supported changes in the canons before the laity did; there was a liturgical movement under way in the Catholic Church, but it was Vatican II that permitted myriad new worship styles. Not all clergy are intellectuals, not by any means. But the ones who are often have progressive tendencies, and they find themselves acting as innova-tors, rather than as conservators of tradition. When innovative clergy find themselves in hierarchies that give them concentrated power, they can liberalize religious traditions more quickly than when their influence is diffuse and occasional.

Finally, we have the Jews. The Jews partook of the most counter-cultural trends, all five discussed, except perhaps gay rights, and many not discussed, including drug culture and mysticism. They sometimes operated within the synagogue structure, but they sometimes split off on their own. They appealed to tradition, when they felt like it. Their house contained so many mansions because Jews had so little to prove: since Jews are Jewish by descent, and can construe themselves nationally instead of religiously, they could hew as close to tradition, or stray as far from it, as suited them. When we consider the centrality of the communion in the Episcopal and Catholic churches, or the importance of unified culture among Unitarians and Southern Baptists, we see that Jews prayed together as Jews for wholly different reasons: because their parents had, or because they found the tradition joyous and meaningful, or maybe out of guilt. But the point is this: because the central fact of their Judaism was uncontested, their reaction to the counterculture was the freest, the least predictable.

In the 1980s, with the rise of a conservative "religious right," American religion was seen to be dividing according to its political alliances, along lines that had nothing to do with theology or actual religious practice. Religion on the coasts was deemed politically liberal, while religion in the South and Midwest was conservative. Religion of the old Standing Order, the Congregationalists and Episcopalians, was liberal, while evangelical religion, comprising Southern Baptists, Pentecostals, some Methodists and Presbyterians, and many independent Bible churches, was conservative. Religion was forced to choose sides in "culture wars" between truth and relativism, or between tradition and moral anarchy. And if a religion would not choose sides, then it would be assigned to a team. The

Catholic Church, for example, is against abortion but also, for the most part, against the death penalty—does that make it liberal or conservative? Political commentators decided, on Catholics' behalf, that they were conservative; the liberals did not want a pro-life ally, and the conservatives were willing to overlook the Catholics' opposition to the death penalty and their support of organized labor.[8]

There is much truth in these generalizations. Religion did become more conservative in the South. Evangelicalism, despite a heritage of abolitionism and pacifism, became more conservative, while liberal churches, like the United Church of Christ, lost their urge to proselytize at all, leaving the evangelical field to the conservatives. These broad categories are products of changes that happened in the Nixon years. Because they have some truth, and are so useful to politicians and pundits, they endure.

But dividing the country along such simplistic lines promotes some faulty conclusions. The paradigm of culture wars, or liberal versus conservative churches, falsely implies that political activism has been the organizing principle in American religious life. Just as most Americans never made long-term commitments to Transcendental Meditation or to countercultural communes, most Americans never directed their religious lives according to the political aims of Jerry Falwell, William Sloane Coffin, Paul Moore, or Marabel Morgan. Rather, the average worshiper served on church committees and read church newsletters. He or she usually did not evaluate a question like the ordination of women as if America's sexual probity were at stake. Episcopalians genuinely wanted to divine the will of God in the matter. Southern Baptist leaders made room for liberal students to speak. Some Catholic priests disliked innovations in the Mass, but others were amenable. Most people sought common ground and tried to avoid conflict. Religion in the Nixon years, like Americans in the Nixon years, only sometimes drifted to the extremes.[9]

Thinking of American religion as an endless struggle between competing political forces also tempts us to imagine that religions are a zero-sum game, with some groups ascending while others inevitably decline. But there are other models worth considering. Perhaps the entire paradigm of decline is based on a short-sighted historical view: after all, the mid-twentieth century was the most religious time in our country's history, more religious by far than revolutionary or Civil War times. Perhaps, as one scholar suggests, the waning power of the mainline churches "may not have been so much an aberration as a restoration, the real aberration being American religion as it reconstructed itself in the late nineteenth and twentieth centuries through the Fifties. In a certain sense, the characteristic Sixties religious style was like a recovery of the more fluid, sentimental, charismatic, psychic, magical, communalistic, and righteous-prophetic style of the first decades of the Republic, perhaps especially the 1840s and 1850s" and afterward, the years of spiritualism, séances, Transcendentalism, and utopian communes.[10]

Religion in the Nixon years reminds us that a clear sense of mission, whether liberal or conservative, can invigorate the laity and bring new streams of membership. No political party, and no one theology, has a monopoly on passion. Just as decline can befall any group, even a conservative one—Promise Keepers came and then went, and where have all the Calvinist Puritans gone?—any religion can be reborn.

The mainline churches survived the strange, strange times of the nineteenth century: times of civil war, brothers killing brothers, more lives lost than in any war since. There was competition from Christian Scientists, Millerites, Latter-day Saints, and, soon, Pentecostals. They were the days of the latter rain, speaking in tongues, gifts of prophesying, and conversations with the dead. Somehow, the old religions survived. They looked different, because Americans looked different. But Catholics still believed in the pope and Episcopalians did not. Unitarians still did not believe that Jesus was God. Baptists did not baptize their young. Jews did not baptize at all. And still, people kept coming. The 1860s couldn't change that. And no, the 1960s couldn't change that either.

Still, all five of our religious groups changed as Americans changed. We got more relaxed in our dress, more slangy our speech, and more lewd in our music. Elvis's swiveling hips and the Beatles' unkempt hair went from being risqué to being mild. People started to go to church in casual clothes. Big, evangelical megachurches learned to use mixed-media light-and-music extravaganzas to lure suburban church-hoppers. Campus Crusade for Christ hired Christian rock bands to perform at colleges.

This aesthetic drift in America, according to which all inventions and innovations of style may be yoked in service to the church, has allowed conservative churches to have a contemporary feel while preaching old-time theology. It has also allowed liberal churches to feel consequential and influential while ignoring theology. Across the ideological divide, even across the rift between Protestants and Catholics and the eschatological gulf between Christians and Jews, we can see that theology in the second half of the twentieth century mattered little. Episcopalian woman priests were fully satisfied that they had changed their church, just as Catholic folk singers were pleased with the changes in theirs, even though official beliefs about the nature of God and the sacrifices required of human beings had not changed at all.

To say that aesthetics is what counts is not to trivialize aesthetics. It can be the most important thing there is. About the pop artist Andy Warhol, one critic wrote, astutely, "Warhol was also the first major postwar artist to put gay identity . . . at the very center of his work. This was in the 1950s and early 1960s, before Stonewall and gay liberation, when to do so meant to be shunned by many of his artist colleagues, gay and straight. Warhol didn't care, or pretended not to, and just by being himself, a public sissy, he automatically became one of the most important political artists of his time."[11] Warhol didn't have to lobby for legislation or even publish a manifesto. He just had to be "a public sissy," in full view of the country. The visual cue told all. In the same way, taking communion from a woman, sitting in a pew next to an openly gay man, saying the Jewish *Amidah* in a ramshackle student apartment still scented by last night's marijuana—when we experience worship so differently, we experience God differently. It's not the same religion at all.

Neither the political left nor the right should claim some hollow victory. These religious changes did not make Americans more reflective about their duties as Americans and children of God. Southern Baptists shed their pacifist heritage, became uncritically jingoistic in times of war, and failed to consider how the capitalism they adore promotes the cultural decay they despise. Meanwhile, the Unitarian penchant for promiscuous toleration allowed New Age silliness to replace, in many of their churches, honored tradition and Scripture. American Catholic bishops for decades allowed priests to continue to molest children; the Jewish Bar Mitzvah ceremony became a celebration of American materialism; and the Episcopal Church began shrinking toward extinction. In the messianic search for heaven on earth, for a new Jerusalem, the road still leads far ahead, and the path looks long and hard.

NOTES

INTRODUCTION

1. Several good books place "the sixties" in historical context and compli-
   cate our notion of those years. See John Morton Blum, *Years of Discord:
   American Politics and Society, 1961–1974* (New York: Norton, 1991);
   David Farber, *The Sixties: From Memory to History* (Chapel Hill: University of North Carolina Press, 1994); Allen J. Matusow, *The Unravel-
   ling of America: A History of Liberalism in the 1960s* (New York: Harper
   and Row, 1984); and Harris Wofford, *Of Kennedys and Kings: Making
   Sense of the Sixties* (New York: Farrar, Straus and Giroux, 1980).

2. George H. Gallup, *The Gallup Poll: Public Opinion, 1935–1971*, vol. 3
   (New York: Random House, 1972), 2,162–2,163; George H. Gallup,
   The Gallup Poll: Public Opinion, 1972–1977, vol. 1 (Wilmington, Del.:
   Scholarly Resources, 1978), 66–67; Maurice Isserman and Michael
   Kazin, *America Divided: The Civil War of the 1960s* (New York: Oxford

University Press, 2000), 268; and David Frum, *How We Got Here: The 70's* (New York: Basic, 2000), xxi.

3. David Gelernter, *Drawing Life: Surviving the Unabomber* (New York: Free Press, 1997), 64, italics in the original.

4. Isserman and Kazin, *America Divided,* 67. This is a good book that unfortunately pays too little attention to culture, far too little to religion. For a good discussion of the historiography of the 1960s, see David McBride, "On the Fault Line of Mass Culture and Counterculture: A Social History of the Hippie Counterculture in 1960s Los Angeles" (Ph.D. diss., University of California at Los Angeles, 1998), 12–82. See Betty Friedan, *The Feminine Mystique* (New York: Norton, 1963); Thomas Crow, *The Rise of the Sixties: American and European Art in the Age of Dissent* (New York: Harry N. Abrams, 1996). Warhol's Campbell's soup can installation opened at Los Angeles's Ferus Gallery in 1962.

5. Rick Perlstein, *Before the Storm: Barry Goldwater and the Unmaking of the American Consensus* (New York: Hill and Wang, 2001); Lisa McGirr, *Suburban Warriors: The Origins of the New American Right* (Princeton: Princeton University Press, 2001).

6. Will Herberg, *Protestant, Catholic, Jew: An Essay in Religious Sociology* (Garden City, N.Y.: Doubleday, 1955). Herberg appears to have borrowed his thesis from Ruby Jo Reeves Kennedy, "Single or Triple Melting Pot? Intermarriage Trends in New Haven, 1870–1940," *American Journal of Sociology* 49, no. 4 (January 1944): 331–339.

7. Robert S. Ellwood, *The Fifties Spiritual Marketplace: American Religion in a Decade of Conflict* (New Brunswick, N.J.: Rutgers University Press, 1997), 5, 103.

8. Alan Watts, *The Way of Zen* (New York: Pantheon, 1957); Christopher Isherwood, *Vedanta and the West* (Hollywood, Calif.: Marcel Rodd, 1945).

9. Stephen A. Kent, *From Slogans to Mantras: Social Protest and Religious Conversion in the Late Vietnam Era* (Syracuse: Syracuse University Press, 2001), 14.

10. Ellwood, *Fifties Spiritual Marketplace,* 99. Suzuki's writings began to appear in the United States in the 1920s and kept coming in various editions. See his *Essays in Zen Buddhism,* 3d series (New York: Rider, 1953).

11. Statistics are taken from Benson Y. Landis, ed., *The Yearbook of Ameri-*

can Churches (New York: National Council of Churches of Christ in the U.S.A., 1963), and subsequent editions. The series was retitled *The Yearbook of American and Canadian Churches* in 1973, when Abingdon Press of Nashville assumed publication. The statistics in the yearbooks come from the church administrations, so if anything tend to overstate the membership. On 1990 to 2000 see the study "Religious Congregation and Membership: 2000," conducted by the Glenmary Research Center and sponsored by the Association of Statisticians of American Religious Bodies. It is cited in Laurie Goodstein, "Conservative Churches Grew Fastest in 1990's, Report Says," *New York Times,* 18 September 2002.

12. George Gallup Jr. and D. Michael Lindsay, *Surveying the Religious Landscape: Trends in U.S. Beliefs* (Harrisburg, Pa.: Morehouse, 1999), 15.

13. When the United Church of Christ was organized in 1957, some Congregational churches did not join the new body, but the vast majority did, and they made up the majority of UCC churches. It seems fair to refer to UCC churches as Congregational. On birth rates, see Wade Clark Roof and William McKinney, *American Mainline Religion: Its Changing Shape and Future* (New Brunswick, N.J.: Rutgers University Press, 1987), 161.

14. Thomas C. Reeves, *The Empty Church: The Suicide of Liberal Christianity* (New York: Free Press, 1996), 159.

15. Some important sociological works are Dean M. Kelley, *Why Conservative Churches Are Growing: A Study in Sociology of Religion* (New York: Harper and Row, 1972); Roof and McKinney, *American Mainline Religion;* Robert Bellah et al., eds., *Habits of the Heart: Individualism and Commitment in American Life* (Berkeley: University of California Press, 1985); Robert Wuthnow, *The Restructuring of American Religion: Society and Faith Since World War II* (Princeton: Princeton University Press, 1988); and Mark Chaves, *Ordaining Women: Culture and Conflict in Religious Organizations* (Cambridge: Harvard University Press, 1997).

16. William G. McLoughlin, *Revivals, Awakenings, and Reform: An Essay on Religion and Social Change in America, 1607–1977* (Chicago: University of Chicago Press, 1978), 202–204. See Carlos Castañeda, *The Teachings of Don Juan: A Yaqui Way of Knowledge* (Berkeley: University of California Press, 1968), and its many sequels.

17. Alan Tobey, "The Summer Solstice of the Healthy-Happy-Holy Orga-

nization," in *The New Religious Consciousness,* ed. Charles Y. Glock and Robert N. Bellah (Berkeley: University of California Press, 1976), 5; Donald Stone, "The Human Potential Movement," ibid., 100.

18. Thomas Piazza, "Jewish Identity and the Counterculture," in Glock and Bellah, *New Religious Consciousness,* 258.

19. Glock and Bellah, *New Religious Consciousness,* 270–271.

20. Reeves, *Empty Church,* 139; Jane Stern and Michael Stern, *Sixties People* (New York: Knopf, 1990), 156.

21. Ludwig Wittgenstein, *Philosophical Investigations,* trans. G. E. M. Anscombe (Oxford: Blackwell, 1999), 1: 67–75.

22. Quoted in Frum, *How We Got Here,* 131.

23. Umberto Eco, "Does Counter-culture Exist?" trans. Jennie Condie, in Eco, *Apocalypse Postponed,* ed. Robert Lumley (Bloomington: Indiana University Press, 1994), 115.

24. Ibid., 124, italics added in the first instance.

   I have greatly simplified Eco's discussion, and anyone deeply interested in the concept of counterculture ought to read the essay, in which Eco offers four different models of counterculture, one of which I have selected for our purposes. He proposes three preliminary definitions of *culture:* "*Culture 1* is counterposed to science, politics, economics and practical/productive activities. It privileges the formation of aesthetic taste. . . . Beethoven is culture, while appreciating the singing of drunks is not, unless in the form of ethnological study, nostalgia, or the snob research of kitsch. . . . *Culture 2* defines itself as a superior attitude of mind set against the bestiality, ignorance and idolatry typical of the masses. . . . A bank manager and a customs officer are equally men of culture. . . . *Culture 3* is the anthropological definition. It comprises the complex of institutions, myths, rites, laws, beliefs, codified everyday behaviour, value systems and material techniques elaborated by a group of humans."

   Each of these three kinds of culture, Eco says, implies its own model of counterculture. *Culture 1,* the aesthetic model, could be opposed by a counterculture that valorized primitive art or anarchic creativity. *Culture 2,* the model of culture as refinement and bourgeois civilized mores, could be opposed by a counterculture that rejected power and integration—a counterculture of oppressed minorities, perhaps Woody Guthrie's riding the boxcars with the hobos. Eco says that draft dodgers also embody this model of counterculture. *Culture 3,* the anthropological model, has for its opposing counterculture simply other cultural models. The culture of pagan Rome saw the emerging Christendom as a counterculture. For Enlightenment liberalism, the Afghan Taliban was a counterculture.

Countercultures of these three types, Eco says, are all doomed as countercultures. They either prevail, like Christendom in Rome, and become the culture itself; or they are assimilated to the dominant taste, like the appreciation of primitive art; or they live forever on the periphery, as hobos and draft dodgers do. But, Eco says, there is one type of counterculture that is more vigorous, and that is religious reform or some other alternative, self-sustaining mode of being, like communism.

25. Ibid., 124, 127.

26. Eco's linking of the intellectual with the counterculture does, of course, exclude most of our university professors from the ranks of the intellectuals. Most university professors guard old knowledge and conserve tradition more than they oppose the culture. The culture wars of the 1990s were fueled by this tension between the conservator intellectuals and the countercultural intellectuals.

27. There are other, more famous definitions of counterculture. Theodore Roszak, whose book *The Making of a Counter Culture* (Garden City, N.Y.: Doubleday, 1969) was widely read, offered this interpretation of the word: "Meaning: a culture so radically disaffiliated from the mainstream assumptions of our society that it scarcely looks to many as a culture at all, but takes on the alarming appearance of a barbaric intrusion" (42). Eco's essay makes clear that Roszak has conflated two aspects of counterculture, that one aspect that is a critique of the dominant culture and another aspect that appears barbaric. Hobos may offer an implicit critique, but they do not seem barbaric; in fact, they seem to be a peripheral but charming component of the society's culture. Drug-peddling gangsters, on the other hand, may seem barbaric but they hardly offer a critique.

28. On the famous October 21, 1967, protest, see Norman Mailer, *The Armies of the Night: History as a Novel, the Novel as History* (New York: Signet, 1968).

29. Jane Kramer, *Allen Ginsberg in America* (New York: Random House, 1969); Tom Wolfe, *The Electric Kool-Aid Acid Test* (New York: Farrar,

Straus and Giroux, 1968); Hunter S. Thompson, *Hell's Angels: A Strange and Terrible Saga* (New York: Random House, 1967).

30. Thompson, *Hell's Angels,* 315, 322–323.

31. Ibid., 313; Stern and Stern, *Sixties People,* 171.

32. Thompson, *Hell's Angels,* 321; Wolfe, *Electric Kool-Aid Acid Test,* 126–127.

33. Sloan Wilson, *The Man in the Gray Flannel Suit* (New York: Simon and Schuster, 1955); William Hollingsworth Whyte, *Organization Man* (New York: Simon and Schuster, 1956).

34. Quoted in William George Thiemann, "Haight-Ashbury: Birth of the Counterculture of the 1960s" (Ph.D. diss., Miami University, 1998).

35. Here I am following Sacvan Bercovitch, who traced the theme of decline in literature from the Puritans onward. See *The American Jeremiad* (Madison: University of Wisconsin Press, 1978).

one. UNITARIANS AND GAY RIGHTS

1. Gene Bridges, "It Seems to Me," *Kukui Lamalana* (newsletter of the First Unitarian Church of Honolulu, Hawaii) 17, no. 17 (29 April 1970), 1. This item is contained in James Stoll's papers, Andover Harvard Theological Library (hereafter Stoll Papers). I also consulted Gene Bridges, interview by author, telephone, 21 January 2002; Emily Champagne, interview by author, telephone, 28 January 2002. According to his sister, James Stoll was born January 18, 1936, in Hartford, Connecticut, where he grew up. (Unitarian obituary records say that he was born in Old Saybrook, Connecticut.) He attended the University of Pennsylvania for a year, then left for San Francisco State University, where he received a bachelor's degree. He received his theological tuition at Starr King School for the Ministry, in Berkeley, California. Jean Stoll Ehinger, interview by author, telephone, 2 September 2002. After providing information about her brother's birth and education, Ehinger declined to answer further questions, and she indicated that her brother Frederick would also refuse to cooperate.

2. This statement must be qualified. The Rev. Troy Perry, a born-again Christian, came out of the closet in 1969 and founded his own denomination, the Metropolitan Community Church. His admission of homosexuality, however, prompted him to create a new church. Stoll acted within an extant faith with which he remained affiliated.

3. For information on Stoll's sexual misdeeds in Kennewick, Washing-

ton, see, for example, Marshall D. Seawell, Howard Hanthorn, and
Marvin M. Hendrickson to Joseph Barth, 8 September 1970, Stoll
Papers. Stoll had been pastor of the Unitarian church in Kennewick
from 1962 to early 1969. About February 1969, armed with evidence
that Stoll had made sexual overtures to two or three boys, one only
twelve years old, church laypeople asked that Stoll resign. The accusa-
tion, which Stoll appears not to have denied, was that he had shown
his penis to the boys and asked them to play with it, and that he had
tried to play with their penises. He resigned, and to most of the community it looked like a voluntary resignation; when church elders
spoke of it, they mentioned Stoll's marijuana use as one of the causes,
but the pederasty never became public knowledge.

Stoll apparently took the occasion of leaving Kennewick to come
out of the closet several months later. Soon after, the Pacific Central
District of the Unitarian Universalist Association voted Stoll "Minister
of the loving revolution," a title which Stoll subsequently employed in
his ill-fated attempts to start a church for oppressed peoples. In speaking appearances, Stoll frequently implied that the church's Department of Ministry was making it impossible for him to find a regular
pulpit because of his homosexuality. It was a rather nefarious ploy,
insofar as he knew that the people in Kennewick, who had hushed up
the reasons for his departure there, would never contradict him by
publicizing the real reasons for his resignation. See "Minister to the
Loving Revolution," *First Church News,* First Unitarian Church,
Chicago, 18 October 1970, Stoll Papers.

4. John C. Godbey, "Unitarian Universalist Association," in *The Encyclo-
pedia of Religion,* ed. Mircea Eliade (New York: Macmillan, 1987), 15:
143–147. See also Charles C. Forman, "Elected by Time," in *A Stream
of Light,* ed. Conrad Wright (Boston: Unitarian Universalist Association, 1975), 3–32, for a description of the early years of the Unitarian
conflict. For its origins see Sydney E. Ahlstrom, *A Religious History of
the American People* (New Haven: Yale University Press, 1972),
388–402; Stow Persons, *Free Religion* (New Haven: Yale University
Press, 1947), 2–17.

5. With regard to Unitarianism as Social Gospel among New England
intellectuals, see Daniel Walker Howe, *The Unitarian Conscience: Harvard Moral Philosophy, 1805–1861,* rev. ed. (Middletown, Conn.: Wes-
leyan University Press, 1988).

6. "Professions from the Past," a broadside produced by the Unitarian Universalist Association, Boston, sometime after 1961, Collection of the Office of Gay, Lesbian, Bisexual and Transgender Concerns, Unitarian Universalist Association (hereafter Unitarian Collection); Godbey, "Unitarian Universalist Association," 145–146. On the Universalists, see David Robinson, *The Unitarians and the Universalists* (Westport, Conn.: Greenwood, 1985); Ann Lee Bressler, *The Universalist Movement in America, 1770–1880* (New York: Oxford University Press, 2001).

7. Derek Slap, interview by author, telephone, 18 December 1995; Richard E. Meyers, "Unitarians, Universalists, and the Bible," *Unitarian Universalist Christian* 27, no. 2 (Summer 1972): 4.

8. John J. McNeill, S.J., *The Church and the Homosexual* (Kansas City, Kan.: Sheed Andrews and McMeel, 1976), ix.

9. Malcolm Boyd, *Take Off the Masks* (Garden City, N.Y.: Doubleday, 1978), 119–34. Boyd's chapter "Coming Out" makes clear how isolated from other homosexual movements the Unitarians were. Boyd's proclamation was occasioned by the 1976 Gay Pride Week in Chicago, where a religious service included members of "Congregation Or Chadash, Metropolitan Community Church, the Methodist Gay Caucus, Lutherans Concerned for Gay People, the Presbyterian Gay Caucus, Integrity, and Dignity"—but no gay Unitarians. It may be that more traditional Protestants did not see gay Unitarians as sufficiently religious to be fighting the same battle. See Boyd, *Take Off the Masks,* 122.

10. James Stoll, interview by Tandi Huelsbeck, telephone, 5 September 1994. Stoll's statement that he "was planning on going on to another church," which offered him a sabbatical first, appears to be a fiction. The only comprehensive account of the Stonewall incident is Martin Duberman, *Stonewall* (New York: Dutton, 1993). It is thorough in its treatment if partisan in its tone.

11. Tom Wolfe, *The Electric Kool-Aid Acid Test* (New York: Farrar, Straus and Giroux, 1968), 187.

12. James Stoll to "My friends (and others) in SRL," ca. March 1970, Unitarian Collection.

13. Richard Nash, interview by author, telephone, 10 February 1995. Gene Bridges, in his interview, says that Stoll had worked with Liberal Religious Youth to support an antiwar resolution at the 1968 General Assembly in Cleveland. Nadine Wharton, "He Preaches for the Rights

of Homosexuals," *Honolulu Star-Bulletin,* 9 May 1970, 4; "Sex, Environment Topics of Sermon," *San Francisco Examiner,* 27 July 1970, 8.

14. Stoll interview.

15. Nash interview.

16. Duberman, *Stonewall.* The gaps in the literature on pre-Stonewall gay and lesbian life remain vast, but see John D'Emilio, *Sexual Politics, Sexual Communities: The Making of a Homosexual Minority in the United States, 1940–1970* (Chicago: University of Chicago Press, 1983); Dudley Clendinen and Adam Nagourney, *Out for Good: The Struggle to Build a Gay Rights Movement in America* (New York: Simon and Schuster, 1999). The most important recent work is George Chauncey, *Gay New York: Gender, Urban Culture, and the Makings of a Gay Male World, 1890–1940* (New York: Basic, 1994).

17. Nash interview.

18. "Gay Religious Liberals to Get Their Thing Together," press release, Gay Religious Liberals Conference Committee, Los Angeles, 8 November 1970, 1–2, Unitarian Collection. See also "Getting Our Thing Together," Gay Religious Liberals Conference, Los Angeles, 12 December 1970, Unitarian Collection.

19. "Discrimination Against Homosexuals and Bisexuals," in *Resolutions on Lesbians, Gay Men and Bisexuals,* ed. Rob Gregson, 1994, Unitarian Collection.

20. "Gay Religious Liberals to Get Their Thing Together," 3.

21. Nash interview.

22. Dick Nash, "Emergence of Gay Consciousness at the 1971 General Assembly," July 1971, Unitarian Collection. Richard Nash sometimes signed his writings as "Dick," and I have retained his usage according to the respective documents.

23. Richard Nash and Elgin Blair to "fellow gay Unitarian Universalists," 10 May 1971, Unitarian Collection; *Unitarian Universalist World,* 1 June 1971, 10.

24. Richard Nash to "fellow gay Unitarian Universalist" [*sic*], 26 May 1971, Unitarian Collection.

25. Thomas Mikelson, "Gay People in Seminaries and Churches," unpublished sermon, 15 February 1981, Unitarian Collection.

26. The membership was not free of homophobia. In a survey taken in 1967 by the Unitarian Universalist Committee on Goals in Boston,

80.2 percent of Unitarians believed that homosexuality "should be discouraged by education."

27. Mikelson sermon.

28. Champagne interview.

29. W. Edward Harris, interview by author, telephone, 22 January 2002.

30. Ibid.

31. Dwight Brown, e-mail to author, 24 January 2002.

32. Fred Campbell, e-mail to author, 20 January 2002. Also of interest David Bumbaugh, e-mail to author, 23 January 2002.

33. Derek Slap, e-mail to author, 13 January 2002.

34. Ken MacLean, interview by author, telephone, 11 January 2002.

35. Nash, "Emergence."

36. "BAC to Disaffiliate," *Unitarian Universalist World,* 1 March 1970, 1–2.

37. Ibid.; Michael Schofield, "BAC Officially Disaffiliates," *Unitarian Universalist World,* 1 May 1970, 1.

38. Schofield, "BAC Officially Disaffiliates."

39. Ghanda di Figlia, *Roots and Visions: The First Fifty Years of the Unitarian Universalist Service Committee* (Cambridge, Mass.: Unitarian Universalist Service Committee, 1990); Richard Nash, interview by author, telephone, 2 May 1995.

40. No reliable list of the original fourteen members survives, but Richard Nash recalls that the caucus included a lesbian couple. Nash interview, 2 May 1995. See "UUWF Steps Up Fight for Abortion Rights," *Unitarian Universalist World,* 15 March 1970, 1.

41. Navias, closeted at the time, had since 1963 been working for the Unitarians' Department of Religious Education; he hired and supervised Deryck Calderwood, who developed the church's sex education curriculum. Navias came out as a homosexual in "1977 or 1978" at a special Arlington Street service—which, sponsored by the Unitarian Universalist Gay Caucus, was yet more evidence that certain churches, like Arlington Street, served as nexuses for multiple progressive movements. Eugene Navias, interviews by Tandi Huelsbeck, telephone, 23 September 1994, 8 October 1994.

42. See, e.g., *UU Christian,* Autumn–Winter 1972, a special issue titled "The Church and the New Feminism." This issue is particularly notable because the *Christian* was popular with the more conservative wing of the denomination. The Navias interviews are also useful.

43. John Preston to Eugene Navias, 23 March 1972, 1, Unitarian Collection.

44. "The Gay Caucus and '*About Your Sexuality*,'" *UU Gay Caucus Newsletter* 2, no. 4 (October 1972): 3.

45. Elgin Blair, "Coming Through: Gay People and the Unitarian Universalist Association," 16 November 1977, Unitarian Collection. *UU Gay Caucus Newsletter* 2, no. 2 (April 1972), e.g., contains a report on the *About Your Sexuality* curriculum, a news item about a Unitarian minister's fight against a judge's censorship of the curriculum, and a promotion for Calderwood's *The Invisible Minority*.

46. Richard M. Fewkes, "Interest in Psi Symposium Increasing," *Unitarian Universalist World*, 15 July 1973; "California UUs Find Unity in ESP Discussion," *Unitarian Universalist World*, probably July 1972.

47. Fewkes, "Interest in Psi Symposium."

48. *UU Gay Caucus Newsletter* 2, no. 4 (October 1972): 4.

49. *UU Gay Caucus Newsletter* 2, no. 5 (December 1972): 5. Unitarians also welcomed gay groups in Cincinnati; Norfolk, Virginia; Brooklyn; and numerous other cities.

50. The original letter is lost. The reply is Eugene B. Navias to Elisabeth Michnick, 15 March 1971, Unitarian Collection.

51. *UU Gay Caucus Newsletter* 2, no. 4 (October 1972): 4.

52. "A Gay Holiday with the Unitarian Universalist Caucus," summer 1973, Unitarian Collection.

53. Blanchon "Skip" Ward, interview by author, telephone, 1 March 1995. Ward went by "Skip" in all correspondence.

54. Blair, "Coming Through," 5.

55. Nash interview, 10 February 1995; Ward interview; *UU Gay Caucus Newsletter* 2, no. 1 (February 1972): 1.

56. A list of the gay caucus's "First Steps" appeared in the inaugural edition of their newsletter. The list is addressed to Norman Benson, head of the Department of Education and Social Concerns, and the list is concerned almost exclusively with educating, and preaching acceptance to, church members. See *UU Gay Caucus Newsletter* 1, no. 1 (September 1971): 1.

57. "Why an Office on Gay Affairs?" Unitarian Universalist Gay Caucus, probably spring 1973, Unitarian Collection.

58. Richard Nash to Robert Wheatley et al., 19 December 1972, Unitarian Collection. According to Richard Nash, "How We Got the Office on

Gay Affairs," June 1973, 1, Unitarian Collection, the five sympathetic congregations were Marin Fellowship in San Rafael, California; Unitarian Fellowship of Alexandria, Louisiana; Unitarian Community Church in Santa Monica, California; First Unitarian Church in Denver; and the Unitarian Fellowship in Baton Rouge, Louisiana. I have not been able to find out which congregation failed to report its sponsorship to Beacon Street.

59. Don Harrington, interview by author, telephone, 3 February 2002. MacLean says that Harrington's granddaughter is a lesbian who has "educated him quite a bit." MacLean interview. The Harris interview is also useful. Nobody seems to have noticed that Harrington's juxtaposition of gay sex with bestiality follows, probably unintentionally, Leviticus 18:22–23, which deals first with homosexuality, then with bestiality.

60. Nash interview, 10 February 1995; Richard Nash, "Report Prepared for the Pacific Southwest District Annual Meeting," 3–5 May 1974, Unitarian Collection. This last piece was written as a resignation from Nash's services as the district's Specialized Minister for Gay Concerns.

61. Robert West, interview by author, telephone, May 2002.

62. This fascinating story was told on the radio show *This American Life,* 11 January 2002, episode 204, written by Alix Spiegel and produced by Chicago Public Radio.

63. The name of the office aroused much debate. "Office of Gay Affairs" might sound like a dating service, but others thought that such fears only reflected stereotypes of homosexuals as sexual predators. Ultimately, caution prevailed.

64. Ward interview.

65. David Frum, *How We Got Here: The 70's* (New York: Basic, 2000), 206; Thomas Reeves, *The Empty Church: The Suicide of Liberal Christianity* (New York: Free Press, 1996), 149.

66. Alfred P. Stiernotte, "Christology and Unitarian Universalists," *The Unitarian Universalist Christian* 28, no. 1 (Spring 1973): 27.

two. ROMAN CATHOLICS AND THE FOLK MASS

1. Annie Dillard, *Teaching a Stone to Talk* (New York: Harper and Row, 1982), 17–18.

2. William F. Buckley Jr., "The Non-Latin Mass: Reflections on the Final Solution," *Commonweal* 87, no. 6 (10 November 1967): 167. Buckley's

allusion to the Nazis' name for the plan to exterminate the Jews (*Endlösung*, final solution) is not, one hopes, intentional, though his ire, deep as it was, may have trumped his tact. Buckley was from a truly unusual family. To take one example, Reid, his brother, moved his family to Franco's Spain to live the dream of a Catholic polity.

3. Garry Wills, *Bare Ruined Choirs: Doubt, Prophecy, and Radical Religion* (Garden City, N.Y.: Doubleday, 1972), 62–63.

4. Andrew M. Greeley, *Come Blow Your Mind with Me* (Garden City, N.Y.: Doubleday, 1971), 26–27. In the literature of the counterculture, only turtlenecks rival brown rice as a signifier of rebellion.

5. Ibid., 79. *Rosemary's Baby* was a 1967 novel by Ira Levin (New York: Random House) made into a 1968 movie starring Mia Farrow and directed by Roman Polanski. Farrow's Rosemary is impregnated with the Devil's child after her husband, a struggling actor, offers his first-born in exchange for a boost to his career.

6. Andrew M. Greeley, *Crisis in the Church: A Study of Religion in America* (Chicago: Thomas More, 1979), 10. "The two percentage points a year decline continued," he writes, "until 1977, when Catholic church attendance reached 42 percent a week, a decline of 30 percentage points in the space of fifteen years." In 1973 weekly attendance was 47 percent, with men at 41 percent, women at 55. For those younger than thirty years old, the rate was 34 percent.

7. Greeley, *Come Blow Your Mind with Me,* 113. Of course, a priest leaving the priesthood for political reasons could be a conservative disappointed in the loss of tradition *or* a liberal disappointed at how little tradition could be lost. Either way, it was a sign of the times. The anecdotal evidence suggests that more liberal priests resigned.

8. William F. Buckley Jr., *Nearer My God: An Autobiography of Faith* (New York: Doubleday, 1997), 92. As Jews, Muslims, and Mormons also know, dietary restrictions, especially because they are linked to our olfactory sense, do substantial devotional work. They remind believers of their separateness and chosenness, and the choice to violate a dietary law one has been raised to obey inevitably feels like something more than a break—perhaps a statement. One could reasonably argue that this action of Paul VI was as powerful as any of the more famous Vatican II documents in unmooring Catholics from tradition; one can still find a Latin Mass, but it has become nearly impossible to find a Catholic who abstains on Friday, and many are unaware

that there ever was such a tradition. On Pope John XXIII, see Thomas Cahill, *Pope John XXIII* (New York: Viking, 2002).

9. Mark S. Massa, *Catholics and American Culture: Fulton Sheen, Dorothy Day, and the Notre Dame Football Team* (New York: Crossroad, 1999), 167. See the editorial "Decree on the Laity," *Commonweal* 83, no. 9 (3 December 1965): 262–263. See also Mark Oppenheimer, "Folk Music in the Catholic Mass" in *Religions of the United States in Practice,* ed. Colleen McDannell (Princeton: Princeton University Press, 2001), 2: 103–111. On Vatican II, see especially Xavier Rynne, *Vatican Council II* (New York: Farrar, Straus and Giroux, 1968).

10. William F. Buckley Jr., *Nearer My God: An Autobiography of Faith* (New York: Doubleday, 1997), 92.

11. For the Waugh quotation, from a letter to Graham Greene, see Barry Spurr, *The Word in the Desert: Anglican and Roman Catholic Reactions to Liturgical Reform* (Cambridge: Lutterworth, 1995), 30. Spurr's is a short and useful account that deals briefly with folk masses. See, too, Joseph A. Komonchak, "Interpreting the Council: Catholic Attitudes toward Vatican II," in *Being Right: Conservative Catholics in America,* ed. Mary Jo Weaver and R. Scott Appleby (Bloomington: Indiana University Press), 25–27; R. Scott Appleby, "The Triumph of Americanism: Common Ground for U.S. Catholics in the Twentieth Century," ibid., 39.

12. See Garry Wills, *Papal Sin: Structures of Deceit* (New York: Doubleday, 2000). In John Cornwell's highly controversial book *Hitler's Pope,* about Pope Pius XII, one argument that even Cornwell's detractors concede is that Pius sought to solidify religious authority in the papacy. Before him, power had been much more diffused throughout the hierarchy. It is sensible, then, to see Vatican II as initiating a power shift back toward the lower rungs of the hierarchy. Pope John Paul II reconcentrated that power, though not with the same ambition shown by Pius XII. See Cornwell, *Hitler's Pope: The Secret History of Pius XII* (London: Viking, 1999).

13. James Terence Fisher, *The Catholic Counterculture in America* (Chapel Hill: University of North Carolina Press, 1989), 19. The quotation within the quotation is from Laver's *The First Decadent.* See also Thomas J. Ferraro, "A Pornographic Nun: An Interview with Camille Paglia," in *Catholic Lives, Contemporary America,* ed. Thomas J. Ferraro (Durham, N.C.: Duke University Press, 1997), 239.

14. In Catholic theology, personalism was refined by the layman Emmanuel Mounier and other editors of *Esprit*, a French journal founded in 1932. Fisher, *Catholic Counterculture*, 43–44. "Personalism," Fisher writes, "was implicit in the Romantic milieu of early twentieth-century French Catholicism and its heroes: the bourgeoisie-hating ungrateful beggar and author, Léon Bloy; the Maritains, Jacques and Raisa, who dramatically converted on the brink of carrying out a double suicide pact; Péguy, and later Gabriel Marcel." See also Jay P. Dolan, *In Search of an American Catholicism: A History of Religion and Culture in Tension* (New York: Oxford University Press, 2002), 152; Massa, *Catholics and American Culture*, 150–151; and Fisher, *Catholic Counterculture*, 48–50. For another example of activity away from the Vatican's directorate, see "The New Priests," *Commonweal* 82, no. 2 (2 April 1965): 49–51.

15. Martin H. Work and Daniel J. Kane, "The American Catholic Layman and His Organizations," in *Contemporary Catholicism in the United States*, ed. Philip Gleason (Notre Dame, Ind.: University of Notre Dame Press, 1969), 349–371.

16. For trends in seminary syllabi, see Louis J. Putz, C.S.C., "Religious Education and Seminary Studies: Some Recent Trends," in Gleason, *Contemporary Catholicism*, 239–265; William A. Osborne, "The Church as a Social Organization: A Sociological Analysis," ibid., 41.

17. See Edward Wakin and Joseph F. Scheuer, *The De-Romanization of the American Catholic Church* (New York: Macmillan, 1966), 76–79, 82. In 1963–1964, American Catholics constituted 25 percent of Americans and about the same percentage of American collegians: 1.07 million of 4.5 million enrolled. See also Greeley, *Come Blow Your Mind with Me*, 168; "Entering the Mainstream," *Commonweal* 81, no. 2 (2 October 1964): 33–37.

18. Gleason, *Keeping the Faith*, 92–96.

19. Osborne, "Church as a Social Organization," 33, 39. Osborne argues that for Catholics attracted to the Mystical Body of Christ doctrine, segregation came to seem untenable, for God united all. John Cogley, *Catholic America* (New York: Dial, 1973), 138; John T. McGreevy, *Parish Boundaries: The Catholic Encounter with Race in the Twentieth Century Urban North* (Chicago: University of Chicago Press, 1996), 143–145. "Shackling the Sisters," *Commonweal* 85, no. 1 (7 October 1966): 5–6; David J. O'Brien, *The Renewal of American Catholicism*

(New York: Oxford University Press, 1972), 9. See also Amy Koehlinger, "From Selma to Sisterhood: Race and the Transformation of Catholic Sisterhood in the 1960s" (PhD. diss., Yale University, 2002); Massa, *Catholics and American Culture,* 172–194.

20. James Fisher, "Clearing the Streets of the Catholic Lost Generation," in Ferraro, *Catholic Lives,* 83–84.

21. For a recent treatment of the sexual revolution, see David Allyn, *Make Love Not War: The Sexual Revolution, An Unfettered History* (Boston: Little, Brown, 2000). And see Cogley, *Catholic America,* 130; Osborne, "Church as a Social Organization," 33, 42.

22. Gertrud Heinzelmann, "The Priesthood and Women," *Commonweal* 81, no. 16 (15 January 1965): 504–508. She goes on to quote the theologian Karl Rahner to the effect that the primitive church need not be an absolute guide, and she argues that the primitive church and early Christianity guaranteed women higher status. Mary Daly, "A Built-in Bias," *Commonweal* 81, no. 16 (15 January 1965): 509, 511. Daly became famous in the 1980s for segregating by sex certain classes she taught at Boston College. See Laura Flanders, "Feminist De-Tenured," *Nation,* 26 July 1999, 5.

23. Gleason, *Contemporary Catholicism,* xiii; Fisher, *Catholic Counterculture,* 205–247; Michael Novak, "The Revolution of 1976," *Commonweal* 86, no. 16 (14 July 1967): 441–443.

24. Thomas Day, *Why Catholics Can't Sing: The Culture of Catholicism and the Triumph of Bad Taste* (New York: Crossroad, 1990), 6.

25. Ibid., 7–9, 18–34.

26. Ralph Thibodeau, "Fiasco in Church Music," *Commonweal* 84, no. 3 (8 April 1966): 74. Jan Michael Joncas, "Psalms, Hymns, and Spiritual Songs: Roman Catholic Liturgical Music in the United States Since Vatican II," Archbishop Gerety Lecture, Seton Hall University, 17 October 1997. Massa, *Catholics and American Culture,* 160–161. Other changes in the Mass: the biblical readings of the liturgy of the Word now could be read, in the vernacular, by a lay lector; the day's readings were now the basis of a homily delivered by the celebrating priest; several of the prayers were now recited by the entire congregation, not just by the choir or the altar boys. In theory, at least.

27. Thibodeau, "Fiasco," 73–78; Buckley, *Nearer My God,* 97–98.

28. See Joncas, "Psalms, Hymns."

29. Joseph Bishop, "Liturgy as Subversive Activity," *Commonweal* 93, no. 13 (25 December 1970): 324–327.
30. Day, *Why Catholics Can't Sing*, 58. Day goes on to tell some pretty wild tales. I don't doubt their veracity, but I wonder whether they were typical: "Members of the folk group would sometimes tell little stories or jokes before each song; sometimes they would have arguments about the music while the priest and congregation watched and waited. [At one mass,] a mother and a father, two singers in a folk group, changed their baby's diaper right in front of the congregation. [At a mass in Connecticut,] while the congregation tried to follow the actions of the Mass, the women in this ensemble—they wore tight clam-digger pants—would writhe in a kind of heated agitation, directly in front of the congregation, and slap tambourines against their ample buttocks, in time with the music." Day also writes of children's masses with celebrants dressed as clowns and of a "basketball mass," during which a local basketball team dribbled balls. He does not cite specific times or places, nor does he give citations. See Day, *Why Catholics Can't Sing*, 32, 59–60.
31. David J. O'Brien, *The Renewal of American Catholicism* (New York: Oxford University Press, 1972), xii–xiii; "The Cool Generation and the Church: A Commonweal Symposium," *Commonweal* 87, no. 1 (6 October 1967): 14. The student was Frank Carling.
32. Charlie Dittmeier, e-mail to author, 4 December 1999. In Joncas, "Psalms, Hymns," we get an even more extensive list of folk singers and composers whose work was used in masses, including Willard Jabusch, Paul Quinlan, Cyril Reilly, Clarence Rivers, Sebastian Temple, James Thiem, the Dameans, and the Montfort Mission. The Catholic charismatic movement, which imported the worship style of Pentecostal and Holiness Protestantism, began about 1967, and some scholars believe that it was influential in breaking the mold of the old Catholic Mass and opening it to folk music and other new music. The evidence for this seems spotty, and estimates of the number of Catholic charismatics—Thomas J. Csordas says 670,000 by 1976—seem inflated. See Csordas, *Language, Charisma, and Creativity: The Ritual Life of a Religious Movement* (Berkeley: University of California Press, 1997), 4, 11, passim. Dan Onley notes, however, that the charismatics were major purchasers of Catholic folk records and that the charismatics' *Song of Praise* songbooks, published by Word of God in

Ann Arbor, Michigan, "spread around more rapidly than anything produced by the major publisher." See Dan Onley, "Parish Folk Musicians: Your Story," posted at http://www.paa2000.com/fmstory.htm.

33. Oppenheimer, "Folk Music in the Catholic Mass," 111.

34. Quoted in Massa, *Catholics and American Culture,* 163; Onley, "Parish Folk Musicians."

35. John McGreevy argues in *Parish Boundaries* that the geographical nature of parish affiliation led Catholics to be more attached to their neighborhoods than other Christians were and thus more likely to see racial integration as a threat to their culture.

36. Minutes of the Community of Hope meeting, White Oak Junior High School, 25 January 1974, Archives of the Archdiocese of Cincinnati (hereafter Cincinnati Archives). Don Olinger of the Community of Hope had been in contact with members of several of these extraterritorial parishes, and he had made tentative plans to invite delegates from these communities to visit the Community of Hope. We do not know whether such meetings ever happened. "Parish Without Bounds: The Community of Christ Our Brother," *Commonweal* 86, no. 19 (25 August 1967): 514–515. Jeff Marlett, e-mail to author, 25 May 2001, also provided input. See also Cogley, *Catholic America,* 126–127; Greeley, *Come Blow Your Mind with Me,* 162; Mary Ellen Leary, "New Liturgy Gives Life to Old Parish," *National Catholic Reporter* 9, no. 26 (27 April 1973): 1, 6. For the Bea Community, Ron Hilvers provided useful information, interview by author, telephone, May 2001.

37. "A History of the Community of Hope," January 1972, Cincinnati Archives, 1. Hilvers interview also provided information. See also Ulmer Kuhn to "All members (present and past) of the Community of Hope," 18 October 1974, Cincinnati Archives.

38. "Statistics as of May 1970," Community of Hope, Cincinnati Archives.

39. With such rapid growth, overcrowding became a problem, and the Community planted a new group at St. Francis Seminary in Mount Healthy, Ohio, which first celebrated Mass on May 9, 1971; others broke off to join a group of celebrants who met at Mount Alverno School for Boys in Delhi, Ohio. But the core group continued to grow. See "History." Ron Hilvers, Ron Discepoli, and Eugene Breyer provided useful information, interviews by author, telephone, May 2001. See also Kuhn to Leibold, 13 August 1970, Cincinnati Archives.

40. Leibold to Kuhn, 14 August 1970, Cincinnati Archives.
41. For more on the radical fringe of worship during this period, see Malcolm Boyd, ed., *The Underground Church* (New York: Sheed and Ward, 1968).
42. Kuhn to Father Provincial and Definitorium, 1 September 1970, Cincinnati Archives; Kuhn to Leibold, 1 June 1971, Cincinnati Archives.
43. Hilvers, Discepoli, and Breyer interviews.
44. Ibid.
45. Breyer interview.
46. Survey results, February 1970, Cincinnati Archives.
47. "Report of Saturday-Sunday Mass Attendance," Fr. Ulmer Kuhn, October 1971, Cincinnati Archives; Rev. Msgr. Henry J. Vogelpohl to Kuhn, 7 May 1973, Cincinnati Archives; Fr. Ulmer Kuhn to Archbishop Paul Leibold, 29 February 1972, handwritten letter, Cincinnati Archives; Kuhn to Leibold, 29 February 1972, typewritten letter, Cincinnati Archives.
48. Besides, Kuhn was a Franciscan, and thus was overseen by his order, not by the archdiocese. Ordered priests sometimes serve as parish priests, but their allegiance and responsibility lie with the superiors of their order. Kuhn had to satisfy the archbishop if he wanted the Community to continue, but as a Franciscan he probably worried less about the archbishop's approval than would a diocesan priest. As for the archdiocese being helpful, here is Eugene Breyer: "The archdiocese was better than just unobtrusive—they were supportive. . . . The two times when we had to find new pastors, they were very helpful and very cooperative. They listed the position, they let us talk to their different folks who were interested." Breyer interview.
49. "The Relocation of the Community of Hope, October, 1972," Cincinnati Archives; Hilvers interview.
50. "Yesterday, Today and Tomorrow: Reflections on the First Ten Years of the Community of Hope," Cincinnati, 1977; Hilvers to Arnold Mann, Kemper American Development Corp, 25 September 1973; Hilvers to Archbishop Joseph Bernardin, 25 September 1973; Hilvers to Mann, 23 October 1973; Hilvers to Rev. James Shappelle, 25 October 1973; "Notice of Special Ballot," 4 November 1973—all from Cincinnati Archives.
51. Hilvers interview.

52. Untitled memo, 1973, giving plans for the move to St. Leo's Church, Cincinnati Archives; Annual Statistical Reports, Community of Hope, Archdiocese of Cincinnati, 1971 and 1972, Cincinnati Archives.

53. "A History of the Community of Hope," January 1972, 1, Cincinnati Archives.

54. "Talents and Resources Directory," sometime in 1972 or 1973 (date based on the address on the letterhead), Cincinnati Archives.

55. Hilvers interview and Breyer interview. In fact, the Community's earliest engagement with a secular political controversy came in 1988, when political correctness was remaking our language. The Community voted to replace "brothers" with "brothers and sisters" or "friends"; also, "Songs where people are represented in the male gender only should not be used." See "Community of Hope: The Inclusive Language Committee Guidelines," 13 April 1988, Cincinnati Archives.

56. Kuhn to "All members (past and present)," Cincinnati Archives.

57. Helen Buswinka, "Adult Christianity Project: An Informal Discussion of the Community of Hope," 30 July 1976, Cincinnati Archives.

58. Ben L. Kaufman, "Catholic Group Finds Its Hope in Its Liturgy," *Cincinnati Enquirer,* 17 May 1982, D1–2; and Christine Wolff, "Catholics Close Doors of Hope," *Cincinnati Enquirer,* 25 June 1989, 1, 14.

59. Kay Brookshire, "Hugs and Happy Singing," *Cincinnati Post,* 2 December 1978; Wolff, "Catholics Close Doors," 14.

60. See *F.E.L Publications, Ltd. v. National Conference of Catholic Bishops,* 466 F. Supp. 1034, 200 U.S.P.Q. 301 (N.D. Ill 1978); "Piracy on the High C's," *America* 135, no. 11 (16 October 1976): 224.

61. Spurr, "Word," 46; Francis J. Guentner, "The Treasury of Sacred Music," *America* 138, no. 7 (25 February 1978): 144.

62. Bella English, "The People Are the Church," *Boston Globe,* 17 July 2002, F1, F6.

three. JEWS AND COMMUNAL WORSHIP

1. Here I rely on the analysis of Michael Alexander, *Jazz Age Jews* (Princeton: Princeton University Press, 2001).

2. By 1986 about 25 percent of all American Conservative and Reform synagogues sponsored havurot; in California and western states, that figure may have been as high as 65 percent, and it was rising. Mark I. Pinsky, "'Quiet Revolution': A New Spirit in Judaism," *Los Angeles Times,* 11 October 1986, 1.

3. Kaplan helped organize the New York Kehillah, which lasted from 1908 to 1922; it was an attempt to bring all of a Jewish life under the guidance of a council of organizations, in loose imitation of the Eastern European *kehillah,* which had provided self-government for unemancipated Jews. See Arthur A. Goren, *New York Jews and the Quest for Community: The Kehillah Experiment, 1908–1922* (New York: Columbia University Press, 1979). Almost simultaneously, Kaplan founded the Jewish Center (1915–1921), a New York synagogue meant to house Jewish social, educational, and religious life in one institution. The kehillah failed, and the Jewish Center is now an orthodox synagogue; but in their time each kindled a democratic spirit that, in Reconstructionism's later guises, strongly informed the havurah movement.

4. Kaplan sought to affect all aspects of the Jew's life, and so he advocated building "synagogue centers," which often had, in addition to sanctuaries, gymnasiums and schools. See Mordecai M. Kaplan, *Judaism as a Civilization: Toward a Reconstructionism of American-Jewish Life* (New York: Macmillan, 1934); Jeffrey Gurock and Jacob Schachter, *A Modern Heretic and a Traditional Community: Mordecai M. Kaplan, Orthodoxy, and American Judaism* (New York: Columbia University Press, 1997). David Kaufman argues that Kaplan has received too much credit for the synagogue center phenomenon. See *Shul with a Pool: The "Synagogue-Center" in American Jewish History* (Hanover, N.H.: University Press of New England, 1999).

5. Peter Margolis, "The Role of the Reconstructionist Movement in Creating 'Havurot' in America, 1920–1970" (M.A. thesis, Hebrew University of Jerusalem, 1993), 23, 25–30.

6. Ibid., 35. See Deborah Dash Moore, *To the Golden Cities: Pursuing the American Jewish Dream in Miami and L.A.* (New York: Free Press, 1994). It was initially called the Reconstructionist Fellowship of Congregations; in 1961, at its conference at Beth Shalom Synagogue in White Plains, New York, the name was changed to the Federation of Reconstructionist Congregations and Fellowships; the following year, it was changed again, to the Federation of Reconstructionist Congregations and Fellowships (Havurot). See Margolis, "Role," 42. Today, the name of the organization has been slightly modified, to the Federation of Reconstructionist Congregations and Havurot. The new name obviously reflects the spread of the havurah ideal.

7. Jakob J. Petuchowski, "Toward a Modern 'Brotherhood,'" *Reconstructionist* 26, no. 16 (16 December 1960): 15.

8. Ibid., 11–12, 18–19; Jacob Neusner, "Fellowship and the Crisis of Community," *Reconstructionist* 26, no. 19 (27 January 1961): 10–11. Around the same time, Neusner also discussed the havurah in "Qumran and Jerusalem: Two Jewish Roots to Utopia," *Journal of Bible and Religion* 18 (October 1959): 284–290, and in "The Fellowship *(havurah)* in the Second Jewish Commonwealth," *Harvard Theological Review* 53, no. 2 (April 1960): 125–142.

9. Neusner, "Fellowship," 14; Margolis, "Role," 43–44, 64, 66. Eisenstein was invited to Washington by Robert Grosse, vice president for havurot of the Reconstructionist Foundation.

10. Margolis, "Role," 45. See also Peter Margolis, "Reconstructionism and Havurah: The Whittier-Schulweis Connection," *Western States Jewish History* 27, no. 4 (July 1995): 217–218.

11. Margolis, "Role," 37; Margolis, "Reconstructionism," 219–221, 223–224; Gerald B. Bubis and Henry Wasserman with Alan Lert, *Synagogue Havurot: A Comparative Study* (Cincinnati: Hebrew Union College, 1983), 8–12.

12. Harold Schulweis, "A Call for Holy Discontent," *United Synagogue Review* 26, no. 4 (Winter 1974): 9. On the Colorado havurot, see Margolis, "Role," 63–64. In 1963 Ira Eisenstein gave a series of lectures on Reconstructionism in Estes Park, Colorado, about two hours from Denver, in which he mentioned the havurah. Intrigued, several of his listeners started a havurah. The next year, after Mordecai Kaplan spoke at Reform Temple Micah in Denver, the Denver Havurah was deluged with potential new members. Rather than expand the existing havurah, they spun off "Havurah B," and supervised the novices on their way to independence. "When 'Havurah C' was subsequently established, the members of the three havurot recognized the need for some form of inter-havurah organization. Thus, in 1967, the Colorado Jewish Reconstructionist Federation was established."

13. Jacob Neusner, *Contemporary Judaic Fellowship in Theory and Practice* (New York: Ktav, 1972).

14. Schulweis, "Call," 8.

15. See Richard Narva, "Judaism on Campus: Why It Fails," in *The New Jews,* ed. James A. Sleeper and Alan L. Mintz (New York: Random House, 1971), 101–119; Bernard Reisman, "The Chavurah: A Jewish

Support Network," *American Behavioral Scientist* 23, no. 4 (March–April 1980): 559–560; Larry Eskridge, "'One Way': Billy Graham, the Jesus Generation, and the Idea of an Evangelical Youth Culture," *Church History* 67, no. 1 (March 1998): 83–106.

16. For more on the configuration of Jewish neighborhoods early in the twentieth century, see Deborah Dash Moore, *At Home in America: Second Generation New York Jews* (New York: Columbia University Press, 1981); see too Sara Feinstein, "A New Jewish Voice on Campus," *Dimensions in American Judaism* 4, no. 2 (Winter 1970): 7; Bill Novak, "The Making of a Jewish Counter Culture," *CCAR Journal* 17, no. 3 (June 1970): 51–52.

17. Sheldon Toib, "Referendum Passes by Wide Margin," *Commentator* 81, no. 7 (27 May 1970): 1. The *Commentator* was the student newspaper of Yeshiva University, the orthodox Jewish university that trains many rabbis. Quoting from Psalm 34, the Rabbinical Assembly of America, and the Central Conference of American Rabbis, the ad answered, of course, yes. See *Jewish Radical* 1, no. 1 (January 1970): 7. The newspaper was published by the Radical Jewish Union of the University of California at Berkeley.

18. Steven Martin Cohen, "American Jewish Feminism: A Study in Conflicts and Compromises," *American Behavioral Scientist* 23, no. 4 (March–April 1980): 524; Novak, "The Making of a Jewish Counter Culture," 54. Edward Hoagland, "On Not Being a Jew," in *The Courage of Turtles* (New York: Random House, 1970), 91–106, originally published in *Commentary* 45, no. 4 (April 1968): 58–62.

19. Philip Roth, *Goodbye, Columbus, and Five Short Stories* (Boston: Houghton Mifflin, 1959); Philip Roth, *Portnoy's Complaint* (New York: Random House, 1969).

20. See Bill Novak, "Philip Roth and Our Situation," *Response* 11 (Fall 1971): 71–87; Sylvia Rothchild and Bill Novak, "On Philip Roth: An Exchange," *Response* 13 (Spring 1972): 147–152. For the story of the Sulzbergers' complex relationship with their Judaism, see Susan E. Tifft and Alex S. Jones, "The Family," *New Yorker*, 19 April 1999, 44–52.

21. "To gloss briefly over the surface of the Jewish counterculture, Israel groups on virtually every campus, *chavurot* in Boston and New York, an increased awareness of and action on behalf on Soviet Jewry, the House of Love and Prayer in San Francisco, freedom seders all over the country, cults build around [Rabbi] Shlomo Carlebach and Elie

Wiesel, in short, a myriad of events and interests taking place *totally outside* of the established America Jewish community." Bill Novak, "Problem and Response," *Dimensions in American Judaism* 4, no. 4 (Summer 1970): 35.

22. McCandlish Phillips, "The Jewish Press Phenomenon," *Challenge* 1, no. 2 (May 1971): 4, orig. pub. *New York Times,* 13 March 1971. *Challenge* was published by the Greater Miami Jewish College Student Union.

23. Sylvia Rothchild, "A Great Happening in Boston: Revolt of the Young," *Present Tense* 3, no. 3 (Spring 1976): 22.

24. Cohen, "American Jewish Feminism," 524; Riv-Ellen Prell, *Prayer and Community: The Havurah in American Judaism* (Detroit: Wayne State University Press, 1989), 78–79, 86.

25. "Jewish Radicals Call for Fast on December 12," *Ha-Orah,* 6 October 1969, 7. *Ha-Orah* was a student newspaper in Los Angeles.

26. J. J. Goldberg, "Radical Concerned Jewish Youth in Action," *Jewish Digest* 17, no. 2 (November 1971): 48. The article was reprinted from *Other Stand,* 12 November 1969, published by the Committee for Social Justice in the Middle East, Montreal. (Goldberg later became the editor of the English-language edition of the *Forward,* the liberal Jewish weekly newspaper in New York City.) We should keep in mind that the active Jewish counterculture—comprising, say, the people who showed up for rallies—was small. One observer estimated that only five hundred of thousands of Jews present marched under the JOP banner at the 1970 peace rally. See Phil Shandler, "When the Cause Stirs Action," *Jewish Digest* 17, no. 2 (November 1971): 40–50.

27. Narva, "Judaism on Campus," 103; Novak, "Problem and Response," 36. Mintz had in fact been international president of United Synagogue Youth.

28. Yosef I. Abramowitz, "The Ongoing Abandonment of Jewish Students," *Response* (Winter 1993): 15; Yosef I. Abramowitz, "To 1969 and Back," *Response* (Winter 1995): 16–26; Rothchild, "A Great Happening," 22; Novak, "Problem and Response," 34–35.

29. Margolis, "Role," 68–69.

30. Stephen C. Lerner, "The *Havurot:* An Experiment in Jewish Communal Living," in *Jewish Radicalism: A Selected Anthology,* ed. Jack Nusan Porter and Peter Dreier (New York: Grove, 1973), 151–152.

31. Ibid., 156.

32. Ibid., 152.
33. George E. Johnson, "New Jewish Consciousness on Campus," *Jewish Digest* 19, no. 3 (December 1973): 16. Johnson's article was a condensed version of "Analysis," no. 30, published by the Institute for Jewish Policy Planning and Research of the Synagogue Council of America.
34. Arthur Green, interview by author, Newton, Mass., 29 February 2000.
35. Bill Novak, "The Havurah in New York City: Some Notes on the First Year," *Response* 8 (Fall 1970): 11–14.
36. Martha Ackelsberg, interview by author, Northampton, Mass., 8 February 2000.
37. Ibid.; Novak, "The Havurah in New York City"; Novak, "Problem and Response," 36.
38. Novak, "The Havurah," 13; Lerner, "The *Havurot,*" 161–162.
39. Jim Sleeper, e-mail to author, 12 November 2001; Ackelsberg interview; Alan Mintz, interview by author, New York, 28 February 2000; Green interview.
40. Gerald Serotta, "Havurah Politics: Toward a New Agenda for the Eighties," *Response* 38 (1980): 43–45.
41. Jacob Neusner, "Further Comments on the Havurot," *Response* 4, no. 3 (Fall 1970): 29–30; Lerner, "The *Havurot,*" 162. Sperling later became a professor at Hebrew Union College in New York City.
42. "JUJ Calendar of Events," *Jews for Urban Justice Newsletter,* May 1969, 7. I doubt the assertion, on the same page, that the seder drew eight hundred people.
43. "Fabrangen," *Jewish Urban Guerilla,* February 1971, 9.
44. "Fabrangen!," *Jewish Urban Guerilla,* April 1971. The article indicates that Carlebach offered a course on Jewish mysticism at the Fabrangen that spring. "Calendar," *Jewish Urban Guerilla,* April 1971.
45. Quoted in Reisman, "The Chavurah," 11.
46. S.R., "Why a *Jewish* Urban Coffeehouse?" *Jewish Urban Guerilla,* February 1971, 4; Reisman, "The Chavurah," 11.
47. Green interview; Kathy Green, interview by author, 29 February 2000, Newton, Mass.; Mintz interview.
48. Quoted in Sara Feinstein, "A New Jewish Voice on Campus," 4–5.
49. M. Jay Rosenberg, "To Uncle Tom and Other Such Jews," *Village Voice,* 13 February 1969, 29, 40. This essay, written by Michael Rosenberg when he was a senior at the State University of New York at Albany,

became a minor classic. It was reprinted often in the Jewish student press, including *Ha-Orah*, 11 April 1969, 1, and *Achdut* 1, no. 2 (January 1971): 4. *Achdut* was a New York City newspaper of Jewish high school activists. Novak, "Problem and Response," 35.

50. Green interview; Rosenberg, "To Uncle Tom and Other Such Jews," 29, 40.

51. Marilyn Fisch, "Jewish Consciousness," *Hakotel* 2, no. 1 (December 1976): 2. *Hakotel* was a publication of Nassau County, Long Island, Jewish student groups. "We Are Coming Home," *Brooklyn Bridge* 1 (February 1971): 1. See Rick Kramer, "Jewish Prejudices Similar to WASP Fears Regarding Black Americans," *Ha-Orah*, 6 October 1969, 2; "E Pluribus Wasp," *Hayom* 2, no. 5 (23 February–9 March 1971): 4 (*Hayom* was published by the Philadelphia Union of Jewish Students); Feinstein, "A New Jewish Voice," 6.

52. Amos Renan, "Israeli Panthers," *Bagolah: In Exile* 1, no. 1 (1970): 1. *Bagolah: In Exile* was published by the Jewish Student Press Collective in Skokie, Illinois. David Bedein and Cheryl Malkin, "Israel's Black Panthers," *Hayom* 2, no. 1 (September 1971): 2. See also Elliot Pisem, "Israel's Black Panthers Expose Social Ills," *Alliance* 1, no. 1 (November 1971): 1. *Alliance* was published by the Jewish High School Alliance. In North America, the term *Sephardi* or *Sephardic* refers to Jews of Iberian descent; they were the first Jews in North America, and in the eighteenth and nineteenth centuries being Sephardic was a mark of prestige. In the Middle East, however, the Sephardim are more properly seen as Mizrachim, or Eastern Jews; they are from Africa or the Middle East, and they are darker and frequently poorer.

53. See *Bagolah*, December 1974, 13–14, 17. *Bagolah* was published by Ichud Habonim, Labor Zionist Youth. "Yeah, Eldridge, You Said It All Right," *Jewish Radical* 1, no. 3 (May–June 1970): 12. The editors also allude, with considerable relief, to philo-Semitic comments in Cleaver's past. Albert Axelrad, "Panthers and Jews," part 2, "Further Comments on the Jewish Imperative," *Response* 12 (Winter 1971–1972): 51–53.

54. M. Jay Rosenberg, "Radical Credo," *Hillel Gate* 2, no. 4 (February 1971): 6. The *Hillel Gate* was published by B'nai Brith of Brooklyn College. See also "Uncle Jake Is Alive and Well and Sitting in Washington!" *Information Bulletin*, March 1971[?], 15. "The Student as Nigger," *Hayom* 3, no. 2 (1–22 November 1972): 5. *The Student as Nigger*

was also the title of a book by Jerry Farber (North Hollywood, Calif.: Contact, 1969).

55. Ackelsberg interview.

56. "The Jewish women's movement emerged against this [havurah] background, beginning in late 1971, when several New York Chavurah women and their friends formed a study group to explore the status of women in Jewish law. Later, they moved to consciousness raising and protest activities. Thereupon they dubbed themselves *Ezrat Nashim* (a Hebrew pun meaning 'help for women' and 'zone for women,' referring to the section of the traditional synagogues set aside for female worshippers)." Cohen, "American Jewish Feminism," 525.

57. Ackelsberg interview. In the interview, Martha Ackelsberg originally quoted Alan Mintz as saying, "I have always loved this, this is really one of my favorite things, it talks about all of these different things awakening and filling up." Mintz's recollections, in an e-mail to the author on 1 September 2002, prompted me to alter the quotation slightly. Mintz also noted in the e-mail that while he had certainly been referring to ejaculation in the sense of sexual climax, he "was also mindful of the fact that the term 'ejaculation' is used figuratively for the act of a sudden outburst of expression."

58. "Chavurot Sisters," *Brooklyn Bridge* 1, no. 4 (June 1972): 4–5; "Giving Up Assimilationist Privilege," *Brooklyn Bridge* 1, no. 4 (June 1972): 17.

59. "Coed Kosher Commune," *Hayom* 1, no. 2 (May 1971): 4. As a junior, Rachel Abramson wrote an article about the Free Minyan, which she had helped found as an alternative to more traditional services.

60. Michael ben Shachar, "The Name's the Same, but the 'Place' Is Different," *Hayom* 2, no. 1 (September 1971), 7. Bob Dylan's real name is Zimmerman, a fact that Jewish students often mentioned in their newspapers. See, among many examples, Mike Masch, "Dylan: Bringing It All Back Home . . .," *Jewish Voice* 2, no. 3 (March 1974): 3, published at Fairleigh Dickinson University; "The Dylan Dilemma," *Nivim: University of Minnesota Journal of Unlimited Jewish Expression*, February 1974, 5–6.

61. "Women Liberate Penn Hillel," *Hayom* 2, no. 2 (October 1971): 5; "The College Student as Jew," *Hayom* 3, no. 6 (19 April–6 May 1973): 1; "The Fabrengen," *Hayom* 3, no. 3 (23 January–13 February 1973): 2; Johnson, "New Jewish Consciousness," 13–14; "Invitation from Shabbat," *Hayom* 5, no. 1 (September 1974): 5; "Jewish Co-op," *Jewish Rad-*

ical 1, no. 2 (February–March 1970): 6[?]; "The Jewish Co-op Speaks," *Jewish Radical* 6, nos. 3–4 (Winter–Spring 1974): 2; Joseph B. Robinson and Julius Schatz, "The Supreme Court and the Havurot," *Congress Bi-Weekly* 41, no. 9 (27 September 1974): 12–14. The latter periodical was published by the American Jewish Congress.

62. Jon Groner, "When Jews Live Together," *Jewish Radical* 6, no. 2 (December 1973): 9–10; Lerner, "The *Havurot*," 160; "Raising the Level of the Havurah," *Reconstructionist* 46, no. 9 (January 1981): 5–6; Jacob Neusner, "The Bar Mitzvah of the Havurot," *United Synagogue Review* 25, no. 2 (Summer 1972): 4–5.

63. In 2003 the New York Havurah and Fabrangen still exist, though with very different feels.

64. Margolis, "Role," 18.

65. Lerner, "Havurot," 148–149.

66. In 2002, of about 1,700 rabbis in Reform Judaism, about 360 were women, according to Florence Thornton of the Central Conference of American Rabbis, in an e-mail to the author, 14 August 2002. One hundred one of 218 Reconstructionist rabbis were women, according to Linda Kaplan of the Reconstructionist Rabbinic Association in an e-mail to the author, 15 August 2002. According to Rabbi Jan Caryl Kaufman of the Rabbinical Assembly, in an e-mail to the author, 28 August 2002, there were 157 female members of the Rabbinical Assembly, a Conservative organization, at the time. Between 1985 and 1997 the Jewish Theological Seminary ordained 111 women, but women ordained elsewhere may join the Rabbinical Assembly. See Deborah E. Lipstadt, "Feminism and American Judaism: Looking Back at the Turn of the Century," in *Women and American Judaism: Historical Perspectives,* ed. Pamela S. Nadell and Jonathan D. Sarna (Hanover, N.H.: University Press of New England, 2001), 305, n.2.

four. EPISCOPALIANS AND FEMINISM

1. On the Episcopal Church, see John E. Booty, *The Church in History* (New York: Seabury, 1979); Robert W. Prichard, *A History of the Episcopal Church,* rev. ed. (Harrisburg, Penn.: Morehouse, 1999); Lawrence L. Brown, "The Americanization of the Episcopal Church," *Historical Magazine of the Protestant Episcopal Church* 94, no. 5 (December 1995): 33–52.

2. Dorothy C. Bass, Afterword, "Episcopalian Women in the Context of

American Religious Life," in *Episcopal Women: Gender, Spirituality, and Commitment in an American Mainline Denomination*, ed. Catherine M. Prelinger (New York: Oxford University Press, 1992), 347; Heather Huyck, "To Celebrate a Whole Priesthood: The History of Women's Ordination in the Episcopal Church" (Ph.D. diss., University of Minnesota, 1981), 4–10. In 1889 the General Convention authorized the "setting apart" of deaconesses by canon, or church law, and in 1920 the Lambeth Conference resolved that the "ordination of a deaconess confers on her holy orders," thus giving women a clerical position inferior, but akin, to that of male priesthood. See Rita Mauchenheimer, "Some Events in Women's Ordination History," 1975[?]. This document, like many cited below, is from the personal collection of Heather Huyck (hereafter Huyck Collection).

3. Begin with Catherine Brekus, *Strangers and Pilgrims: Female Preaching in America, 1740–1845* (Chapel Hill: University of North Carolina Press, 1998). Continue with Ronald L. Numbers, *Prophetess of Health: Ellen G. White and the Origins of Seventh-Day Adventist Health Reform,* rev. ed. (Knoxville: University of Tennessee Press, 1992); Stephen J. Stein, *The Shaker Experience in America: A History of the United Society of Believers* (New Haven: Yale University Press, 1992); Edith L. Blumhofer, *Aimee Semple McPherson: Everybody's Sister* (Grand Rapids, Mich.: Eerdmans, 1993); Stephen J. Stein, "Retrospection and Introspection: The Gospel According to Mary Baker Eddy," *Harvard Theological Review* 75 (1982): 97–116. Ann Braude's *Radical Spirits: Spiritualism and Women's Rights in Nineteenth Century America* (Boston: Beacon, 1989) discusses spiritualism, a movement instigated and sustained by women but quite peripheral by the twentieth century.

4. For a classic essay on Bishop James Pike, see Joan Didion, "James Pike, American," in *The White Album* (New York: Simon and Schuster, 1979), 51–58. Huyck, "Celebrate," 12, 18; *Journal of the General Convention of the Protestant Episcopal Church of the United States of America* (hereafter *Convention Journal*), Houston, 11–22 October 1970, 19.

5. With regard to the race question, the Episcopal Church comes across in one article as well-meaning but rather ineffectual, too timid perhaps. See Charles F. Rehkopf, "Reactions to the Events of the '60s and '70s," *Historical Magazine of the Protestant Episcopal Church* 47, no. 4 (December 1978): 453–462. In 1969 women joined blacks in South

Bend, Indiana, to picket the church's House of Deputies. See Sue Hiatt, "Organization for Ordination of Women to the Priesthood," 1974[?], Huyck Collection. There is a charming passage from "Negro Priest Named to Beauty Pageant Board," from the conservative Episcopal magazine *Living Church* 157, no. 8 (25 August 1968): 7: "A Negro priest will have a role in the selection of the next Miss America. The election of the Rev. Kenneth E. MacDonald, rector of St. Augustine's Church, Atlantic City, to the beauty pageant's board of directors marks the first time a Negro has served in such a position."

With regard to Vietnam, see "St. Paul's and Antiwar Protest," *Living Church* 156, no. 1 (1 January 1968): 5, in which it is reported that both the vicar of St. Paul's Chapel and the rector of Trinity Church, New York, of whose parish St. Paul's was a part, denied permission for antiwar protesters to use St. Paul's for a protest service in which draft resisters would turn in their draft cards. The service was held instead at the Evangelist Lutheran Church in Brooklyn. On Clergy and Laymen Concerned About Vietnam, see Mitchell K. Hall, *Because of Their Faith* (New York: Columbia University Press, 1990). Betty Bone Schiess referred to the Episcopal Peace Fellowship, of which she was a member, as "a marginal group of liberal folk who believed in peace." Betty Bone Schiess, interview by author, telephone, 16 November 2002. See, too, Betty Bone Schiess, *Why Me, Lord: The Story of One Woman's Ordination* (Syracuse, N.Y.: Syracuse University Press, 2003).

6. "Holy Hippie Matrimony," *Living Church* 157, no. 2 (14 July 1968): 6–7; "Drugs Discussed," *Living Church* 156, no. 1 (7 January 1968): 11.

7. "Rock Group Performs in Church," *Living Church* 157, no. 24 (15 December 1968): 5–6; Lester B. Singleton, "Folk Mass Phenomenon," letter to the editor, *Living Church* 159, no. 2 (13 July 1969): 3; Trevor Wyatt Moore, "Speaking to the Lord in Rock," *Episcopalian* 134, no. 2 (February 1969): 44; George Silliman, "The Folk Mass Phenomenon," *Living Church* 158, no. 24 (15 June 1969), 29; "Mass Marks 'Hair's' Anniversary," *Living Church* 162, no. 24 (13 June 1971), 12; Alla Bozarth-Campbell, *Womanpriest: A Personal Odyssey* (New York: Paulist, 1978), 89; Leonard Freeman, "A Cathedral in the Works," *Episcopalian* 138, no. 7 (July 1973): 3–4.

8. "Homosexual-Oriented Service Held," *Living Church* 162, no. 11 (14 March 1971): 24; Emily C. Hewitt and Suzanne Hiatt, *Women Priests: Yes or No?* (New York: Seabury, 1973), 81.

9. Louis Cassels, "A Woman's Place . . . ?" *Episcopalian* 136, no. 7 (July 1971): 19.

10. Huyck, "To Celebrate," 18; "A Summary of the General Convention Actions," *Episcopalian* 135, no. 12 (December 1970): 13; Hewitt and Hiatt, *Women Priests*, 14–15; "Priests, Deacons: Two Orders," *Living Church* 164, no. 13 (26 March 1972): 13; the Rev. Charles Wheeler Scott, letter to the editor, *Living Church* 164, no. 18 (30 April 1972), 113.

11. See the Proceedings of the Special Meeting of the House of Bishops, 1971, in the *Convention Journal*, Louisville, Ky., 1973, 1,064.

12. Episcopal Women's Caucus to Presiding Bishop John E. Hines, 30 October 1971, Archives of the Episcopal Church USA (hereafter Episcopal Archives); "The Episcopal Women's Caucus: A Brief History and a Beginning," *Ruach* 1, no. 1 (May 1972), 1; Special Meeting of the House of Bishops, 1972, *Convention Journal*, 1973, 1,130–1,131.

13. Huyck, "To Celebrate," 73–74; Appendix C, "Report of Special Committee of the House of Bishops, on the Ordination of Women," *Convention Journal*, 1973, 1,127.

14. *Convention Journal*, 1973, 224–225.

15. Paul Moore, interview by author, Stonington, Conn., 26 May 2002.

16. "Statement read by the Rev. Carter Heyward [deacons use the title Reverend] during ordination service, Dec. 15, 1973, Cathedral of St. John the Divine, New York City," Episcopal Archives.

17. Episcopal Women's Caucus, "Where Did We Come From?" 24 October 1976, Huyck Collection.

18. Huyck, "To Celebrate," 105–106, 108; Schiess interview.

19. The Rt. Revs. Daniel Corrigan, Robert DeWitt, and Edward R. Welles II, "An Open Letter," 20 July 1974, Episcopal Archives.

20. Suzanne Hiatt, interview by author, Cambridge, Mass., 22 October 2001.

21. Mark Oppenheimer, "Episcopal Priestesses," *Christian Century* 119, no. 1 (2–9 January 2002), 7–8.

22. On Carter Heyward, see Muffie Moroney, "And the Walls Came A-Tumblin' Down: Moments from the Life of a Lesbian Feminist Episcopal Priest," posted at http://www.outsmartmagazine.com/issue/i09–01/walls.html.

23. Eleanor Blau, "11 Women Ordained Episcopal Priests; Church Law Defied," *New York Times*, 30 July 1979, 1, 17; "Eleven Women Ordained

to the Priesthood!" *Genesis III* 4, no. 2 (June–July 1974): 1. The eleven women were Jeannette Piccard, Alla Bozarth-Campbell, Betty Bone Schiess, Merrill Bittner, Emily Hewitt, Marie Moorefield, Carter Heyward, Suzanne Hiatt, Katrina Swanson, Alison Cheek, and Nancy Hatch Wittig.

24. "Eleven Women Ordained," 2.

25. The Rt. Rev. Arthur A. Vogel to Katrina Swanson, 31 July 1974, Episcopal Archives; Ellen Biggs et al., *Statement of Clarification and Concern from the Steering Committee of the Episcopal Women's Caucus,* 2 August 1974, Episcopal Archives; *Convention Journal,* Minneapolis, 1976, B-199–201; "Two Resignations Result," *Genesis III* 4, nos. 3–4 (August–September and October 1974): 3; "Women Priests Will Celebrate Eucharist," *Genesis III* 4, nos. 3–4 (August–September and October 1974): 1; and Huyck, "To Celebrate," 143.

26. See *Convention Journal,* 1976, B-251, B-255–256; Huyck, "To Celebrate," 135.

27. "WON: The Voice of Women's Ordination," probably early 1975; Mary Ann Peters to Helen Havens, 22 February 1975, Episcopal Archives.

28. "Women Mark First Year of Disputed Ordinations," *Episcopalian* 140, no. 8 (September 1975): 8; "Four More Women Illegally Ordained," *Living Church* 171, no. 13 (28 September 1975): 6; *Convention Journal,* 1976, B-311–B-317; United Press International, "Rector Who Let Women Officiate Won't Be Tried," 3 June 1975, reprinted in *Episcopalian* 140, no. 7 (July 1975): 13; Janette Pierce, "D.C. Court Recommends Wendt Admonition," *Episcopalian* 140, no. 7 (July 1975): 4, 13; Huyck, "To Celebrate," 157.

29. Heyward to Sue Hiatt et al., 31 January 1976, Suzanne Hiatt Papers, Archives of Union Theological Seminary (hereafter Hiatt Papers). The caucus, too, continued to exist. In December 1975 it had 189 women and 55 men. Episcopal Women's Caucus to Board Members, 11 December 1975, Episcopal Archives. On relations between WON and the coalition, see Huyck, "To Celebrate," 215.

30. Heather Huyck, interview by author, Williamsburg, Virginia, 29 September 2001.

31. *Convention Journal,* 1976, B-54; *Daily of the General Convention of the Episcopal Church* (hereafter *Convention Daily*), 17 September 1976, 1.

It is interesting to note that region seemed to matter little in the vote; most of the deep South, for example, was for ordination.

32. Bozarth-Campbell, *Womanpriest,* 83–84; *Study Guide on the Ordination of Women to the Priesthood,* McWON, Minneapolis, April 1976, 5, Huyck Collection.

33. Betty Friedan, *The Feminine Mystique,* rev. ed. (New York: Norton, 1974), 351–353.

34. Huyck, "To Celebrate," 66–67.

35. Hewitt and Hiatt, *Women Priests,* 24.

36. The Rt. Rev. Philip F. McNairy to the Rt. Rev. David E. Richards, 9 December 1974, Huyck Collection; Jane Wolf to the Rev. William W. Eastburn, 4 March 1976, Episcopal Archives.

37. For example, Women's Ordination Now, "WON: A History," *WON: The Voice of Women's Liberation,* probably early 1975, 1, Huyck Collection.

38. Helen Claire, "I Need Women Priests," *De-liberation* 2, no. 1 (November 1975): 6.

39. Betty B. White to Dean [Harvey] Guthrie and the Faculty of Episcopal Theological School, 20 May 1970, Episcopal Archives.

40. Carter Heyward, *A Priest Forever* (New York: Harper and Row, 1976), 6.

41. Letty M. Russell, *Human Liberation in a Feminist Perspective: A Theology* (Philadelphia: Westminster, 1974); Rosemary Radford Ruether, *Religion and Sexism: Images of Woman in the Jewish and Christian Traditions* (New York: Simon and Schuster, 1974); Mary Daly, *The Church and the Second Sex* (New York: Harper and Row, 1968); Mary Daly, *Beyond God the Father: Toward a Philosophy of Women's Liberation* (Boston: Beacon, 1973); Leonard Swidler, "Jesus Was a Feminist," *Southeast Asia Journal of Theology* 13, no. 1 (1971): 102–110. According to Paula Hyman, many Jewish feminists considered this article anti-Semitic.

42. Study Guide, McWON, 1976, Huyck Collection; the Rev. David Gracie, "The Episcopal Peace Fellowship and the Ordination of Women," probably late 1973, Episcopal Archives; and "Project W," sermon by the Rev. William L. Dois Jr., Immanuel Church-on-the-Hill, Alexandria, Virginia, 23 February 1975, Episcopal Archives. Immanuel was the church of Pat Park, one of the leaders of the coalition.

43. Betty B. White, memo to the Episcopal Theological School Community and Parishioners of Christ Church, Cambridge, and Other Inter-

ested People, 12 May 1970, Episcopal Archives; Betty B. White, "Discrimination Against Women in the Episcopal Church," 31 May 1970, Episcopal Archives.

44. Heyward, *A Priest Forever,* 73; Susan [*sic*] Hiatt, "The Female Majority: Can Sisterhood Survive?" *Focus,* November 1971, 1–2. Emphasis Hiatt's.

45. "Hiatt Symposium: Suzanne Hiatt remarks," 12 November 12 1985[?], Hiatt Papers.

46. Mary Dona, letter to the editor, *Living Church* 165, no. 23 (3 December 1972): 3; Eleanor Lewis, "To Iron a Shirt," undated, Huyck Collection; Heyward, *A Priest Forever,* 121. The letter to Heyward was written by a Nebraska laywoman in 1975.

47. Mary Ann Peters to Helen Havens, 22 February 1975, Episcopal Archives. See Huyck, "To Celebrate," 65, on one woman's description of the "abusive militancy advocated by some women's groups."

48. "Statement from the Reverend Merrill Bittner at a meeting of the clergy of the Dioceses of Rochester, Central New York and Western New York about the ordination of women to the priesthood, February 20, 1973," Episcopal Archives; "Priest Hasn't Joined Cause," *Philadelphia Daily News,* 17 September 1975, 13.

49. "Behind the Marriage Canons," *Living Church* 158, no. 18 (4 May 1969), 9; Review of Frances M. Bontrager, *The Church and the Single Person,* in *Living Church* 158, no. 20 (18 May 1969): 20; Jan Dilbeck, for the Houston chapter of NOW, to the National Coalition for the Ordination of Women to the Priesthood and Episcopacy, 14 October 1975, Hiatt Papers. Dilbeck does say that her NOW chapter had voted on 8 October to endorse the coalition's efforts. The Bloomington, Indiana, chapter of NOW invited Carter Heyward to speak in 1975. See Anne Bruce Stoddard to Heyward, 31 July 1975, Episcopal Archives. Katrina Swanson asked a woman she had met at a NOW convention to help find Suzanne Hiatt a job. See Katrina Swanson to "Lee," 11 October 1974, Episcopal Archives. A NOW weekend retreat in October 1971 had a session about women and religion. See "Women in the Seventies: The New Feminism," NOW conference program, 9–10 October 1971, Episcopal Archives.

50. Linda Van Vlack to Carter Heyward, 8 March 1975, Episcopal Archives; anonymous letter to Suzanne Hiatt, undated, Hiatt Papers.

51. "A Group of Concerned Women Gathered Together at Graymoor

April 24–26, 1970, and Formulated this Resolution," Huyck Collection.

52. Heyward, *A Priest Forever*, 17–18.

53. The Rev. Suzanne R. Hiatt, "Why I Believe I Am Called to the Priesthood," in *The Ordination of Women, Pro and Con*, ed. Michael P. Hamilton and Nancy S. Montgomery (New York: Morehouse-Barlow, 1975), 37. Schiess noted that while she was a member of NOW, she worried about more radical feminism: "They are talking about things like abolishing marriage, which I am not ready to accept." Lois Vosburgh, "Changes in the Church," *Syracuse Herald-American*, [between May and August 1968]. Ellen Barrett, "The Women's Witness at Trinity Institute," Episcopal Archives.

54. Judy Mathe Foley, "Dealing with a Manifesto," *Episcopalian* 134, no. 7 (July 1969): 11–12; James Foreman, "The Black Manifesto," *Living Church* 159, no. 15 (12 October 1969): 20–24; James Patrick, "Love, Trust, and Marxism at GCII," *Living Church* 159, no. 17 (26 October 1969): 16–17; "Stringfellow on Reparations," *Living Church* 159, no. 20 (16 November 1969): 7; "Roy Wilkins on Reparations," *Living Church* 160, no. 2 (11 January 1970): 13; "The New Black Leadership," *Episcopalian* 134, no. 10 (October 1969): 28.

55. *Newsweek*, 13 March 1972, 101.

56. Betty Bone Schiess to Pauli Murray, undated, Episcopal Archives; Betty B. White, "Discrimination Against Women in the Episcopal Church"; Hewitt and Hiatt, *Women Priests*, 19; Pauli Murray, "Black Theology and Feminist Theology: A Comparative View," *Anglican Theological Review* 61, no. 1 (1978): 3–24; Pauli Murray to the Rt. Rev. Anson P. Stokes, Bishop of Massachusetts, 19 October 1969, Episcopal Archives; Pauli Murray to the Rt. Rev. John Burgess, Bishop of Massachusetts, 28 February 1973, Episcopal Archives.

57. Heyward, *A Priest Forever*, 50–51; "Eleven Women Ordained to the Priesthood!" 1; Martin Luther King Jr., *Letter from Birmingham City Jail* (Philadelphia: American Friends Service Committee, 1963); Bernard Haldane to Helen Havens, 14 September 1976, Episcopal Archives; Alla Bozarth-Campbell, "It's No Joke," *Gynergy* (Minneapolis: Wisdom House, 1978), 24.

58. "Project W," sermon by the Rev. William L. Dois Jr., Immanuel Church-on-the-Hill, Alexandria, Virginia, 23 February 1975, Episcopal Archives; Heyward, *A Priest Forever*, 56–57; Schiess interview.

59. Jill Johnston, *Lesbian Nation: The Feminist Solution* (New York: Simon and Schuster, 1973); Gabriel Chase, "Preferences for Priesthood," letter to the editor, *Living Church* 164, no. 3 (26 March 1972): 5.

60. Carter Heyward to Suzanne Hiatt et al., 31 January 1976, Hiatt Papers; Helen Havens to "Kathy," July 1976, Episcopal Archives. I have not been able to determine who Kathy was.

61. *Convention Daily,* 21 September 1976, 2; William R. MacKaye, "Gays Pleased with Convention," *Convention Daily,* 22 September 1976, 3.

62. *Convention Journal,* 1976, D-139, B-157.

63. James W. Wickliff to Helen Havens, 26 October 1976, Episcopal Archives; "Ron" to Helen Havens, 18 October 1976, Episcopal Archives.

64. Huyck interview.

65. Shulamith Firestone, *The Dialectic of Sex: The Case for Feminist Revolution* (New York: William Morrow, 1970), 33.

66. Heyward, *A Priest Forever,* 23, 28–29, 78; Bozarth-Campbell, *Womanpriest,* 136, 195; Hewitt and Hiatt, *Women Priests,* 36.

67. See Philip Rieff, *The Triumph of the Therapeutic: Uses of Faith After Freud* (New York: Harper and Row, 1966).

68. Alla Bozarth-Campbell, from *Gynergy,* "Discipline Means to Teach, Not to Break," 11; "Rape Poem," 14; and "Women Loving Women," 18.

69. Heyward, *A Priest Forever,* 32–33.

70. Hewitt and Hiatt, *Women Priests,* 28–29.

71. The Rev. Thomas Davis, "Deaconesses Are Different," letter to the editor, *Living Church* 162, no. 11 (14 March 1971): 9; "Deaconesses," *Living Church* 164, no. 6 (6 February 1972): 7.

72. Emily Hewitt, "Women, Ministry, and Education," probably 1975, 8–10, Episcopal Archives; Malcolm Boyd, "Who's Afraid of Woman Priests?" *Ms.,* December 1974, 47–51; Bozarth-Campbell, *Womanpriest,* 167, 169; and "Grass-Roots Organizing in Your Parish," Episcopal Women's Caucus Midwestern Regional Workshop, 14 September 1974, Huyck Collection.

73. Dorothy A. Faber, "The Defiant Women: Doing Their Own Thing," *Christian Challenge* 14, no. 1 (January 1975): 4–6; Emily Gardiner Neal, letter to the editor, *Living Church* 164, no. 5 (30 January 1972): 3–4.

74. Bozarth-Campbell, *Womanpriest,* 125; Sue Moody to Hiatt and Heyward, 30 April 1975, Hiatt Papers.

75. C. S. Lewis, "Priestesses in the Church?" in *God in the Dock: Essays on*

Theology and Ethics, ed. Walter Hooper (Grand Rapids, Mich.: Eerdmans, 1970), 234–239.

76. The Rev. John Saward, "Why Is the Ordination of Women So Wrong?" Coalition for the Apostolic Priesthood, New York, undated, Huyck Collection; Huyck, "To Celebrate," 59–60; the Rev. Robert S. S. Whitman, letter to the editor, *Living Church* 164, no. 3 (16 January 1972): 3.

77. John Askins, "How a Woman Priest Figures the Opposition," *Detroit Free Press,* 12 May 1975, 1C, 4C. Feminist theologians focused also on the Eucharist as a locus of male privilege. See Ruth Tiffany Barnhouse, "An Examination of the Ordination of Women to the Priesthood in Terms of the Symbolism of the Eucharist," in *Women and Orders,* ed. Robert J. Heyer (New York: Paulist Press, 1974), 15–37; Rosemary Radford Ruether, "Why Males Fear Women Priests," *Witness* 63 (July 1980): 19–21.

78. Hewitt and Hiatt, *Women Priests,* 95.

79. "Bishops Reverse Action," *Convention Daily,* 23 September 1976, 1.

80. "Mother of Four Is First Woman Episcopal Priest," *Rocky Mountain News,* 2 January 1977, 34; "First Woman Regularly Ordained to Episcopal Priesthood," Diocesan Press Service, 6 January 1977, Episcopal Archives; Episcopal Diocese of Rochester, press release, 3 January 1977, Episcopal Archives; "A Celebration of the Feast of the Epiphany and Recognition of the Priesthood of the Church for the Rev. Dr. Alla Bozarth-Campbell and the Rev. Dr. Jeannette Piccard," Cathedral Church of St. Mark, Minneapolis, 6 January 1977, Huyck Collection; http://www.episcopalchurch.org/women/seven/statistics.htm; *Anglican Advance* 111, no. 3 (June–July 1998): 7.

81. Merrill Bittner, "Statement to the Clergy," 17 January 1975, Huyck Collection.

82. On the 1979 Book of Common Prayer, see Michael Moriarty, *The Liturgical Revolution: Prayer Book Revision and Associated Parishes, a Generation of Change in the Episcopal Church* (New York: Church Hymnal Corporation, 1996).

five. SOUTHERN BAPTISTS AND VIETNAM WAR PROTEST

1. The Rev. Jim Greene, e-mail to author, 18 May 2000; Lelia Routh Cothen, interview by author, telephone, 24 September 2002.

2. Walker Knight, e-mail to author, 18 May 2000; *Biblical Recorder* (North Carolina) 135, no. 48 (6 December 1969): 13.

3. Alex Vaughn, "North Carolina Baptist Students Debate Vietnam," Bap-

tist Press press release, 9 May 1966, Southern Baptist Historical Library and Archive (hereafter Baptist Archive); *Biblical Recorder* (North Carolina) 134, no. 46 (23 November 1968): 4, 7; *Baptist State Convention of North Carolina,* (Raleigh, N.C., 1968), 79–80; *Baptist State Convention of North Carolina* (Fayetteville, N.C., 1969), 165–166.

4. Terry Nichols, interview by author, telephone, 7 October 2002.

5. Stuart Sprague, "A Case of Nostalgia: Houston 30 Years Later," *Baptists Today* 16, no. 8 (20 August 1998), 25–26.

6. Greene, e-mail; Sprague, "A Case of Nostalgia," 25; Sprague, e-mail to author, 22 August 2002.

7. John Finley, "The 1968 Statement Concerning the Crisis in Our Nation," posted at EthicsDaily.com, 24 July 2002.

8. "A Statement Concerning the Crisis in Our Nation," *Annual of the Southern Baptist Convention* (Nashville, Tenn.: Southern Baptist Convention, 1968), 67.

9. Stuart Sprague, interview by author, telephone, 2 May 2000.

10. Sprague, "A Case of Nostalgia," 25; Jim Newton, "Students Urge SBC to Face Issues; Pastors Say Don't Leave," Baptist Press press release, 3 June 1968, Baptist Archive.

11. Stuart Sprague, interview by author, telephone, November 1999; Sprague, "A Case of Nostalgia," 25–26; Sprague, e-mail, 22 August 2002; "Baptist Students Picket SBC, Offer Resolutions for Change," Baptist Press press release, 11 June 1969, Baptist Archive.

12. Roger Sharpe, interview by author, telephone, 2 May 2000; Tom Graves, interview by author, telephone, 2 May 2000. It is not clear that Graves's draft board was allowed to make this decision for him.

13. Graves interview; Sprague, "A Case of Nostalgia," 25.

14. Greene, e-mail.

15. Graves interview; Routh interview.

16. Stuart Sprague, e-mail to author, 2 May 2000; Knight, e-mail.

17. William G. McLoughlin, *Isaac Backus and the American Pietistic Tradition* (Boston: Little, Brown, 1967).

18. Quoted ibid., xii; emphasis in the original.

19. Rhys Isaac, *The Transformation of Virginia, 1740–1790* (New York: Norton, 1988), 163–164.

20. Nancy Ammerman, *Baptist Battles: Social Change and Religious Conflict in the Southern Baptist Convention* (New Brunswick, N.J.: Rutgers University Press, 1990), 31–32.

21. John Lee Eighmy, *Churches in Cultural Captivity: A History of Social Attitudes of Southern Baptists,* with a revised introduction, conclusion, and bibliography by Samuel S. Hill (Knoxville: University of Tennessee Press, 1987), 19–20.

22. Eighmy, *Churches in Cultural Captivity,* 48.

23. Ammerman, *Baptist Battles,* 42.

24. See, among others, Donald Mathews, *Religion in the Old South* (Chicago: University of Chicago Press, 1977); Charles Reagan Wilson, *Baptized in Blood: The Religion of the Lost Cause* (Athens: University of Georgia Press, 1980); Christine Leigh Heyrman, *Southern Cross: The Beginnings of the Bible Belt* (New York: Knopf, 1997).

25. "Baptist Response to Camille Voted Top SBC Story of 1969," Baptist Press press release, 23 December 1969, Baptist Archive; "Cartoonist Explains Theology Behind the Great Pumpkin," Baptist Press press release, 15 November 1971, Baptist Archive.

26. Victor B. Howard, "The Baptists and Peace Sentiment During the Mexican War," *Quarterly Review* 38, no. 3 (April–June 1978): 68–84; Ken Sehested, "Conformity and Dissent: Southern Baptists on War and Peace Since 1940," *Baptist History and Heritage* 28, no. 2 (April 1993): 3. Sehested, it should be noted, was a Southern Baptist peace activist, not a professional historian; the article has an interested tone. "Statements on World Peace by the Southern Baptist Convention," prepared by the Christian Life Commission, Nashville, Tenn., 1958[?], Baptist Archive.

27. Bill Sumners, "Swords into Plowshares: Southern Baptists, World War I, and the League of Nations," *Quarterly Review* 41, no. 3 (April–June 1981): 79; Sehested, "Conformity and Dissent," 3.

28. Sehested, "Conformity and Dissent," 3.

29. For more on how the abortion issue became so prominent, see Susan Friend Harding, *The Book of Jerry Falwell: Fundamentalist Language and Politics* (Princeton: Princeton University Press, 2001).

30. Annual of the Southern Baptist Convention (Nashville, Tenn.: Southern Baptist Convention, 1971), 72. On Nixon's "Vietnamization" policy, see his speech of 3 November 1969.

31. Annual of the Southern Baptist Convention (Nashville, Tenn.: Southern Baptist Convention, 1969), 74. One example that places the SBC comfortably within the mainstream of American opinion on race is an editorial written by T. B. Maston, a seminary professor generally

considered a liberal. He writes, "There is comparatively little basis for the prevalent fear concerning interracial marriage," yet such unions are still "not wise." "Interracial Marriage," Christian Life Commission (Nashville: Southern Baptist Convention, 1974), Baptist Archive.

32. "Maryland Baptist Church Accepts Negro as Member," Baptist Press press release, 28 February 1966, Baptist Archive.

33. "Southern Baptists Elect First Negro Staff Member," Baptist Press press release, 10 May 1968, Baptist Archive.

34. Walker L. Knight, "Survey Shows SBC Messengers Here Have 'Hawkish' Attitudes," Baptist Press press release, 1 June 1967, Baptist Archive; *Annual of the Southern Baptist Convention,* 1969, 75.

35. "500 Baptist Pastors Surveyed: Nixon, Wallace Favored By Most," Baptist Press press release, 5 August 1968, Baptist Archive; "Secular City Challenges Baptists to New Strategy," Baptist Press press release, 10 July 1967, Baptist Archive.

36. Jack R. Noffsinger, "Churches Seeking to Bridge the Generation Gap," *Proceedings,* 1969 Christian Life Commission Seminar, Chicago, 31 March–2 April 1969, 51–54, Baptist Archive.

37. John D. Carter, "Pop Festivals Produce New Problems for Society," Baptist Press press release, 12 September 1969, Baptist Archive.

38. "Kentucky Convention Slaps College for Allowing Dancing," Baptist Press press release, 15 November 1968, Baptist Archive; Floyd A. Craig, "Tennessee Baptists Ask College Trustees to Rescind Dancing Rule," Baptist Press press release, 13 November 1970, Baptist Archive; "Survey Shows Most Baptists Willing to Restrict Rights," Baptist Press press release, 16 December 1971, Baptist Archive.

39. "Texas College Opposes Campus Demonstrations," Baptist Press press release, 9 February 1968, Baptist Archive.

40. On Finlator, see G. McLeod Bryan, *Dissenter in the Baptist Southland: Fifty Years in the Career of William Wallace Finlator* (Macon, Ga: Mercer University Press, 1985).

41. Dallas Lee, "Take a 'Trip' with God, Evangelist Tells Hippies," Baptist Press press release, 6 June 1968, Baptist Archive; Mary Burns, "Baptists Scratch Itch to Reach Youth with Coffeehouse Ministry," Baptist Press press release, 28 October 1969, Baptist Archive.

42. Roger C. Palms, *The Jesus Kids* (Valley Forge, Penn.: Judson, 1971), 21, 31.

43. John D. Carter, "New Orleans Hippies Get the Word on Soul Power,"

Baptist Press press release, 18 June 1969, Baptist Archive; "Baptist Leader's Son Turns Off Drugs, On to Jesus," Baptist Press press release, 7 July 1971, Baptist Archive.

44. Anson Mount, "The Playboy Philosophy—Pro," *Proceedings,* 1970 Christian Life Commission Seminar, Atlanta, 16–18 March 1970, 25, Baptist Archive.

45. William M. Pinson Jr., "The Playboy Philosophy—Con," ibid., 29.

46. Clarence W. Cranford, "Forks in the Road," ibid., 12–14.

47. Joseph Fletcher, "Situation Ethics," ibid., 18–20. Key texts of situation ethics included Gabriel Vahanian, *The Death of God: The Culture of Our Post-Christian Era* (New York: George Braziller, 1961); Joseph Fletcher, *Situation Ethics: The New Morality* (Philadelphia: Westminster, 1966); O. Sydney Barr, *The Christian New Morality: A Biblical Study of Situation Ethics* (New York: Oxford University Press, 1969).

48. Walker L. Knight and Everett Hullum Jr., "The Jesus Movement: What Is It, and Why?" special issue of *Home Missions,* June–July 1971; Billy Graham, *The Jesus Generation* (Grand Rapids, Mich.: Zondervan, 1971). The most sober treatment of the Jesus Movement is Ronald M. Enroth, Edward E. Ericson, and C. Breckinridge Peters, *The Jesus People: Old Time Religion in the Age of Aquarius* (Grand Rapids, Mich.: Eerdmans, 1972).

49. "Statement on Vietnam and World Peace," *FCNL Washington Newsletter* (Friends National Service Committee), no. 259 (April 1965): 1; "Moral Dilemma: Vietnam," a special issue of the United Church of Christ's *Social Action* 33, no. 7 (March 1967), probably published by its Council for Christian Social Action; *Social Progress* 58, no. 4 (April 1968), published by the Office of Church and Society of the Board of Christian Education of the United Presbyterian Church (USA), a special issue titled "Vietnam: This Troubling War"; *Concern* 7, no. 17 (1 October 1965), published by the General Board of Christian Social Concerns of the Methodist Church, a special issue whose cover, a map of Vietnam, said it all. The National Council of Churches, an umbrella organization of liberal mainline churches, pressed a record album meant to encourage debate on America's role in the Vietnam conflict. The album contains speeches from Arthur S. Flemming, the council president, and Robert S. Bilheimer, director of the council's International Affairs Program; side 2 is a recording titled "Action Steps for the Local Church: An Iowa Congregation Talks About Its Involvement."

The cardboard casing offers optimistic tips on how to use the record to spark discussion. See "A Multi-Media Album to Encourage Debate and Action on Vietnam," New York, National Council of Churches, ca. 1967, Baptist Archive. And see R. H. Edwin Espy to the Rev. Clifton J. Allen, 27 December 1966, Baptist Archive.

50. Wayne Dehoney, "Viet Nam Servicemen Need Spiritual Help," Baptist Press press release, 8 February 1966, Baptist Archive.

51. Untitled press release, Baptist Press, 4 March 1966, Baptist Archive; "Baptist Chaplain Contends with Noise in Vietnam," Baptist Press press release, 16 March 1966, Baptist Archive; "Baptist Chaplain Awarded Silver Star for Bravery," Baptist Press press release, 19 April 1966, Baptist Archive.

52. "Baptists Send 48-Lb Packet to Vietnam," Baptist Press press release, 25 March 1966, Baptist Archive; "South Carolina Church Helps Vietnam Children," Baptist Press press release, 30 April 1967, Baptist Archive; "SBC Seminary Collecting Books for Vietnam Seminary," Baptist Press press release, 5 March 1968, Baptist Archive; "Vietnamese Children Learn English in Saigon Church Program," Baptist Press press release, 31 December 1970, Baptist Archive.

53. William M. Dyal Jr., "The 'Silent Shriek' of Baptists on Vietnam," Christian Life Commission press release, Nashville, Tennessee, 13 December 1966.

54. District of Columbia Baptist Convention (Washington, D.C.: Ninety-first Session), Silver Spring, Maryland, 20–21 November 1967, 57–58, Baptist Archive.

55. Roy Jennings, "SBC President Supports U.S. Policy in Viet Nam," Baptist Press press release, 14 March 1966, Baptist Archive; Gainer E. Bryan Jr., "Baptist Missionaries Say Most Support Vietnam War," Baptist Press press release, 24 January 1968, Baptist Archive.

56. "Vietnam and the American Conscience," *California Southern Baptist,* 14 September 1967, 4; Chauncey R. Daley, "Which Way in Vietnam?" *Western Recorder* (Kentucky) 142, no. 6 (8 February 1968): 4; "The War in Vietnam," *Maryland Baptist* 49, no. 10 (10 March 1966): 8. See also a column run by the magazine: Henlee H. Barnette, "Should the United States Get Out of Vietnam?" *Maryland Baptist* 51, no. 35 (5 September 1968): 3. Barnette was a highly respected ethicist at Southern Baptist Theological Seminary in Louisville. Jim Newton, "Baptist State Conventions Act on Education, Doctrine, Vietnam," Baptist

Press press release, 25 November 1969, Baptist Archive; "Let's Get Out," *Arkansas Baptist* 66, no. 32 (17 August 1967): 3.

57. Resolution no. 4: On Peace, *Annual of the Southern Baptist Convention* (Nashville, Tenn.: Southern Baptist Convention, 1967), 75; resolution no. 10: On Peace, *Annual of the Southern Baptist Convention* (Nashville, Tenn.: Southern Baptist Convention, 1968), 80–81; resolution no. 3: Resolution on Peace, *Annual of the Southern Baptist Convention* (Nashville, Tenn.: Southern Baptist Convention, 1970), 71.

58. See Baptist Press press release, 1 June 1971, Baptist Archive, and *Annual of the Southern Baptist Convention* (Nashville, Tenn.: Southern Baptist Convention, 1971), 73, item no. 162. The Baptist Press's annual survey of top Baptist news stories placed the Jesus movement, the nondenominational prayer amendment defeated in Congress, and racial reconciliation in the top ten. The Vietnam War appeared nowhere at all. "*Becoming* Controversy Voted Top Baptist News Story of '71," Baptist Press press release, 30 December 1971, Baptist Archive. For the Criswell story, I am indebted to Nancy Ammerman, e-mail to author, 28 June 2002.

59. Nancy Ammerman, in *Baptist Battles,* offers the best discussion of the strife that has riven the Southern Baptist Convention in the past twenty years.

60. In 1976 Southern Baptists generally supported Jimmy Carter, one of their own, for president. But in 1979 Jerry Falwell, a Baptist (though not Southern Baptist) preacher from Virginia, famous for his *Old Time Gospel Hour* on television, helped found the Moral Majority, the organization most influential in aligning religious Protestants with the right wing of American politics. See Sara Diamond, *Roads to Dominion: Right-Wing Movements and Political Power in the United States* (New York: Guilford, 1995); Michael Lienesch, *Redeeming America: Piety and Politics in the New Christian Right* (Chapel Hill: University of North Carolina Press, 1993).

CONCLUSION

1. Percy Bysshe Shelley, *A Defense of Poetry,* ed. Albert S. Cook (Boston: Ginn, 1891), 25; Friedrich Nietzsche, *The Birth of Tragedy,* in *The Basic Writings of Nietzsche,* trans. Walter Kaufmann (New York: Modern Library, 1968), 33–46. I am also following Camille Paglia, *Sexual Per-*

sonae: *Art and Decadence from Nefertiti to Emily Dickinson* (New Haven: Yale University Press, 1990), ch. 3.

2. Jane and Michael Stern, *Sixties People* (New York: Knopf, 1990), 114.
3. Ibid, 4.
4. Martha Ackelsberg, interview by author, Northampton, Mass., 8 February 2000.
5. Beverly Swaren, "'Aggiornamento' Lost," *America* 131, no. 7 (21 September 1974): 129.
6. On the influence of civil rights and Black Power on other liberal movements, see Sara Evans, *Personal Politics: The Roots of Women's Liberation in the Civil Rights Movement and the New Left* (New York: Knopf, 1979); Alice Echols, "Nothing Distant About It: Women's Liberation and Sixties Radicalism," in *The Sixties . . . from Memory to History,* ed. David Farber (Chapel Hill: University of North Carolina Press, 1994), 165–166; Maurice Isserman and Michael Kazin, *America Divided: The Civil War of the 1960s* (New York: Oxford University Press, 2000), 172.
7. In traditional Judaism, Jewish membership is inherited through the mother's side. Reform Judaism has decided to recognize patrilineal descent, so that one with a Jewish father but not a Jewish mother may be considered Jewish.
8. The classic sociological work about religion in modern America is Robert Wuthnow, *The Restructuring of American Religion: Society and Faith Since World War II* (Princeton: Princeton University Press, 1988). Wuthnow ably shows not only how religious commitment has declined, but also how denominationalism has declined, special purpose groups have grown in influence, and higher education has contributed to a divide between religious and political liberals and conservatives. A more alarmist and ideological view, but one that is in many respects correct if we are talking about the politically interested, educated elite, is James Davison Hunter, *Culture Wars: The Struggle to Define America* (New York: Basic, 1991). A sensible distillation of all these conclusions is given in Alan Wolfe, "Under God, Not Indivisible," *New York Times,* 27 February 2000.
9. Wade Clark Roof is a leading scholar of alternative religion and nondenominational religious structures, but he is the first to admit that "clearly the local congregation, or religious assembly, remains the most common religious form in the United States. It is the vehicle

through which most of what is identified as religious is nurtured and the means through which most voluntary religious activity and service is channeled. It is the key structure around which stable religious life is sustained and passed from one generation to the next." *Spiritual Marketplace: Baby Boomers and the Remaking of American Religion* (Princeton: Princeton University Press, 1999), 298. In fact, what makes Roof's work so compelling is his recognition of how religious creativity and countercultural trends can exist in denominational religion. A book like Stephen J. Stein's *Alternative American Religions* (New York: Oxford University Press, 2000), while a useful guide to nondenominational religion, leaves one with no sense of how relatively marginal such alternative communities are. "In fact," he writes, "alternative religions constitute perhaps the most innovative, creative, and productive portion of the religious scene in the contemporary United States." Stein is writing about "the closing decades of the twentieth century," and it is clear from the scope of his book that he is including the Nixon years; his statement is as much an overstatement for 1970 as it is for 2000.

10. Robert S. Ellwood, *The Sixties Spiritual Awakening: American Religion Moving from Modern to Postmodern* (New Brunswick, N.J.: Rutgers University Press, 1994), 335–336.

11. Holland Cotter, "Everything About Warhol but the Sex," *New York Times,* 14 July 2002.

INDEX